ALICE

ALICE

GRAND DUCHESS OF HESSE

PRINCESS

OF

GREAT BRITAIN AND IRELAND

LETTERS TO HER MAJESTY THE QUEEN

NEW AND POPULAR EDITION

WITH

A MEMOIR BY H.R.H. PRINCESS CHRISTIAN

WITH PORTRAIT

LONDON

JOHN MURRAY, ALBEMARLE STREET

1885

All rights reserved

LONDON: PRINTED BY
SPOTTISWOODE AND CO., NEW-STREET SQUARE
AND PARLIAMENT STREET

PREFACE TO POPULAR EDITION

OF

PRINCESS ALICE'S LETTERS TO THE QUEEN

*WITH MEMOIR BY HER SISTER
PRINCESS CHRISTIAN.*

IN PUBLISHING a new and revised edition of my dear Sister's Letters, some extracts from my Mother's Journal have been added, and the Memoir translated from the German has been replaced by a short biographical sketch written by myself, in which I have tried to tell the story of my dear Sister's life as simply as I could, and to picture her as she was, the loving Daughter and Sister, the devoted Wife and Mother, and a perfect, true Woman.

It would have been premature and out of place to attempt anything like a complete picture of a character so many-sided, or of my Sister's ideas on the affairs of Europe, in which she took the deepest interest, and on which she formed opinions remarkable for breadth and sagacity of view. The domestic side of her nature might alone for the present be freely dealt with. There was no thought at first of making these letters public, but they were found to be so beautiful, and to be so true an expression of what my Sister really was, that, in compliance with the request of the Grand Duke her husband, they were allowed to be translated into German and published, so that her subjects might see in them how great reason they had to love her whom they had lost.

The letters in their original form are now given to the English public, and I am sure that all who read them will feel thankful to my Mother for thus granting them a closer insight into my dear Sister's beautiful and unselfish life.

They will see in them also, with satisfaction, how devoted she was to the land of her birth,—how her heart ever turned to it with reverence and affection as the country which had done and was doing for liberty and the advancement of mankind more than any other country in the world. How deep was her feeling in this respect was testified by a request, which she made to her husband in anticipation of her death, that an English flag might be laid upon her coffin; accompanying the wish with a modest expression of a hope, that no one in the land of her adoption could take umbrage at her desire to be borne to her rest with the old English colours above her.

I feel confident that the perusal of these letters must deepen the love and admiration which has always been felt for my beloved Sister in this country, where she ever thanked God that her childhood and youth had been tended with a wise love, that had fostered and developed all those qualities and tastes which she most valued and strove to cultivate in her later years.

HELENA.

CUMBERLAND LODGE:
January 1885.

CONTENTS.

1862

Departure from England — Reception at Darmstadt — Daily routine—Visits to Coburg and Auerbach—Festival at Giessen—The Ludwigstag—Visits to Worms and Baden—Prince Arthur at Darmstadt—Return to England . . . 54

1863

At Marlborough House—Visit to Mayence—Summer residence at Kranichstein—Jugenheim—Reading and domestic employments—First large dinner party—Visits to Lich, Frankfort, and Homburg—Return to Kranichstein—Tour through the Grand Duchy—Second visit to England (Aug.)—Return to Darmstadt (Nov.)—The Holstein Question—Visits to the hospitals—Visit to Amorbach— Christmas festivities . 69

1864

Birth of Prince Albert Victor (of Wales)—The Schleswig Holstein Question—Daily routine—Visiting the poor—Visit to Munich—Wedding of Princess Anna of Hesse—Third visit to England (May to Aug.)—Visit to Darmstadt of the Emperor of Russia, of the Crown Prince and Princess of Prussia—Birth of Princess Elizabeth (Nov. 1)—Dr. Macleod comes to Darmstadt 85

1865

PAGE

Smiles's Lives of the Engineers—Dean Stanley's sermon—Visit to Berlin—Return to Darmstadt—Masked ball—Plans for a journey—Death of Princess Anna and of the Cesarewitch—Robertson's Sermons—Prince Louis invested with the Garter—Seeheim—Pauli's History of England—Travelling in Switzerland—Fourth visit to England—Betrothal of Princess Christian—Illness and death of the King of the Belgians   98

1866

Organisation of Bazaar for the Idiot Asylum (Jan. 14)—Visit to Gotha—Opening of Parliament by the Queen in person—Completion of the new palace at Darmstadt—War between Austria and Prussia imminent—Death of Queen Marie Amélie—Mobilisation of the army (May)—Prussians enter Darmstadt (June)—Organisation of field hospitals—Prince Louis' division ordered to the front—Death of Prince Sigismund of Prussia—Sadowa (July 3)—Birth of Princess Irène (July 12)—The Prussians in Darmstadt—Horrors of civil war—Prince Louis appointed to the command of the Hessian troops—Residence at Nierstein—Conclusion of peace (Sept.)—Christening of Princess Irène (Sept. 12)—Visit to the fields of Frohnhofen and Laufach—Visit to Wald Leiningen—General Grey's 'Early Years of the Prince Consort'—Carlsruhe—Establishment of the Frauenverein   125

1867

The lessons of Sorrow—Charitable works—Rumours of war with France—Visit to Paris—Attempt on the life of the Czar—Return home and departure for St. Moritz (Aug.)—Excursions among the Alps—Piz Languard—Pontresina—Livigno—Bormio—The Stelvio—Münsterthal—Return from Switzer-

CONTENTS. [9]

PAGE

land—Visit to Arenenberg—Wiesbaden—Visit of the Prince and Princess of Wales to Darmstadt—Want of companions—Christmas presents 162

1868

Theatricals—Illness of Prince Leopold—Birth of Prince Waldemar of Prussia—Neuralgia—Reminiscences—Continued ill-health of Princess Alice—Death of Jäger—Fifth visit to England (May to August)—Osborne—Return home—Kranichstein—The Queen's visit to Switzerland—Rumours of war with France—Birth of Prince Ernst (Nov. 28)—Presents from England . 181

1869

Death of the only son of the King of the Belgians—Confirmation of Prince Leopold—Recollections of the Prince Consort—Anxiety about the children—The Irish Church Question—Visit to Potsdam—Gewerbe-Museum at Berlin—Fischbach—Dresden — Kranichstein — Friedberg — The Ludwigstag—Gewerbe-Ausstellung at Mayence—Prince Louis' tour to the East with the Crown Prince—Princess Alice goes to Cannes—Return of the Princes (Dec.)—Return home—Christmas arrangements 195

1870

Illness of the children—Prince Louis has scarlet fever—Princess Victoria also—and Prince Ernst—Entertainment to the civil authorities—Death of General Grey—of Sir James Clark—and of Lord Clarendon—Education—Outbreak of war with France—National enthusiasm—Continued ill-health—Weissenburg—Suspense and anxiety—Prince Louis at the front—Care of the wounded—German victories—The miseries of war—Prince Louis receives the Iron Cross—Princess Alice suffering from inflammation of the eyes—General longing for

1878

Love of England—Conduct of the Opposition in Parliament—Heinrich von Angeli at Darmstadt—Tenth and last visit to England—Eastbourne—Visit to the Albion Home at Brighton—Letter to Mrs. Vicars—Return home—Weariness and failing strength—Outbreak of diphtheria—Recovery of Princess Victoria and Princess Alix—Illness of Princess May, of the Grand Duke, Prince Ernest, and Princess Irène—Death of Princess May—Sympathy—Faith the only support in sorrow—The end 307

A WATCHER BY THE DEAD 317

SKETCH OF THE LIFE OF PRINCESS ALICE. By Sir Theodore Martin 325

INDEX 333

PORTRAIT OF PRINCESS ALICE IN 1860 . *Frontispiece*

Memoir of Princess Alice.

By her sister

Princess Christian.

On the 25th of April, 1843, at Buckingham Palace, a second daughter and third child was born to the Queen and Prince Consort—Alice Maud Mary—who ever since has been known and loved in the country of her birth as 'Princess Alice.' She was christened on the 2nd of June. The Queen, in a letter written at the time to her uncle the King of the Belgians, describes the ceremony as having been 'very imposing,' and mentions that 'little Alice behaved extremely well.'

Her childhood was, like that of all her brothers and sisters, a very happy one. Indeed, few children can ever have been more blessed in their home life. 'When she was a year old, her father mentions her as the " beauty of the family, and an extraordinarily good and merry child," and her mother adds, " she was a very vain little person."'

She had the brightest, happiest nature, and was a great favourite with all around her.

At the age of two years, the Queen mentions Princess Alice in her Journal as follows:

'Alice is really a treasure, the dearest, sweetest, funniest little pet I ever saw; so little, and so fat, and so active and dear and gentle, with such a funny long little face, and such a sweet little voice.'

And, writing again a year later, the Queen says:

'Dear little Alice comes to me every morning while I am dressing, and she really is the dearest little bijou I ever saw, and our very great pet. She has such little independent, winning ways, she talks so plain and says so dearly, "Let me kiss you, dear mama."'

The education and training, both mental and bodily, of their children, was an object of unceasing solicitude to the Queen and the Prince Consort, who themselves chose with the utmost care those persons who, under them, were to carry out their plans. The Queen, in a memorandum dated the 4th of March, 1844, writes as follows: 'The greatest maxim of all is, that the children should be brought up as simply and in as domestic a way as possible, that (not interfering with their lessons) they should be as much as possible with their parents, and learn to place their greatest confidence in them in all things.'

On leaving the nursery the children were entrusted to the care of an English governess and of a German and a French governess. These again were under a lady superintendent.[1]

---

[1] Lady Lyttelton from 1842 to 1851; and then Lady Caroline Barrington, who remained with the Royal Family till her death.

It was the governesses who directed the children's studies, accompanied them in their walks, and watched over them in their playtime. The Queen and the Prince Consort were kept informed of the minutest details of their education by these ladies, in whom they had the utmost confidence, and who were allowed at all times direct communication with them.

Princess Alice learnt with great facility, and showed great talent for music and drawing. 'Her copy-books were always neatness itself, and she wrote a very pretty hand.' 'Fresh, blooming, and healthy, escaping most of the illnesses of childhood. Cheerful, merry, full of fun and mischief.'

Such are her eldest sister's words when mentioning her as a child.

She excelled in skating and gymnastics, and was especially devoted to riding. At the age of four the Queen writes of her as follows:

'November 12, 1847.

'The children rode on the rocking-horse with great delight, and Alice really distinguished herself by riding upon it and making it go very high, and sitting on one side without any pommel or stirrup, and without being held on.'

I myself well remember her devotion as a child to a silver *bonbonnière* in the shape of a horse's head, in which she kept a piece of the tail and mane of her favourite horse, and used to put it under her pillow when she went to bed at night.

Her romps and games with her brothers were what she particularly loved; and, though so fearless and bold, she was full of gentleness, kindness of heart, and consideration for others.

It was the custom among the Royal Children to celebrate in some way or other all anniversaries in the family, often preparing charming surprises for their parents. In the little theatrical pieces which they performed, Princess Alice never failed to distinguish herself. Her rendering of the part of 'Joad the High Priest' in Racine's *Athalie* was most remarkable.

The following account of the Princess's acting in Racine's piece is from the Queen's own Journal:

'February 10, 1852.

'At six the children performed their fragment from *Athalie*. Vicky,[2] "Athalie;" Alice, "Joad the High Priest" and "Josabeth" (she acted two characters); "Agar, *suivante* of Athalie," Lenchen;[3] "Joas," Affie;[4] "Abner, *un officier*," Bertie;[5] "Zacharie, the boy of Josabeth," Louise. The dresses were extremely pretty and simple and graceful. Vicky looked extremely well, and spoke and acted her long and difficult part (the celebrated scene describing her dream, which is Rachel's great part) really admirably, with immense expression and dignity, and with the true French emphasis, which indeed they all did. She looked very well, Lenchen lovely, and Affie beautiful in his little white tunic-robe and long hair. Little Zacharie was dressed just alike. Alice was *méconnaissable* as the priest with a white beard and hair, and very handsome in her second character: she acted beautifully; Affie very nicely; Bertie very well. He and Alice appeared in the first scene: the curtain

[2] Princess Royal. [3] Princess Helena.
[4] Prince Alfred. [5] Prince of Wales.

then dropped to enable Alice to change her dress, and the music from Mendelssohn's *Athalie* was played. The scenery used was that from *Julius Cæsar*.

'Mama and Lady Anna Maria,[6] the Ladies, Stockmar, Phipps, and children, Colonel Grey and Sybil, Lady Caroline and daughter, and Mr. Wellesley were there.

'My beloved Albert was much pleased and surprised, for he had no idea of it.'

Baroness Bunsen in her *Mémoires* of her husband also gives a description of one of these performances, which took place on the anniversary of the Queen and Prince Consort's wedding day, February 10, 1854. On this occasion a tableau of the Four Seasons had been arranged by the Royal Children as a surprise for their parents.

'First appeared Princess Alice as the Spring, scattering flowers, and reciting verses, which were taken from Thomson's *Seasons*; she moved gracefully, and spoke in a distinct and pleasing manner with excellent modulation, and a tone of voice sweet and penetrating like that of the Queen.'[7]

An extract from the Queen's Journal on this subject will be read with interest :

'At near six we went over with the whole party to the Rubens Room, where the children had kindly arranged a charming surprise for us. The room was entirely darkened. There were five tableaux. Four of these represented the Seasons. 1. Alice as Spring recited some very pretty verses from Thomson's *Seasons*. 2. Vicky as Summer, with dear little Arthur asleep near some sheaves; she also recited

[6] Lady Anna Maria Dawson, Lady in Waiting to the Duchess of Kent.
[7] Bunsen's *Life*, ii. 328.

verses. 3. Affie as Bacchus, representing Autumn, also reciting verses. 4. Bertie with a long icicled beard and snowy cloak, and Louise in a sort of Russian dress sitting before a fire, as Winter: this was the prettiest almost. Bertie also recited some verses: all were taken and adapted from Thomson's *Seasons*. The fifth and last tableau combined the four others as they had each been separately represented, and in the clouds at the back stood dear little Lenchen and recited, as the spirit of the Empress Helena, very pretty verses written on the occasion by Mr. Martin Tupper. Lenchen spoke beautifully, and looked lovely. The scenery was admirably adapted to each tableau; appropriate music was played between each. The children spoke well (Alice beautifully), and looked very pretty. All were so anxious to do their best. Mr. Corbould,[8] Miss Hildyard,[9] and Mr. Gibbs[1] had the merit of the whole arrangement.

'We were all delighted.'

As years went on, her intellectual faculties and those rarer qualities of her character became more and more apparent; above all, a wonderful sweetness of disposition which endeared her to all around. She had a great power of observation and a remarkable gift of making herself attractive to others.

With all this she continued merry, full of fun and mischief, and always a great favourite with her brothers and sisters.

It is often maintained that none but those who live in comparative retirement really know the blessings of a home life. Certainly the contrary was proved in this royal

---

[8] The Princes and Princesses' drawing-master.

[9] Princesses' English governess.

[1] Prince of Wales's and Prince Alfred's tutor.

English family, and none knew better how to appreciate this than Princess Alice. The happy daily intercourse with her parents; the many walks, drives, journeys with them and her brothers and sisters; the various occupations and amusements, all watched over and shared in by the Queen and the Prince Consort, make up the sum of a most perfectly happy childhood and youth. Her adoration for her father became the one leading star through all her life; it influenced her every thought and action, and to the end of her short stay on earth she strove to act up to what he would have thought right. He was her highest ideal of all that was perfect, beautiful, and good, and even on her deathbed his loved name was the last she ever uttered.

After the Princess Royal's marriage [2] Princess Alice had to assume the position of eldest daughter in the house, and this brought with it more responsibilities and more duties. She had hitherto shared all joys and sorrows, all studies and recreations, with her sister. Now her intercourse with her parents became a much more intimate one, and, under the guidance of her father, she soon showed her appreciation of all that was purest and noblest in art, whether in painting or in music. The Prince Consort strove at all times to imbue his children with that honesty and thoroughness of purpose without which ' it was impossible to fill one's position in life happily, worthily, and with dignity.' [3]

The Revolution of 1848–1849, the Crimean War, and

---

[2] Princess Royal was married on the 25th of January, 1858, to Prince Frederick William of Prussia.

[3] Baron Stockmar.

other political disturbances throughout Europe, happening as they did at a time when the Princess was just old enough to appreciate their importance, laid the foundation of that keen interest and clear understanding she showed later in all political events.

Princess Alice's Confirmation took place on the 21st of April, 1859. She had been prepared for it by the Dean of Windsor (the Honourable and Very Reverend G. Wellesley). The Prince Consort had also read with her every evening for the previous few months. The following extract from the Queen's own Journal gives an account of those eventful days:

'April 20, 1859.

'At a quarter past four dear Alice's examination took place by the Dean in the presence of ourselves, the Archbishop, and Miss Hildyard. It lasted more than half an hour in her own room. She answered extremely well, without any hesitation or agitation, better than either of the others, and seemed so relieved when it was over, as she said she was so frightened. She behaved admirably.'

'April 21.

'We gave dear Alice a pretty Prayer Book. At twelve all was ready. The two little girls and Arthur were present. Albert went to fetch dear Alice. She looked very nice and pretty in a muslin dress trimmed with lace over white silk, her pearl necklace her only ornament. Albert led her into the chapel; Ernest Coburg, me; George, Mama. We two and the three children stood on one side; Ernest, Mama, &c., opposite. Music very fine, the whole very moving, reminding me so much of dear Vicky, three years ago.[4] Dear

---

[4] Princess Royal's Confirmation, which took place at Windsor, the 20th of March, 1856.

Alice seemed much moved when we came out and kissed her.

'We went to the "King's rooms," where were all Alice's presents.

'We talked with the company, including Lord Clarendon, who hoped things were coming right. Vain hope! At that very moment Albert was called out by Lord Derby, whose face told nothing but *bad news*. He soon returned with the distressing news that Austria had sent a summons to Sardinia to disarm, giving them three days' time to answer, at the end of which time the Austrians would march on Turin. Terribly distressed and *bouleversée* on such a day and at such a moment.'

'April 22.

'Dear Alice breakfasted with us. We took the Sacrament with her, Ernest, Lady Gainsborough, Miss Hildyard, and Fräulein Bauer. Immediately after it we walked out with Alice, and found it very hot and beautiful, all so green, birds singing beautifully.

'We and all the children attended evening service.'

'April 25.

'To-day is our dear and sweet Alice's sixteenth birthday! I can hardly believe it possible. She is a great treasure and a child who only is a comfort and pleasure to us. May God leave her long with us, and may she ever be blessed, preserved, and protected! We wished one another warmly joy. Put on a new dress. When dressed we went to fetch our dear Alice, gave her a nosegay, and took her with all the children to the breakfast room.'

It was in June 1860 that Princess Alice first made the acquaintance of her future husband. The Queen and Prince Consort always received many guests at Windsor Castle during the Ascot race week, and this year amongst others were Prince Louis and Prince Henry of Hesse.

It soon became evident to her parents that the Princess and Prince Louis had formed a 'mutual liking for one another,' and they had but little doubt 'that it would lead to further advances from the young gentleman's family.' Even that little doubt was soon removed, and Prince Louis of Hesse returned to Windsor Castle during the month of November 1860.

On the 30th of November the Queen wrote as follows in her Diary:

'. . . After dinner, whilst talking to the gentlemen, I perceived Alice and Louis talking before the fireplace more earnestly than usual, and when I passed to go to the other room, both came up to me, and Alice in much agitation said he had proposed to her, and he begged for my blessing. I could only squeeze his hand and say "Certainly," and that we would see him in our room later. Got through the evening as well as we could. Alice came to our room . . . agitated, but quiet. . . . Albert sent for Louis to his room; he went first to him and then called Alice and me in. . . . Louis has a warm noble heart. We embraced our dear Alice, and praised her much to him. He pressed and kissed my hand, and I embraced him. After talking a little, we parted; a most touching, and to me most sacred, moment.'

The marriage gave general satisfaction, and from being one entirely of mutual affection [5] there was every reason to

---

[5] 'Alice and Louis are as happy as mortals can be, and I need scarcely say this makes my heart as a father glad.'—*Prince Consort's Letter to the Crown Princess.*

think that a very bright and happy future was in store for the Princess.

March of 1861 brought the first great sorrow to the bright and happy home. The Duchess of Kent, the beloved mother and grandmother, was taken to her rest. She had been ailing for some time, but her condition had become much more serious since the commencement of the year, and though she was as full of life and interest as ever, and apparently unchanged, all those near her felt that her state was most precarious.

On the 16th of March, 1861, the Duchess of Kent gently breathed her last. The Queen and Prince Consort and Princess Alice were with her, and it was then that the young Princess first showed that wonderfully tender sympathy, and that perfect unselfishness of her nature, which but a few months later, when a far bitterer sorrow fell on her family, proved the comfort and solace of her broken-hearted mother.

The Queen writes in her Diary at that time:

'Dear good Alice was full of intense feeling, tenderness, and distress for me.' And again: 'Good Alice was with us through all.'

In the spring the Queen announced to Parliament Princess Alice's engagement; and when, later on, 'the Princess's settlement of a dowry of 30,000*l.* with an annuity of 6,000*l.* was brought before the House of Commons, it was voted unanimously.'[6] Her father, writing on this subject to Baron

---

[6] *Prince Consort's Life.* Sir Theodore Martin.

Stockmar, mentions, that as the Princess's income would not be a large one, she 'would not be able to do great things with it.'

Prince Louis of Hesse paid several visits to England during the year—one of the last being to the Highlands. Balmoral had ever been peculiarly dear to the Princess, and in her letters to the Queen after her marriage she gives constant proof of her love for her Scotch home.

On the return of the Court to Windsor Castle, the preparations for the Princess's marriage were being carried rapidly forward, her father himself directing and settling all. It was whilst engaged on these that he was taken ill with typhoid fever, and died on the 14th of December, 1861.

The light and sunshine seemed to have gone out of that hitherto so happy home. Though utterly crushed by the loss of the father whom she so adored, all thought of herself was put aside, and she only lived for her mother. What she was to her in those first terrible weeks is well known; and it was at that time that an article appeared in the *Times*, from which the following extract is taken:

'It is impossible to speak too highly of the strength of mind and self-sacrifice shown by Princess Alice during these dreadful days. Her Royal Highness has certainly understood that it was her duty to be the help and support of her mother in her great sorrow, and it was in a great measure due to her that the Queen has been able to bear with such wonderful resignation the irreparable loss that so suddenly and terribly befell her.'

In every way in her power the Princess strove to guard her mother from all that was painful, to help her over all that was unavoidable. Since her father's death she had developed a force of character, combined with tact and judgment, truly admirable, settling and arranging everything for the Queen with Ministers and officials, and sustaining her mother by her own firmness and skilfully ministered sympathy; and when it was decided, at the urgent desire of the King of the Belgians, that the Queen must leave Windsor for Osborne but a few days after the Prince's death, it was the Princess's gentle influence which induced her mother to make that great sacrifice. 'She also gained at this time that practical knowledge for organising, and the desire for constant occupation, which in her public as in her private life became a part of herself.'[7]

Princess Alice's marriage took place at Osborne on the 1st of July, 1862. The following most touching accounts of the wedding and the days after it, from the Queen's own Journal, will be read with the deepest interest.

'July 1, 1862.

'A very bad night, very little sleep, and towards morning heard the knocking for the arrangements for the sad marriage. When dear Alice got up and came and kissed me I gave her my blessing and a Prayer Book, like the one dear mama gave me the day of our happy marriage, and another very pretty book. Got up a little earlier, and breakfasted with dear Alice. . . . Went with Colonel Biddulph to look at the dining-room arranged as a chapel,

---

[7] By the Grand Duchess of Baden.

with the altar just under our dear family picture. A dark blue velvet cloth and cushions, and chairs covered with dark blue cloth, rails in a circular form, like at our blessed wedding and Vicky's; the furniture taken out of the room. Then the breakfast for the Royal personages in the Council Room, where our marriage picture was placed (the deer-stalking one had been taken away for the Exhibition, and I had this brought from Windsor on purpose).

'Took a very short drive with Lenchen, and then sent for dear Louis, who was much overcome when I kissed him and wished him joy; and so was I. Dear Alice was dressed by a little before one. She looked lovely in her bridal attire. Unlike Vicky she had no train, and had a berthe and half-long sleeves. The deep flounce of Honiton lace and the veil to correspond were chosen by my beloved angel, he having seen last spring the designs and ordered a new one to be made, as that first sent was "so unmeaning." Ever his precious taste!

'Darling Alice had her order on, the beautiful opal cross and brooches of her adored papa, and Bertie's bracelet and the one with our pictures in it. She looked most lovely, with rather a full wreath of orange flowers and myrtle. The dress of crystalline silk, no more flowers but round the bottom of the dress. The four bridesmaids, our three girls and Anna,[8] were in sprigged net over white, with grey silk ribbon trimming. The time came. I, in my sad cap, as dear Baby calls it—most sad on such a day—went down with our four boys, Bertie and Affie leading me. It was dreadful; and yet I felt him very near. No one in the room except the Archbishop of York (the Archbishop of Canterbury not being strong enough), the Dean, and Mr. Prothero. Felt very nervous when I heard the doors open and the different people one after another walk in, though

---

[8] Prince Louis' sister.

no one could see me, for I sat the whole time in an armchair near the altar, and Bertie and Affie stood close to my right and hid me; the little boys to my left. The parents and Wilhelm [9] stood opposite to me, and the Augustuses [1] and Nemours next to them. Another painful pause and Louis came in, conducted by Lord Sidney, and followed by Heinrich.[2] Again a still more painful pause, and in complete silence in came the dear dear bride on her uncle's arm, followed by her bridesmaids—a touching sight—and the service began. The Archbishop read most impressively, solemnly. Dear Alice answered sweetly, distinctly, and in her harmonious voice, full of dignity and self-possession. Louis answered very distinctly and plainly. I restrained my tears (poor dear Affie cried terribly all through) till the words which I never could bear, and which have been fulfilled in an earthly sense, "till death us do part," were pronounced, and then I had a violent struggle to prevent a complete outburst. I feel he is near me as ever, and his beloved picture [3] where he stretches out his hand as though he blessed us.

'All over! Dearest Alice, who was wonderfully calm, embraced *me*, who was *all* she had, while Louis embraced his parents, who were much affected. Then I embraced dear Louis and his parents. I then left the room, shook Ernest's [4] hand and kissed him, and dearest Feodore [5] came and embraced me. When all had left I got up and went as I had come, and took and pressed the Archbishop's hand as I passed him, the tears rolling down his cheeks. Went at once with the boys to the Horn Room, where I cried bitterly,

[9] Prince William of Hesse.
[1] Prince and Princess Augustus of Saxe-Coburg and Gotha.
[2] Prince Henry of Hesse.
[3] Family picture by Winterhalter. The altar was arranged underneath the picture.   [4] Duke of Saxe-Coburg and Gotha.
[5] Princess Hohenlohe Langenburg.

and clasped dear Affie in my arms, who sobbed very much, and was terribly overcome; the little boys too. Alice and Louis then came in, and Prince and Princess Charles, who were very much upset, and Prince Charles so kind, saying he felt so much for me. Good dear Fritz [6] came to kiss me, and was very much moved. The Dean then arrived with the three registers, which we signed, and which took a long time; after which the young couple left the room. Heinrich, Wilhelm, and Anna [7] as well as the other bridesmaids, came in also. Darling Baby cried very much. Then in succession the Cambridges, most feeling, and other Princes, came in, including Nemours. I took leave of all, and then went upstairs, followed by the dear young couple, who lunched with me and Baby in the schoolroom, all the others lunching below.

'Mr. Thomas made a slight sketch of Alice in her dress, and then she went into her dear papa's room and changed, putting on a white muslin de soie. Her calmness and composure continued. They both went over to wish the Prince and Princess good-bye, who then came with their children to wish me good-bye, after which they all left. Ernest went with them to town, to return on Thursday. Dear Alice and Louis came to me, and I talked a little to her. . . . At five she put on her white tulle bonnet with orange flowers, and I took leave of her, and blessed them both, and saw them from the stairs drive off to St. Clare—Jane Churchill, General Seymour, and Baron Westerweller following them.'

'July 3, 1862.

'At twenty minutes to three started with Feodore, the two girls, Bertie, the Duchess of Athole, and Mademoiselle de Schenck, for St. Clare,[8] going a long way round to avoid

---

[6] Crown Prince of Prussia.   [7] Prince Louis' two brothers and sister.
[8] Villa near Ryde belonging to Colonel and Lady Catherine Harcourt.

Ryde, and to arrive there a little before six. Most strange it seemed to see dear Alice and Louis and their people at the door. But oh! to come alone, without my own blessed one, the incredibility of which, when I think of so many years—of last year—was too dreadful, and gave all a sad, sad tinge. Dear Alice had rather a cold, but seemed well and happy, very quiet and *posée*, but yet sad too. They gave us tea. We left a little before seven.'

'July 4.

'Went to Alice and Louis's rooms. At half-past seven o'clock they arrived; took them to their room—the same Vicky had, and Prince and Princess Charles had, but they have been fresh done up. New carpets with orange flowers and wreaths of flowers, and their cyphers. They dined with me, and are very nice together.'

'July 5.

'After luncheon gave dear Louis the Garter. Of course only put it over his shoulder. He was very much pleased, and said, "Ich hoffe ich werde mich immer würdig zeigen."'[9]

'July 6.

'Feodore dined with me, and after it the others came up. Bertie and Affie went to play billiards, and Louis remained with us. Alice read aloud the *Lady of Shalot*.'

'July 7, 1862.

'Alice came over to me and played a few of our chapel hymns. Alice drove me, and it again turned showery—Louis and the others riding. Went with Alice to her room; she and Louis dined with me. After dinner the boys went down to play at billiards again. Took Alice to her room, being her last night, and she began to cry bitterly; and I strove to cheer her by the prospect of an early return, but

[9] 'I hope I shall ever prove myself worthy of it.'

she said, "It is my home," and its being so sad made no difference in it, she loved it so much : she loved me, poor dear child !'

'July 8, 1862.

'Went out with Alice and Louis, first walking to play with the monkey, and then driving in little Sardinian pony carriage, Louis sitting behind. Alice received an immense number of pretty presents from all the household, chiefly ornaments for the table, china, &c.—really beautiful things. She and Louis came over to my room, and while she was seeing Dr. Becker[1] in the next room, Louis remained with me, and talked very sensibly of Alice's health, &c. I feel quite satisfied as to her happiness; nothing can be nicer than their tone together, or more truly satisfied and happy, though Alice is serious; but I feel anxious about her health, she is grown very thin again. Louis is extremely unselfish, and made so little fuss about keeping her to himself, and is very affectionate to me; and Alice praises him so much, finds him so sensible, not narrow-minded or prejudiced.

'Baby and Leopold to luncheon. Soon after Alice again came to me, and I afterwards went over to her room and saw her put her things on, and at half-past four took her over to our side and here had to take leave. She was very much overcome, but I tried to bear up as much as I could and not to cry too violently. Blessed her, and felt (D.V.) we should meet again at the end of October.

'Louis was excessively upset. I told him I gave Alice to him in perfect confidence. I joined their hands again, and embraced them, and then they left, and I felt *all alone*.'

On the 8th of July the Princess and her husband left for her new home. Many were the earnest prayers, and

---

[1] Princess Alice's private secretary, who had formerly been private secretary and librarian to the Prince Consort.

many were the loving wishes, that accompanied her on her leaving her English home—that home to which she clung even more passionately as years went on.

> 'Dear to us all by those calm earnest eyes,
>   And early thought upon that fair young brow;
>   Dearer for that where grief was heaviest, thou
> Wert sunshine, till He passed where suns shall rise
> And set no more: thou, in affection wise
>   And strong, wert strength to Her who even but now
>   In the soft accents of thy bridal vow
> Heard music of her own heart's memories.
>
> 'Too full of love to own a thought of pride
> Is now thy gentle bosom; so 't is best:
>   Yet noble is thy choice, O English bride!
> And England hails the bridegroom and the guest
>   A friend—a friend well loved by him who died.
> He blessed your troth: your wedlock shall be blessed.'
>
> Punch.

July 1862.

MARRIED LIFE.

The young married couple met with a most enthusiastic reception on their arrival at Darmstadt. From far and near the people had flocked together to do honour to their young Prince's bride. The Princess created the very best impression, and all were captivated by her great simplicity and grace, and at the same time by the wonderful dignity of her demeanour.

The first few weeks after their arrival were fully occupied by the official duties of their position. In the autumn the Princess had the joy of meeting her mother and several of her brothers and sisters, who had come to Germany (to Rheinhardsbrunn in Thuringia, a shooting castle of the Duke of Coburg's) for a few weeks.

Prince and Princess Louis decided to come to England at the beginning of the winter and spend some months with the Queen. This they did, and on Easter Sunday, the 5th of April, 1863, a little daughter[2] was born to the Prince and Princess at Windsor Castle, and was christened there a few weeks later.

Early in the summer they returned to Germany, spending the hottest months at Kranichstein, a shooting castle

[2] Victoria, married, April 30, 1884, to Prince Louis of Battenberg.

of the Grand Duke's near Darmstadt, beautifully situated among large beech woods. Here the Princess lived a most quiet, happy life, much occupied with ideas and plans of how she could best prove her love and interest for her adopted country and its people.

'The Congress' of crowned heads and princes of Germany (which took place at Frankfort in August 1863 under the auspices of Austria, the King of Prussia declining to be present) called forth afresh the Princess's interest in politics. Her letters of that time show how keenly she entered into the great questions which were then stirring Germany to its very core—foremost among them the Schleswig-Holstein question, which soon became one of European importance, and out of which sprang the war of 1866.

A second daughter [3] was born at Darmstadt on the 1st of November, 1864. During that and the previous years the Princess superintended the building of her own palace, which she had planned herself. She had hitherto lived in a very small house adjoining the palace of her parents-in-law, Prince and Princess Charles of Hesse, and it was felt to be impossible, with an increasing family, for her and the Prince to continue living there; besides, they were quite unable to receive the society of Darmstadt—in fact, to fulfil the social duties of their position.

Much of the Princess's time was always taken up in organising and carrying out various schemes for the good and welfare of the people at Darmstadt, and in Hesse generally. This was no easy task, for she met with many

[3] Elizabeth, married, June 1884, to the Grand Duke Sergius of Russia.

difficulties and had to combat many prejudices. The mere fact of her being an Englishwoman with broad and liberal views excited suspicion in a certain set. She felt this very keenly from the first, but more so as time went on. Yet the great love and respect universally felt for her in her new home, deeply appreciated by her, encouraged her to persevere in her efforts.

Some time in each year was spent in England with the Queen, and though so thoroughly happy in her husband's country, each return to the old home only strengthened the Princess's passionate attachment to it.

The death of the King of the Belgians, December 1865, who had been the kindest and tenderest of uncles, was a great grief to the Princess, who felt deeply what an irreparable loss the death of this wise, devoted friend and counsellor would be to the Queen.

The year 1866 was an eventful one for Germany. To the Princess it brought alike joys and sorrows, and, great as were the anxieties through which she had to pass, she felt in the end she had also much cause for thankfulness.

In the spring of the year a bazaar which she had herself arranged in her 'new palace' took place with the most satisfactory results. This undertaking was for the purpose of raising funds to found an Idiot Asylum in Darmstadt. She had previously attended some lectures on the subject; and knowing the want of such an institution, she determined to found one herself.[4] At the outset she found herself much hampered by the different views prevailing on the subject;

[4] See the Princess's letter of the 2nd of January, 1866.

but with tact and patience, and with the help of kind friends, the Princess secured the success she so fully deserved. The Idiot Asylum founded by her is now doing its work nobly, and is carried out on the principles laid down by her. The proceeds of the bazaar amounted to 16,000 florins.

In June the war between Austria and Prussia broke out. The Princess was 'such a true German' that she could not but be affected by it most nearly. It was a struggle between Germans and Germans, or, as she herself writes to her mother, of 'brother against brother, and friend against friend.' She knew but too well how Prince Louis and his country would suffer by it; she knew, too, that her husband must soon take the field with his division against Prussia. The Grand Duke of Hesse naturally went with the 'Bund' (the German Confederation), and the Princess with her clear foresight saw how South Germany must suffer in the end through the struggle. The mere idea that her husband should stand opposed to the Crown Prince of Prussia (her brother-in-law) was bitter pain to her.

In the midst of this most trying time, the Princess gave birth to a third daughter on the 12th of July, 1866. By the merest chance Prince Louis had returned to Darmstadt for a few hours the very day the child was born, and she had the comfort of having him with her. On the 21st of July the Prussian General von Göben entered Darmstadt with his troops. The Princess, though barely recovered from her confinement, was aware of what took place, and was the comfort and stay of all at that time.

In August Prince Louis came home for a few days.

As soon as the Princess was sufficiently strong, she and her husband visited the wounded and endeavoured to organise means for their relief. On the 12th of September the baby Princess was christened at Darmstadt. The sponsors were the brigade Prince Louis commanded: 'as a remembrance that he and they had stood in the field together for their first campaign, he asked these two regiments, officers and men, to stand sponsors to Baby, as she was born during that time, and they are delighted, but wish the child to have one of their names.'[5]

The Princess had felt throughout the late war the necessity for a general and widespread organisation 'for aid to the sick and wounded in times of war.' A society had existed since 1865 in Hesse for this purpose, Prince and Princess Charles of Hesse being at its head. It had been established on the principle of the German Red Cross Society. Princess Alice, who was very much interested in the movement, and in all that had to do with nursing, &c., resolved to found a 'Ladies' Union,' in which ladies and women of every rank and denomination should join. A committee was formed in 1867, consisting of seven ladies and four doctors, with Princess Alice at the head. Branch committees were to spring from it and be spread all over the country, to assist 'the nursing and supporting of troops in times of war, and in times of peace to train nurses to assist other hospitals, and to help among the poor or to nurse the rich.'[6]

---

[5] The Princess received the names Irène Louise Marie Anna.
[6] See the Princess's letter of the 21st of December, 1866.

At the same time that Princess Alice founded the 'Ladies' Union for Aid to Sick and Wounded,' she had turned her attention seriously to the subject of 'the improvement of the condition of poor unmarried women and girls.' Fräulein Louise Büchner, a distinguished philanthropist, proved a most efficient help to the Princess, and aided her in establishing a 'Committee for the Encouragement of Female Industry.'

The 'Alice Bazaar' (a permanent one) was founded on the 25th of November, 1867, 'for the object of receiving and selling articles of needlework, and for obtaining employment for women of all classes.'

The year 1867 was not without its anxieties. There were rumours of war with France, which, however, passed off. The Princess, with her clear-sighted judgment, recognised that this could only be for a time. In a letter to her mother she writes as follows:

'Darmstadt: April 21, 1867.

'... How I wish you may be right in *not* believing in war. I always fear it is not Luxemburg, but the intense jealousy of the French nation, that they should not be the first on the Continent, and that Germany is becoming independent and powerful against their will. Then, again, the Germans feel their new position, and assert their rights with more force because unanimous, and neither nation will choose to give in to the other.

'The war would be totally useless, and sow no end of dissension and hatred between the two neighbour countries, who, for their own good as for that of mankind, ought to live in peace and harmony with each other.

'We seem drifting back to the Middle Ages, as each question is pushed to the point of the sword. It is most sad. How dear Papa would have disapproved of much that has happened since 1862!'

The new Convention[7] entered into by the Grand Duchy of Hesse with Prussia was at first a great source of trouble to Prince Louis. He had every reason to fear that the Grand Duke, with his aversion to the new state of affairs, would never give a very hearty allegiance to it. Under these circumstances Prince Louis felt it incumbent on him to resign his command in the Hessian army, not wishing to appear in constant opposition to his uncle.

For some time there was great doubt whether the Grand Duke would agree to what was inevitable. The first condition under which the Prince considered it would be possible for him to retain the command was that he should have a Prussian officer at his side, and the Grand Duke had said he would rather lose his country than consent. However, finally, to the surprise of all, he gave in to the Prince's wishes rather than lose his services.

During this year (1867) the strain of her life seemed to tell greatly on the Princess's health. She wrote in May to the Queen: 'I am not up to very much. I don't always feel quite strong; but the change [to England] will do me good.' A year or two before she had written: 'From being always so well and strong, I feel a slight indisposition more than most people.' As the years went on, this feeling

---

[7] Through which the Hessian army was placed under the King of Prussia's command.

of bodily weakness and the looking forward to change and rest recurred with more and more frequency.

The year 1868 brought great joy to the Prince and Princess and the whole country, in the birth of a son [8] and heir, on the 25th of November. During the autumn of the following year the Prince and Princess were for the first time separated for some months. Prince Louis accompanied the Crown Prince of Prussia on his tour to the East. Writing to the Queen at that time, the Princess says: [9] 'I am very glad you approve of Louis' journey, which I know will be so useful and interesting to him, though it was not possible to attain this without parting from each other, which is of course no small trial to us who are so unaccustomed to being separated.' The thought of what was best and what was most likely to benefit and fit the Prince for his future high position was ever her first thought, however great the personal sacrifice to herself. The Princess spent the time of her husband's absence with her sister the Crown Princess at Cannes. Prince Louis returned at Christmas, and the New Year saw them safe home at Darmstadt.

It was in the beginning of 1870 that Princess Alice became intimately acquainted with the great theological writer Frederick David Strauss. He was staying at Darmstadt at the time, and often spent some hours with the Princess reading aloud to her and conversing. This gave rise to a proposal, made by the Princess, that Strauss should make notes on Voltaire, whose works they had been discussing together, and then that he should read them to her, and to

[8] Ernst Ludwig.   [9] Darmstadt, October 3, 1869.

a select circle of friends, Mr. (now Sir Robert) Morier being amongst them. This plan, however, was never carried out, as Prince Louis was attacked by scarlet fever. The Princess then intimated to Strauss how glad she would be if he would come and read his lectures to her alone, provided he did not fear the risk of infection in coming to the palace. Strauss agreed to this most willingly. At the time he first took up the idea of writing these lectures on Voltaire for the Princess, he had hoped that when they were printed he might be allowed to dedicate them to her. He, however, quite gave up the idea when he had completed his book. He shrank from making the request, for fear it should place the Princess in a difficult position, owing to the views he held. After some discussion on the point, the Princess, with the full approbation of Prince Louis, accepted the dedication of the book in the terms in which it now stands published. Her intercourse with him has excited much comment, and been the cause of much misconception. The Princess at all times loved to gather around her people of distinction, of whatever denomination. To discuss abstruse subjects with them, and become acquainted with their opinions, was her great delight. She had a peculiar talent in drawing others out, and an inclination to enter, for the time at least, into their thoughts. It was not strange, therefore, that she should have been attracted by one so gifted as Strauss, nor was it strange that, at a time when the Princess was passing through a phase of mental struggle as to her own religious views, this intercourse and real friendship with Strauss should have exercised a considerable influence on her opinions. It was, however, but a phase, out of which she passed triumphantly; not, alas, without much suffering to herself, but only, as we now know from her own letters, to become in the end more trustful and strong in the most perfectly childlike faith.

She carried away from her own home that perfect fearlessness which has always been the true reward of pure motives and true faith. The Princess had had occasion to learn how unjust public clamour could be, even in a free country; but she had also learnt the sacredness of the duty never to join in such clamour, or to countenance it in any way, without a conscientious examination of the grounds on which it professed to rest.

In Germany the opinions of Strauss were looked upon with such dislike and distrust, that it required no small courage on the part of the Princess to make his acquaintance. To many people this would no doubt have proved a dangerous experiment, and even to her it was, as we know, a painful trial. As the true child of her father, she wished to prove everything, and to retain what was best; and she had her reward. What seemed a loss became to her a real gain, and in the future no page in her life will probably be read with deeper sympathy, no sacrifice that the Princess ever made will prove, it may be, a greater blessing to many 'sick and wounded' in spirit, than her noble courage in facing a danger from which so many shrink, and the triumph of that childlike faith which in the end helped her to bear burdens which seemed almost too heavy to be borne.

Though in course of time she ceased to agree with Strauss in his views, she ever felt and acknowledged his rare gifts and the perfect sincerity of his nature.

In June 1870, France declared war against Germany, and on the 1st of August Prince Louis was ordered to the front with his division, which formed part of the Second Army, commanded by Prince Frederick Charles of Prussia.

The Princess had been much urged by her sister, the Crown Princess, to pass the time of her husband's absence with her; but she determined to stay at Darmstadt. She considered that her parents-in-law, who had all their sons in the war, had the first claim upon her; and moreover, though she knew all the comfort and advantage it would be to her to be with her sister, it was a satisfaction to her to be in her husband's home, nearer to him, and where he would have wished her to stay. She was living at Kranichstein with her children, and drove in every morning early to Darmstadt to attend the meeting of the 'Society for Aid to the Sick and Wounded,' which she allowed to have its 'head-quarters' at her palace. She daily went to the hospitals and ambulances, directing and organising the best means of relief, and bringing comfort and brightness wherever she went, proud to work like the wife of a German officer whose only thought during her husband's absence was to relieve as much as possible the misery and suffering of the wounded soldiers. 'The Alice Society for Aid to Sick and Wounded' did grand work all this time. The Princess established a 'depôt' at her own palace of all hospital necessaries, and organised committees of ladies who served out refreshments day and night at the railway station to the wounded who were constantly passing through Darmstadt on their way home. She was indefatigable, never a thought given to herself, and though almost distracted with anxiety about the Prince, it was she who 'kept others up,' who kept her presence of mind, who directed, guided, advised, who comforted the bereaved, and gave hope to many ready to despair. But what tried her the most sorely was the heartrending sight of the crowds of mothers, wives, sisters, pressing round her carriage after the first intelligence of a great battle: all came to her for news, and yet she was often unable to tell them anything but 'that the loss had been enormous.'

The strain on her health was intense, but she would not give in. In answer to one of her sisters writing to her at that time and begging her to spare herself, she said: 'I must work only not to be able to think. I should go mad if I had to sit still and think;' and this, too, was shortly before her second boy's birth, which took place on the 6th of October.[1] After it, to help her recovery, she was persuaded by her parents-in-law to go for three weeks to her sister at Berlin. There is no doubt that the perpetual mental anxiety and the great physical strain of that terrible time told permanently on the Princess's health.

The christening of the little Prince had been deferred as long as possible in the hopes of Prince Louis being able to return home, at least for a short time, which hope had

[1] Frederic William.

been strengthened by the fact that an armistice had been concluded between Germany and France. However, the Princess was doomed to disappointment, and the baby boy, whom his father had never yet seen, was christened on the 11th of February, 1871. The Princess writes to her mother as follows on the very day:

'Darmstadt: February 11, 1871.

'To-day our little son is to be christened, but only the family will be present, and my ladies and the two wounded gentlemen, who can get about on crutches now. When I think that the one owes his life to being here, it always gives me pleasure.

'How I shall miss dear Louis to-day! The seven months will be round ere we meet, I fear, and he has never seen his dear little boy. It always makes me sad to look at him, though now I have every reason to hope—please God—that I shall have the joy of seeing Louis come home, and of placing his baby in his arms. My heart is full.

'I will tell Christa[2] to write an account to you of the christening, for Leopold to see also, as he will be godfather. Frederic William Augustus (after the Empress) Victor (victory) Louis will be his names. Fritz and Vicky, the Empress and Fritz Carl, are godparents.'

On the 21st of March Prince Louis at last returned home, though only for a short time; but the beginning of June saw the end of that long and trying separation. The Prince and Princess went to Berlin to be present at the entry of the troops on the 16th of June.

The Prince and Princess spent the autumn with the Queen at Balmoral. She had not seen her mother since

[2] Baroness von Schenck, Lady in Waiting to the Princess.

the war; and she much needed rest and quiet, somewhat to restore her after all she had gone through. In November she went to Sandringham, where, soon after her arrival, the Prince of Wales was taken ill with the same terrible illness that, ten years before, had proved fatal to the life of the Prince Consort. The Princess remained with her sister-in-law during that time, sharing with her the fearful anxieties of those dark days, and, as ever, helping when need was greatest. The end of January 1872 saw her home at Darmstadt, having left her beloved brother entirely convalescent.

In June of that year a fourth daughter[3] was born. The year was passed quietly and peacefully. The Princess continued her indefatigable exertions for the welfare of the people at Darmstadt, and more especially turned her attention to bettering the condition of women, and to extending their sphere of employment. The following letter will explain the objects of the great work the Princess had undertaken, and the proceedings of the 'Frauentag,' or Ladies' Diet, which held its meeting at Darmstadt. At that moment England had sent several delegates to it.

'Darmstadt: October 13.

'... A few words about our doings here may be of interest to you. The meeting went off well, was very large, the subjects discussed to the purpose and important, and not one word of the emancipated political side of the question was touched upon by anyone. Schools (those of the lower, middle, and higher classes) for girls were the principal theme; the employment of women for post and

---

[3] Victoria Alix Helena Louise Beatrice.

telegraph offices, &c.; the improvement necessary in the education of nursery maids, and the knowledge of mothers in the treatment of little children; the question of nurses and nursing institutes.

'The public meeting on the following day lasted from nine to two with a small interruption; a committee meeting in the afternoon; and that evening all the members and guests came to us—nearly fifty in number. The following day the meetings lasted even longer, and the English ladies were kind enough to speak—only think, old Miss Carpenter, on all relating to women's work in England (she is our guest here). Her account of the Queen's Institute at Dublin was most interesting. Miss Hill (also our guest), about the boarding-out system for orphans. Miss C. Winkworth, about higher education in England.

'There was a good deal of work to finish afterwards, and a good many members to see. They came from all parts of Germany—many kind-hearted, noble, self-denying women. The presence of the English ladies—above all, of one such as Miss Carpenter, who has done such good work for the reformation of convicts—greatly enhanced the importance of the meeting, and her great experience has been of value to us all. She means still to give a lecture on India and the state of the native schools there, before leaving us.'

In November of that year a monument erected to the memory of the Hessian troops who had fallen in the war was unveiled at Metz, the Prince and Princess being present, 'besides deputations of officers and men, and the Generals from Metz.'[4]

In the spring of 1873 Princess Alice at last saw one of her fondest daydreams realised—a visit to Italy. She had

[4] Princess Alice's letter to the Queen, November 12, 1872.

never really got over the effects of the strain to her health during the time of the great war, and had moreover lately been in much anxiety about little Prince Fritz, so that a complete change was thought essential. Her great love of Art had always made her long to see Rome and Italy, and now that this wish was to be realised she could scarcely believe it. She writes to her mother just before starting:

'Rome is our first halting-place in Italy, and for years it has been my dream and wish to be in that wonderful city, where the glorious monuments of antiquity and of the Middle Ages carry one back to those marvellous times.

'I am learning Italian, and studying the history and art necessary to enable me, in the short time we have, to see and understand the finest and most important monuments. I am so entirely absorbed and interested in these studies just now, that I have not much time for other things.'

No journey was ever so enjoyed, or so thoroughly appreciated; but the Princess returned home much fatigued in body, though thoroughly refreshed in mind.

Whilst still in the midst of her joy and thankfulness at being safe home again, and at finding her dear ones 'all well and flourishing,' a terrible misfortune befell that hitherto so happy home, which for a time seemed to crush the whole brightness out of it. Prince Fritz—the Princess's 'darling little Frittie'—was killed by a fall from the window on the 29th of May.

Her husband had left her that very morning on a tour of military inspection. The hour of his departure being so early, the Princess had remained in bed, contrary to her usual habit. The two little Princes came to wish her good morning, and were left alone with her, as she always tried to accustom her children from their earliest years to be as independent as possible. The two brothers were playing at 'hide and seek.' The Princess's sitting-room had a large bow window, from which it was possible to look into one of the bedroom windows. The Princess always supposed that the little brothers had wished to look at each other from the opposite windows; suffice it to say, the elder ran into the sitting-room, and little Prince Fritz to the bedroom window as 'hard as he could tear,' and the impetus must have shot him out, the windows being half open and giving way with him. He fell about twenty feet on to a stone balustrade below. He was picked up insensible, but outwardly unhurt beyond a small bruise at the side of his head. The Princess's scream on seeing her child disappear from her sight has never been forgotten by those who heard it. Doctors were called hurriedly, and the first comers were full of hope; but when the Princess's own medical adviser arrived he shook his head. His familiar acquaintance with the child's fragile nature made him fear the worst, and in the evening suffusion of blood on the brain ended that precious little life.

Alone, but calm and collected as ever, the broken-hearted mother had sat all day near that little bed, watching the life so dear to her ebbing slowly away. There was no smile of recognition, but, thank God, there was no struggle and no pain, as the child passed from her care to that of the loving Heavenly Father, who would for ever shield him from all pain and suffering.

Prince Louis, though sent for at once, only reached home after all was over.

The sympathy was universal; and if anything could have brought comfort and solace to the Princess's aching heart, it was the love shown her at that time. Prince Fritz was buried in the mausoleum at the Rosenhöhe, near Darmstadt, on the evening of Whit Sunday, the 1st of June.

The Princess never entirely recovered from this fearful shock—indeed, all her own family felt it had been her 'death-blow.' A more tender, self-sacrificing mother never lived. All her thoughts were centred in the welfare of her children; and though so full of loving care, she was wonderfully wise in her system of training and education. As she says herself:

'. . . I always think that in the end children educate the parents. For their sakes there is so much one must do: one must forget oneself, if everything is as it ought to be. It is doubly so, if one has the misfortune to lose a precious child. Rückert's lovely lines are so true (after the loss of two of his children):

'Nun hat euch Gott verliehen, was wir euch wollten thun,
Wir wollten euch erziehen, und ihr erzieht uns nun.
O Kinder, ihr erziehet mit Schmerz die Eltern jetzt;
Ihr zieht an uns, und ziehet uns auf zu euch zuletzt.'[5]

---

[5] Now unto you the Lord has done what we had wished to do;
We would have train'd you up, and now 't is we are train'd by you.
With grief and tears, O children, do you your parents train,
And lure us on and up to you, to meet in heaven again.

Though so utterly crushed by the death of her child, and feeling, like so many that have suffered, 'that one grows to love one's grief as having become part of the thing one loved,' still she did not weakly give way to it, but she tried to find a blessing in the hour of trial and grief; she threw herself with energy into her work, and her courage and self-sacrifice were not without a reward; she found indeed, as she so truly said, 'the day passes so quickly when one can do good, and make others happy.' The visit to England in the autumn did much towards comforting her, and the quiet and rest seemed to restore her to some of her former strength. In the May of the following year, a fifth daughter[6] was born, and though momentarily disappointed at its not being a boy, this child henceforth became her mother's 'sunshine' and comfort.

The years 1875 and 1876 brought outwardly little change in the Princess's life. She continued to take a great interest in politics and in all her favourite schemes; she was able to fulfil her social duties, but her health became gradually but steadily worse. Change of air always seemed to restore her for the time, and she apparently benefited much by visits to England and Scotland, and also to the Black Forest, but the close observer could not fail to see that the improvement was never more than temporary. She herself was fully aware of this, and was often very despondent as to the future. She had over and over again at different times mentioned to one of her sisters[7] her conviction that she would not live long.

In 1877 the apparent lull in her life was broken by the

---

[6] Marie Victoria Feodora Leopoldine.   [7] Princess Christian.

great strain caused by the illness and death of her father-in-law, whom she dearly loved, followed closely by that of the Grand Duke.

Prince Louis succeeded his uncle as Grand Duke Louis IV. As ever, it fell to the Princess to share the full burden of the trial, and the new life of responsibilities and duties, which came upon her when her physical strength was at a very low ebb, tried her most severely, for with her high sense of duty she could not accept lightly her new position of 'Mother of the country' (Landesmutter).

In July of 1878 the Princess came to England with the Grand Duke and children, and spent some weeks at Eastbourne. The doctors had insisted on a thorough change. During her stay there she endeared herself to high and low. She took the liveliest interest in all local institutions, helping where she could, and showing her personal sympathy with the poor by visiting their cottages. Before leaving Eastbourne she made the acquaintance of Mrs. Vicars, the founder of the Albion Home at Brighton. She herself paid a visit to that Home, and afterwards became its patroness. She had at first refused to do so, not that she did not take the deepest interest in that good work and long to help it on, but because she knew the prejudices existing against such homes. She was deeply impressed by Mrs. Vicars' 'wonderful knowledge and practical power, and by her loving gentle ways towards those poor girls;'[8] and this eventually induced her to take the Home under her protection. She wrote as follows to Mrs. Vicars:

[8] Princess Alice's own words.

'Dear Mrs. Vicars,   'New Palace, Darmstadt.

'I have returned from visiting the Home, so convinced of your excellent management of it in every respect, that, if you still feel my becoming Patroness of the Home (and of the Ladies' Association connected with it) can further the good and noble work, I am most willing to comply with your request. The spirit of true, loving, Christian sympathy in which the work was begun by you, and with which it is carried out; the cheerfulness you impart, the motherly solicitude you offer to those struggling to return to a better life, cannot fail to restore in a great measure that feeling of self-respect so necessary to those voluntarily seeking once more a virtuous life, and by so doing regaining the respect of their fellow-creatures. "Inasmuch as ye have done it unto one of the least of these my brethren, ye have done it unto Me." In this spirit may the Home, as well as the Association connected with it, continue its good work. My entire sympathy and good wishes will ever be with it.

                                  'Ever yours truly,
                                           'ALICE.'

After having settled at home again, the Princess threw herself with renewed zeal into her work. During her last visit to England she was full of admiration for Miss Octavia Hill, whose acquaintance she had made in England in 1877, and entirely entered into the spirit of her great undertaking, sharing her view 'that we must become the friends of the poor to be their benefactors.' The Princess was anxious to work on 'the same lines' as Miss Hill, and to see similar efforts made in improving the dwellings and condition of the poor at Darmstadt.

Several of the Princess's own family visited her at Darmstadt during the autumn, the very last of them being Prince Leopold. Her happiness at having what she called 'a bit of home and of England' with her always seemed to give her fresh strength. But she had scarcely had time to realise how great the happiness of those visits had been before an awful and sudden calamity broke in upon her. On the 8th of November, Princess Victoria was seized with diphtheria; Princess Alix took it next, then little Princess May, after her Princess Irène, then Prince Ernest and the Grand Duke.

The following touching and beautiful account of those dark days will speak for itself, and will only deepen the love and admiration already felt for the beloved Princess. The account is written by a great personal friend of hers, Miss Macbean, who never left her during that dreadful time, and whose devotion to her cannot be too much appreciated. Miss Macbean's family had settled at Darmstadt. The Princess and the Grand Duke were very intimate with them, and always considered them amongst their best and truest friends. Princess Alice's own lady-in-waiting happened to be away on leave when the illness broke out, and Miss Macbean was, as often previously, doing the duty for her.[9]

---

[9] Miss Macbean left the Princess, to return to England, at the Princess's express wish, after the Grand Duke and Prince Ernie were convalescent. The Princess was anxious her dear friend should have a thorough change and rest after all she had gone through. This is only another proof of the Princess's unselfish thought for those who were about her.

'We were having five o'clock tea on Tuesday afternoon, the 5th of November, 1878, the Grand Duke and Duchess and myself—they were both in particularly good spirits—and afterwards we all sat some time talking, the Princess as usual on her sofa. She said, "Katie, you have had the mumps; isn't it awful pain? I believe Victoria is going to have them; she has got such a stiff neck, and her glands seem giving her great pain. Fancy if we are all ill with the mumps, because I believe it is very infectious." Then she called in Princess Victoria, who was reading to all her sisters and Prince Ernie in the next room. Princess Victoria did not hear the call, and I got up and went to tell her. I saw her sitting on the sofa, with Princesses Ella, Irène, Alix, and May, and Prince Ernie in a circle close round her, listening intently to a story she was reading to them. I thought Princess Victoria looked flushed and not very well; she said her neck was rather painful, and she couldn't move her head comfortably about. The subject was then dropped, as little Princess May was asking her mother ("Mother dear," as Her Royal Highness was teaching her to call her) for some cake and a little tea, and then she begged me to play, for them all to dance. Her Royal Highness was reading *Sarchedon*, and I asked her if it would disturb her, but she said no, she enjoyed it; so I sat down to the piano and played every description of thing I could remember, over and over again, and the children all danced in the next room for about half an hour. They were then all sent to bed, Princess Victoria not being allowed to kiss the others on account of the "mumps." . . . The next morning Miss Jackson,[1] Herr v. Dadelsen,[2] and I were in the schoolroom, when the Princesses came up from breakfast. Princess Victoria came up to me, and we talked for some time, each of us perched on the

---

[1] Governess to the young Princesses.
[2] Tutor to the Hereditary Grand Duke.

edge of the table; she kept on whispering to me and telling me "secrets." I noticed she looked rather strange, and her neck was so stiff she could not move her head, but she said nothing. The Grand Duchess sent for me, and I ran downstairs. She at once said, "I can't think what is the matter with Victoria; at breakfast just now it was such pain to her to swallow that it made her cry, and her throat was so painful she ate nothing." The doctor came that morning, and at once ordered her to be shut up away from the others, and towards luncheon-time we heard it was diphtheria. The Grand Duchess was much alarmed, as Princess Victoria got much worse in the afternoon (that was Wednesday, the 6th of November), and also because, as they had all been at breakfast together, the fear was that she had given it to the other children. Thursday and Friday she continued very ill. Friday the doctor told the dear Grand Duchess he hoped to pull her through. Then the illness did not strike one in its horrible strength, hers being the first case, and the doctor not saying very much about it to Her Royal Highness. I hardly left her those days; she had the children a great deal with her, and I don't think she took in that the little ones, her pets, could be taken ill. We went to church as usual on Sunday morning; we were then all taking disinfectants, and no one was allowed to come into the palace on account of infection, nor was I allowed to go home.

'The Grand Duchess and I went out driving as usual on the following Monday, the 11th of November, and that evening we were rather uneasy about Princess Alix, as she did not appear to be very well, and on coming down to Her Royal Highness's room the next morning, she told me that she had been called up to see her at two o'clock in the morning, and on looking at her throat had seen large patches of white membrane; she had at once sent for the doctor, who declared she had taken it in a very violent form. Her Royal Highness was dreadfully anxious, as one of the little ones had got it, and her great fear was that Princess May should have the horrible illness. The little one came into Her Royal Highness's bedroom at about half-past eight, and rushed up to her mother, clambered on to the bed, and kissed her. I sat on the floor, and we played a long time, close to Her Royal Highness's bed, and she watched us and kept on saying "My sweet Maysie." The little one climbed all over me, on my back and shoulders. I thought I had never seen her look so well or in such high spirits, or such a dear sweet little thing as she was that morning romping with me. After breakfast the Princess and I went out, and on going downstairs we saw Princesses Ella, Irène, and May, and Prince Ernest all at the top of the stairs going down also for their drive. Little Princess May smiled and looked so sweet in the little blue hat and ulster she nearly always wore, with her little face covered with dimples and looking the picture of health. At about 12 A.M. Joey[3] came into Her Royal Highness's sitting-room, and said Princess May did not seem at all well. Her Royal Highness gave me a look that said what she had feared had come; she started up at once and went to the nursery, and there was little Princess May in high fever and spots in her throat. Her Royal Highness was very quiet though deadly anxious, but the little thing was so strong naturally, and in such good health, that we hoped and almost believed she would be spared. She had it so badly from the first that all our thoughts were given to her. The Princess Alix was very ill. That was Tuesday. On Wednesday morning I was writing a note about half-past nine, when Her Royal Highness came in; she looked *so* ill and worn and wretched, and threw herself down into a chair, and burst into tears, and said, "Oh, if only my little May is left to me, my little pet, my darling with her precious dimples and loving ways!"

---

[3] Nurserymaid.

She was utterly miserable, but so good and patient. Dr. Eigenbrodt said I ought to go home, but I would not. Her Royal Highness said she was so thankful to have me. Princess Ella and Miss Jackson had been sent the day before to Princess Charles', and Prince Ernie with M. von Dadelsen on the Wednesday. She had ordered the pony carriage at eleven, and then we drove to the Exercirplatz, because she thought the air was so good there. She was so dear and sweet, and said how changed she was in her way of thinking on religion, and how now she was able to bear things much more patiently. All that day Princess May became worse. Every morning the doctor looked at our throats—she said, "just to be on the safe side. I am quite sure I shall not take the illness."

'The next morning, Thursday, Princess Irène was down with the diphtheria; she had been taken ill in the middle of the night, and about ten o'clock the same day Prince Ernie was brought back to the palace, down with the illness too. Princess Victoria was now recovering. After breakfast Her Royal Highness and I drove to her hospital to get a cold-water cushion for Princess May, as her fever was so dreadfully high. Fräulein Helmsdörfer tried to comfort Her Royal Highness in saying that they had had many as bad a case and had cured them, but Her Royal Highness was very anxious; she went often to the door of Princess May's room, but was not allowed in. Princess Ella was quite well, but kept entirely away from the palace. On Thursday evening Her Royal Highness and I went to the service in the English church; special services they were having every day now, and in the other churches the same. They had nearly all her favourite hymns, and when we got home she made me mark them for her in her hymn-book. The last two or three evenings she had sent for Mr. Sillitoe [4]

---

[4] English chaplain at Darmstadt.

to read prayers in her room, and she found it such a comfort, she said—she did not think she could have borne it all without them; they were some beautiful prayers for strength for the sick. Friday was an awful day; all the day the little one continued to get worse, and though very quiet and calm, the Princess was nearly mad with anxiety and fear, but even then always thinking of others and what she could do for them. God gave her wonderful strength to bear it all. All that day we feared the worst, and Princess May's life, and Princess Irène's as well, were hanging on a thread. I had luncheon with the Grand Duke and Duchess, as I had for the last three days, and he was in a wild state of what seemed excitement; he was dreadfully flushed and hot, and said he couldn't swallow, but kept on whistling and singing all the time. We thought it looked very bad, but Her Royal Highness tried to laugh at him, and told him the port he had been drinking had flushed his face, and some hazel nuts he had been eating that morning were the cause of his sore throat. However, he laughed, and said he was going to be ill, teasing me very much all the time. He sent for a housemaid and had a fire made in the next bedroom (the Crown Princess's bedroom), and directly after lunch went and lay down, saying he was going to sleep. Her Royal Highness said, "Well, Katie, you and I are the only ones now left who are not ill, and we must not be ill, there is so much to be done and seen after."

Whenever she was not going about seeing after the others, she was lying on her sofa, but too anxious to read or do anything, and I always sat on a chair by her. That evening the little one was almost hopelessly ill, but at about half-past seven she improved a little; she always said, "If my little one is only left me! What should I do if she were taken away?" I stayed with her till late that night. She looked so sad and worn.

'Next morning, at about five o'clock, Frau Kantner[5] came to my door and said the Grand Duchess wished me to go down to her room. I went down, and straight up to her bed; she was half sitting up, her face ghastly white; she put out both her arms, and drew me to her, and whispered, "She is gone; my little darling is dead," and then burst into tears. And then she told me how it was: that in the middle of the night Dr. Eigenbrodt had come into her room and said there had been an accident, a piece of membrane had crossed the windpipe of the little one, choked her, and in a moment she was gone; that she (the Grand Duchess) had rushed into the nursery, but that it was too late; she sat by the little one a long time, then kissed her and left her, and had spent those hours of misery by herself, and then sent for me. She said, "It is God's will, but oh that He should have taken that one, my greatest joy and delight in life my sweet, sweet little May-flower! Do you remember the last time we saw her well, at the top of the stairs before going out driving, and her face covered with those bewitching little dimples?" She continued talking about her for some time, and what she dreaded was having to tell the Grand Duke, which she thought she must do almost directly, as he kept on asking after Princess May. She was very quiet after we had talked about the little one for some time, and made an effort to remain calm; at last she said, "I must go and tell him; you remain here," and sat up in bed saying, "Come and kneel down, and let us ask God for strength for me to tell him and bear it." Then she got up quite quietly, and went to the Grand Duke's room, where she stayed about a quarter of an hour, after which she came back and got into bed again. She told me that when she had told him, at first he would not believe it, and he then gave a great cry. She said it was heartrend-

[5] Princess's own housemaid.

ing to see his awful grief, and then she herself broke down afresh. She said, "My little darling! I have said they are not to dress her out, and have told Orchy[6] only to put on her little nightgown, and have given one of my lace handkerchiefs for her feet." She spoke about it quite quietly, and seemed to make an effort to do so, and then said, "She was so especially beloved because she was the baby and the nearest to me, and used to kiss and pet me as none of the others do, I suppose because they are older."

'I don't quite know how we got through that day. She had Herr von Westerweller, and arranged all about the funeral. It was a sort of quiet despair, and she did not seem to comprehend or take it in that "the little one" was gone. That whole day, and for some days after, Prince Ernie's life hung on a thread; and she used to say, "Only not him too; if my boy is taken I shall die too; surely it is enough to give up *one* child, my best loved little one;" and she would lie with clasped hands and closed eyes quite quiet for a long time, till I roused her. Prince Ernie did not improve, but continued almost getting worse, and the suspense was dreadful. She was not able to tell the other children, as they were not strong enough, and she dreaded so having to tell them, especially Prince Ernie, as little Princess May was his special favourite, and they all kept talking of her and sending her their toys. All Saturday and Sunday passed, I don't know how; I never left her except to write letters for her, and she said she wished to have no one with her but me. The service and funeral was to be that (Monday) afternoon, a short private service taking place in the palace at three o'clock. I asked her in the morning if it would not be a great relief when the day was over, and she said, "Oh no, why should it be? It will be worse after to-day; it is her last day at home, and to-day they take her

---

[6] Nurse, who had been with the children since 1866.

away from me altogether." She was very quiet, almost cheerful, and told me at the service I was to stand directly behind her, and follow after her next into the room. She said two or three times, "I am so glad it is such a fine bright day for her to go out there (to Rosenhöhe), such bright sunshine, and the birds singing like a spring day—just such a day as she always liked so much." She spoke very little, and always with her eyes fixed on the sky, and then they would fill with tears; and once she said, "Fancy having *two* up there in that blue sky, two of my little angels. I wonder if they know that 'mother dear' is looking at them, and if my two sweet little loves are looking down at me! Only no more, not Ernie. I could not bear that; it would kill me to have to give him up too." She then went into her room, putting on the long crape veil that was customary for funerals. Frau Strecker and Fräulein Helmsdörfer were waiting outside in the passage; and just before it was time to go down to the service she sent the maid out of her room, and turned round to me, and said, "It is *so* hard to bear, but let us ask God to give me strength. My Maysie, my sweet little flower, they take my heart away with you this afternoon—away for ever! Never to see her face again, or to feel her sweet kisses on my face, all blank and dreary!" Then she was quite calm, and said, "Now we must go down; keep close to me all the time, and if I kneel down be ready to help me up, as I feel so weak."

'It was a lovely afternoon, and the sun streamed in through the glass front door. At the bottom of the staircase, and in rows facing us as we went down, stood all the gentlemen of the Court, and gentlemen filling official posts, and on each side of the staircase her servants. Past them you saw into Prince Alfred's room where they had put her "little one," the curtains of the room drawn, and in the centre the coffin raised and quite buried in masses of white flowers, on either side large candles burning, and at the head great palm plants. She walked into the room, her face looking like a mask, and I kept close to her during the service; on the other side of the room were all the gentlemen who had moved in. Just after the clergyman had finished the service she knelt down close by the coffin and prayed for a few minutes, then took up a corner of the white satin pall in her hands and kissed it, and got up and walked upstairs again; halfway up she turned round and looked into the hall and said, "They are going to take her out of that door, where she has often gone, but after to-day she will never come in or go out again." The carriage (Her Royal Highness's own) was waiting outside in the porch, and they were carrying the flowers out as fast as they could. She then went to the top of the stairs and told me to watch till they brought "her" out, and then tell her, which I did, and she knelt down and looked (and *how* she looked!) through the banisters, and watched them putting her into the carriage; and then she and I went into the Grand Duke's sitting-room, and watched it all going out of the gates. After that she was wonderfully quiet, and went and saw the Grand Duke.'

The Princess seemed to feel with renewed keenness the loss of Princess May after Prince Ernest began to recover. Whilst he was so ill she had to keep from him the death of his favourite little sister, and the mere fact of having to do so seemed to help her over those first sad days; for her only thought, then as ever, was to try and help the loved husband and children, whom she would so gladly have sheltered from all suffering and grief.

On the 6th of December the Grand Duke and Prince Ernest were sufficiently recovered to go out in a close carriage, and it was on that day too that Princess Alice wrote for the last time to her mother. It was the intention that the whole family should go in a few days to Heidelberg for change of air. The Princess herself was most anxious for this move, and had personally made all the arrangements for it. On the afternoon of the 7th of December, hearing that the Duchess of Edinburgh would pass through Darmstadt with her children on her way to England, Princess Alice went to the station to see her. She had complained all day of a very bad headache, but did not seem otherwise more than usually ailing. That evening, however, the first symptoms of that fatal illness declared themselves, and the next morning the doctors confirmed the fact of its being diphtheria. The case was a most severe one from the first, and the Princess's weakened delicate state made all specially anxious as to the course it would take.

When first taken ill she had quite given up all hope of her recovery, and she occupied herself in writing numerous directions down on slips of paper for the Grand Duke, also several wishes in case of her death. As the illness, however, assumed a more and more hopeless aspect, the Princess herself said she felt better, and also that she was convinced she would 'get through it.' She suffered terribly, but through it all her patience, gentleness, and unselfishness, as ever, made themselves felt; there never was a thought for herself, only sympathy and consideration for all around.

The Grand Duke was still so weak that he could not be as constantly with her as he would have wished, but she was tended with untiring devotion by her nurses, her lady in waiting, and mother-in-law. On Friday morning, the 13th, the doctors gave up all hope, and broke it to the poor husband. All that day she remained perfectly conscious, and, as it seemed, unaware of her extreme danger. She was able to see her mother-in-law that afternoon, and derived much pleasure from her visit. Her joy, too, when the Grand Duke entered her room, was most touching to see, and she bade him 'good night' with her usual bright smile and with tender words of inquiry after his health. He knew but too well those were the last words he would ever hear from her loved lips, and yet, fearful of agitating her or causing her pain, he bade her 'good-night' as if he should meet her on the morrow. She slept off and on through the day, and took all the nourishment given her, yet all was in vain; all the skill and the untiring efforts of the doctors could not save that precious life. Almost the last thing she did was to read a letter from her mother brought her that afternoon by Sir William Jenner (who had been sent over by the Queen); she then composed herself to rest, saying, 'Now I will go to sleep again.' From that sleep she passed into unconsciousness, murmuring to herself as a tired child would do, 'From Friday to Saturday—four weeks—May—dear papa!' Those were her last words, and early on the morning of the 14th of December she passed away in her sleep from the world where she had suffered so much, yet where she had been so happy and so blessed, to that home above where 'God shall wipe away all tears from their eyes; and there shall be no more death, neither sorrow nor crying, neither shall there be any more pain, for the former things are passed away.'

On the following Tuesday evening, the 17th of December, the loved remains of the Grand Duchess were taken to the chapel in the 'Schloss' (Grandducal castle), and the next evening to the mausoleum at the Rosenhöhe. (Her two brothers the Prince of Wales and Prince Leopold, as well as her brother-in-law Prince Christian of Schleswig-Holstein, were present.) There she rests between those two children she had loved so well and lost awhile.'

LETTERS.

1862

Beloved Mama,   Royal Yacht : July 9.

Before leaving the yacht I must send you a few lines to wish you once more good-bye, and to thank you again and again for all your kindness to us.

My heart was very full when I took leave of you and all the dear ones at home; I had not the courage to say a word—but your loving heart understands what I felt.

                                           Darmstadt : July 13.

Yesterday, after we reached Bingen, all the Hessian officers of state received us. At every station we received fresh people, and had to speak to them. At Mayence also the beautiful Austrian band played whilst we waited, in pouring rain, which only ceased as we reached Darmstadt. The station before, the Grand Duke, Prince and Princess Charles with their children, Prince Alexander and his wife, received us—all most kind and cordial.

At the station we were again received; the whole town so prettily decked out; the Bürger [Burgesses Escort] rode near our carriage; countless young ladies in white, and all so kind, so loyal: in all the speeches kind and touching allusions were made to you, and to our deep grief. I believe the people never gave so hearty a welcome. We two drove together through the town; incessant cheering and showering of flowers. We got out at Prince and Princess Charles's house, where the whole family was assembled.

We then went to our rooms, which are very small, but so prettily arranged, with such perfect taste, all by my own dear Louis; they look quite English.

We then drove to Bessungen for dinner *en famille*. . . .

We were listening to twelve Sängervereine [Choral Unions] singing together yesterday evening—two hundred people; it was most beautiful, but in pouring rain. Some came upstairs dripping to speak to us. The Grand Duke gave me a fine diamond bracelet he and his wife had ordered for me, and showed me all over his rooms.

To-morrow we receive the Standesherren [Princes and Counts] and the gentlemen of both Houses.

My thoughts, rather *our* thoughts, are constantly with you, beloved Mama. Please give my love to all at home; it is impossible to write to them all.

July 16.

. . . It is extremely hot here. The last two days we rode out at eight in the morning in the wood, where the air is very pleasant, near the ground where the troops are drilled. On Monday we looked on, and the soldiers were so much flattered.

At half-past one on Monday we received the gentlemen of the Upper House, then the Lower House, then the Flügeladjutanten [aides-de-camp], then the Stadtvorstand [Town Council], then about seventy officers, then a deputation of the English here. All these people I had to speak to *en grande toilette*, and at four we drove to a large dinner at the Schloss. The Grand Duke led me, and I always sit near him.

Yesterday at three the whole family drove to Seeheim,

a lovely place in the mountains, to dinner with the Grand Duke. In the two villages we passed, flowers were showered upon us, and the Pfarrer [clergyman] made a speech.

I am really deeply touched by the kindness and enthusiasm shown by the people, which is said to be quite unusual. They wait near the house to see us, and cheer constantly—even the soldiers.

We then drove for tea, which is always at eight, to Jugenheim to Prince Alexander, whose birthday it was, and did not get home till ten.

The whole family are very amiable towards me, and Prince Alexander is most clever and amusing.

Darling Louis is very grateful for your kind messages. We talk and think of you often, and then my heart grows very heavy. Away from home I cannot believe that beloved Papa is not there; all is so associated with him.

Beloved Mama, July 19.

Many thanks for your last kind letter, and all the news from home; dear Baby [Princess Beatrice] is the only one you have mentioned nothing of, and I think of her so often.

Some people are coming to us at one, and then the whole Ministerium [Administration]. It is really so difficult to find something to say to all these people, and they stand there waiting to be spoken to.

Yesterday we received a deputation from Giessen, with a very pretty dressing-case they brought us as a present.

On Thursday we went incognito with Prince Alexander and his wife to Frankfurt. The town is decked out most beautifully, and countless Schützen [riflemen] are walking about in their dress. We dined at the Palais and then sat in the balcony.

I have just taken leave of dear Lady Churchill and General Seymour.[1] They have made themselves most popular here, and the people have been very civil to them.

Louis and I have begun reading *Westward Ho!* together.

The Grand Duke went all the way to Kranichstein for me the other day, and walked about till he was quite hot. He has forbidden my visiting the other places until his return, as he wishes to lead me about there himself. I do not see very much of the other relations save at meals; and, having our own carriages, we two drive together mostly alone. We have tea usually out of doors in some pretty spot we drive to.

These lines will find you in Windsor. I went out this morning and tried to find some of those pretty wreaths to send you, but could get none. Please put one in St. George's[2] from me. It is the first time you go to that hallowed spot without me; but in thought and prayer I am with you. May God strengthen and soothe you, beloved Mama, and may you still live to find some ray of sunshine on your solitary path, caused by the love and virtue of his children, trying, however faintly, to follow his glorious example!

I do strive earnestly and cheerfully to do my duty in my new life, and to do all that is right, which is but doing what dear Papa would have wished.

July 20.

Thousand thanks for your dear long letter of the 18th just received. How well do I understand your feelings! I was so sad myself yesterday, and had such intense long-

---

[1] Afterwards Marquis of Hertford, who died on the 25th of January, 1884.

[2] St. George's Chapel, Windsor, where the Prince Consort rested until removed to the Mausoleum at Frogmore.

ing after a look, a word from beloved Papa! I could bear it no longer. Yet *how* much worse is it not for you! You know, though, dear Mama, *he* is watching over you, waiting for you. The thought of the future is the one sustaining, encouraging point for all. 'They who sow in tears shall reap in joy;' and great joy will be yours hereafter, dear Mama, if you continue following that bright example. . . .

We usually get up about a quarter or half-past seven, and take some coffee at eight. Then we either go out till ten or remain at home, and till twelve I write and arrange what I have to do.

At one, when we return from breakfast, we usually read together. I have still a great many people to see, and they usually come at two.

At four is dinner, and at half-past five we are usually back here, and occupy ourselves till six or seven, then drive out somewhere for tea at eight, walk about, and return at a quarter or half-past ten. We do not waste our time, I assure you, and Louis has a good deal to do at this moment.

Mr. Theed's bust of dear Papa must be very lovely. I am curious to hear what you think of Marochetti's.[3] It will be very sad for you to see.

A fortnight already I am here, and away from my dear home three weeks! How much I shall have to tell you when we meet. My own dear Mama, I do love you so much! You know, though silent, my love and devotion to you is deep and true. If I could relinquish part of my present happiness to restore to you some of yours, with a full heart would I do it; but God's will be done! God sustain my precious mother! is the hourly prayer of her loving and sympathising child.

[3] The recumbent statue of the Prince Consort, now in the Mausoleum at Frogmore.

July 24.

. . . You tell me to speak to you of *my* happiness—our happiness. You will understand the feeling which made me silent towards you, my own dear bereaved Mother, on that point; but you are unselfish and loving and can enter into my happiness, though I could never have been the first to tell you how intense it is, when it must draw the painful contrast between your past and present existence. If I say I love my dear husband, that is scarcely enough—it is a love and esteem which increases daily, hourly; which he also shows to me by such consideration, such tender loving ways. What was life before to what it has become now? There is such blessed peace being at his side, being his wife; there is such a feeling of security; and we two have a world of our own when we are together, which *nothing* can touch or intrude upon. My lot is indeed a blessed one; and yet what have I done to deserve that warm, ardent love which my darling Louis ever shows me? I admire his good and noble heart more than I can say. How he loves you, you know, and he will be a good son to you. He reads to me every day out of *Westward Ho!* which I think very beautiful and interesting.

This morning I breakfasted alone, as he went out with his regiment. I always feel quite impatient until I hear his step coming upstairs, and see his dear face when he returns.

Yesterday, and the previous night, I thought of you constantly, and of our last journey together to dear Balmoral. Sad, painful though it was, I liked so much being with you, trying to bear some of your load of sorrow with you. From here I share all as if I were really by your side; and I think so many fervent prayers cannot be offered to a merciful loving God without His sending alleviation and comfort.

Please remember me to Grant, Brown, and all of them at home in dear Scotland, and tell them how much I wish, and Louis also, that we were there, changed though everything is.

Darmstadt: August 1.

... My heart feels ready to burst when I think of such sorrow as yours. I pray my adored Louis may long be spared to me. If you only knew how dear, how loving he is to me, and how he watches over me, dear darling!

To-morrow we go to Coburg, which was an old promise. Dear Uncle[4] sent only two days ago to say he left Coburg on the 5th, and would we not come before? You will understand that, happy beyond measure as I am to go there, a lump always comes into my throat when I think of it—going for the first time with Louis to dear Papa's house, where but recently he showed us everything himself.[5] Dear Mama, I think I can scarcely bear it—the thought seems so hard and cruel. He told us as children so much of Coburg, spoke to us of it with such childlike affection, enjoyed so much telling us every anecdote connected with each spot; and now these silent spots seem to plead for his absence.

To see the old Baron [Stockmar] will be a great happiness, and that Louis should make his acquaintance.

Calenberg bei Coburg: August 4.

Once more in dear Coburg, and you can fancy with what feelings. Everything reminds me of beloved Papa and of our last happy visit.

---

[4] Duke of Saxe-Coburg Gotha.
[5] This was in the autumn of 1860.

We are living here, and yesterday we spent all the afternoon and dined at the Rosenau. It was a lovely day, and the view so beautiful. We went all over the house and walked about in the grounds. We walked to dear Papa's little garden, and I picked two flowers there for you, which I enclose.

Every spot brought up the remembrance of something dear Papa had told us of his childhood; it made me so sad, I can't tell you. Uncle Ernest was also sad, but so kind and affectionate, and they both seemed so pleased at our having come.

Everything about dear Papa's illness, and then of the sad end, I had to tell. I lived the whole dreadful time over again, and wonder, whilst I speak of it, that we ever lived through it.

At nine o'clock Church service was in the pretty little chapel. Holzei read, and Superintendent Meyer preached a most beautiful sermon, the text being where our Saviour told His disciples they must become as a little child to enter into the kingdom of heaven. He spoke with his usual fervour, and it was most impressive. I saw him afterwards, and he inquired very much after you.

We are going after breakfast to the Festung, and then Louis and I are going to see the dear Baron [Stockmar].

August 9.

Next Monday we are going to Auerbach, to live there for a little time. It lies in the Bergstrasse, and is very healthy. The Grand Duke allows us to inhabit one of the houses.

August 16.

... How I long to read what Mr. Helps has written about Papa! What can it be but beautiful and elevating, if he has rightly entered into the spirit of that pure and noble being?[6]

Oh, Mama! the longing I sometimes have for dear Papa surpasses all bounds. In thought he is ever present and near me; still we are but mortals, and as such at times long for him also. Dear good Papa! Take courage, dear Mama, and feel strong in the thought that you require all your moral and physical strength to continue the journey which brings you daily nearer to *Home* and to *Him*! I know how weary you feel, how you long to rest your head on his dear shoulder, to have him to soothe your aching heart. You will find this rest again, and how blessed will it not be! Bear patiently and courageously your heavy burden, and it will lighten imperceptibly as you near him, and God's love and mercy will support you. Oh could my feeble words bring you the least comfort! They come from a trusting, true and loving heart, if from naught else.

Auerbach: August 16.

. . . We do feel for you so deeply, and would wish so much to help you, but there is but One who can do that, and you know whom to seek. He will give you strength to live on till the bright day of reunion. . . .

Auerbach: August 21.

. . . Our visit to Giessen[7] went off very well. The people were most loyal. We went to see the Gymnasts, and Louis walked about amongst them, which pleased them very much. He is very popular there, and I am very glad we both went, for it made a good impression.

[6] This refers to Mr., afterwards Sir, Arthur Helps's Introduction to the *Collected Addresses and Speeches of the Prince Consort*, which was then about to be published (Murray, 1862).

[7] During a Musical and Gymnastic Festival.

We drove to Louis' property, Stauffenberg, a beautiful (alas! ruined) castle, which by degrees he is having restored, and which will be a charming house for us, if it is finished, which can only be done gradually.

Auerbach: August 23.

. . . Try and gather in the few bright things you have remaining and cherish them, for, though faint, yet they are types of that infinite joy still to come. I am sure, dear Mama, the more you try to appreciate and to find the good in that which God in His love has *left* you, the more worthy you will daily become of that which is in store. That earthly happiness you had is indeed gone for ever, but you must not think that every ray of it has left you. You have the privilege, which dear Papa knew so well how to value, in your exalted position, of doing good and living for others, of carrying on his plans, his wishes into fulfilment, and as you go on doing your duty, this will, this must, I feel sure, bring you peace and comfort. Forgive me, darling Mama, if I speak so openly; but my love for you is such that I cannot be silent, when I long so fervently to give you some slight comfort and hope in your present life.

I have known and watched your deep sorrow with a sympathising, though aching heart. Do not think that absence from you can still that pain. My love for you is strong, is constant; I would like to shelter you in my arms, to protect you from all future anxiety, to still your aching longing! My own sweet Mama, you know I would give my life for you, could I alter what you have to bear!

Trust in God! ever and constantly. In *my* life I feel that to be my stay and my strength, and the feeling increases as the days go on. My thoughts of the future are bright, and this always helps to make the minor worries and sorrows of the present dissolve before the warm rays of that light which is our guide.

Auerbach: August 25.

. . . To-day is the Ludwigstag, a day kept throughout the country, and on which every Ludwig receives presents, &c.; but we spend it quite quietly. Louis' parents and the others are coming to breakfast, and remain during the day. Louis is out riding. We always get up early. He rides whilst I write, and we then walk together and breakfast somewhere out of doors.

We went to the little church here yesterday, which is very old, and they sang so well.

I drew out of doors also, as it was very fine; but it is very difficult, as it is all green, and the trees are my misfortune, as I draw them so badly. I play sometimes with Christa;[8] she plays very well.

August 26 [Prince Consort's Birthday].

With a heavy heart do I take up my pen to write to you to-day—this dear day, now so sad, save through its bright recollections. I cannot bear to think of it now, with no one to bring our wishes to, with that painful silence where such mirth and gaiety used to be. It is very hard to bear, and the first anniversary is like the commencement of a new epoch in our deep sorrow.

When your dear present was brought to me this morning, I could not take my eyes from it, though they were blinded with tears. Oh, those beautiful, those loved features! There wants but his kind look and word to make the picture alive! Thousand thanks for it, dear Mama.

How trying this day will be for you! My thoughts are

---

[8] The Princess's lady, Baroness Christa Schenck.

constantly with you, and I envy the privilege the others have in being near you and being able to do the least thing for you.

The sun shines brightly in the still blue sky; how bright and peaceful it must be where our dear Spirit dwells, if it is already so beautiful here.

September 5.

... Two days ago, Louis and I went to Worms. Whilst he went to his regiment, which the Grand Duke came to inspect, I went to the Dom, which is most beautiful; and then went in a little boat on the Rhine, which was charming. It took us, driving, an hour and a half from Auerbach to Worms.

Auerbach: September 7.

... For Louis' birthday we are going to Darmstadt; it is getting cold and damp here, and the house is small. We take our meals in another house, and it is cold to walk over there of an evening. Think of us on the 12th. It was such a happy day last year.[9]

I have such *Heimweh* [yearning] after beloved Papa; it is dreadful sometimes when I think of him and of our home. But he is so happy in his bright home, could we but catch a glimpse of him there. Dear Grandmama [the Duchess of Kent], too, is constantly in my thoughts lately. I can see her before me—so dear, kind, and merry. As time goes on, such things only mingle themselves more vividly with one's usual life; for it is their *life* which is nearest us again, and not their *death*, which casts such a gloom over their remembrance.

Auerbach: September 11.

... How beautiful Heidelberg is! we went all over the Castle, and with such glorious weather. There is one

---

[9] Prince Louis was then at Balmoral.

side still standing, built and decorated by a pupil of Michael Angelo, which dear Papa admired so much. How do I miss not being able to talk to beloved Papa of all I see, hear, feel, and think! His absence makes such a gap in my existence.

Darmstadt: October 13.

. . . Our visit to Baden was charming, and dear Fritz and Louise [1] so kind! Louis and I were both delighted by our visit. The Queen, the Duchess of Hamilton, and Grand Duchess Hélène were there, besides dear Aunt [Princess Hohenlohe], and Countess Blücher. The two latter dear and precious as ever.

We left yesterday morning; spent three hours with Grand Duchess Sophie,[2] who is the most agreeable, clever, amiable person one can imagine. It gave me real pleasure to make her acquaintance. Aunt Feodore's house, though small, is really very pretty, and her rooms are hung full of pictures. I saw Winterhalter also, in his lovely new house, which he has gone and sold, saying it was too good for him. He has painted a most beautiful picture of the Grand Duchess Hélène—quite speaking.

. . . I am going to make my will before leaving. I do not like leaving (for England) without having done something.

Darmstadt: October 17.

First of all, thousand thanks from Louis and me for your having allowed dear Arthur[3] to come to us. I cannot tell you what pleasure it has been to me to have that dear child a little bit. He has won all hearts, and I am so

---

[1] Grand Duke and Grand Duchess of Baden.
[2] Grand Duchess of Baden, mother of the reigning Grand Duke.
[3] Duke of Connaught, then twelve years old.

proud when they admire my little brother, who is a mixture of you and adored Papa.

Darmstadt: October 23.

... We intend probably leaving this on Saturday, the 8th, remaining until the 10th at Coblenz, from whence we go direct in eleven hours and three-quarters to Antwerp, leaving Antwerp the morning of the 12th, to reach Windsor that evening or the next morning.

We always continue reading together, and have read *Hypatia*, a most beautiful, most interesting, and very learned and clever book, which requires great attention.

I have the great bore to read the newspapers every day, which I must do; see Dr. Becker[4] from eleven to twelve; then I write, and have constantly people to see, so that I have scarcely any time to draw or to play. I also read serious books to myself.

Louis would like to go to Leeds and Manchester from Osborne, as he wants to go to London from Windsor. I shall accompany him sometimes.

October 25.

As you come later to Windsor, we shall not leave till the 10th, remain the 11th with the Queen, then go direct to Antwerp. If the weather is bad we shall wait. Then on the 14th or 15th we shall be at Windsor, which we prefer to coming to Osborne. We hope this will suit you.

All are full of lamentations at our departure, and for so long, which is most natural; but they are very kind. We have a family dinner in our little room to-day, which is large enough for a few people. The Grand Duke has quite lost his heart to Arthur, and Bertie [Prince of Wales] pleased him also very much.

In talking together last night, Louis said what I feel so

---

[4] The Princess Alice's private secretary.

often, that he always felt as if it must come right again some time, and we should find dear Papa home again. In another *home* we shall.

October 30.

The Grand Duke was quite overcome when I gave him the photographs, and with Baby's [Princess Beatrice's] he is quite enchanted, and wishes me to tell you how grateful he is, and how much he thanks you. You cannot think *how* pleased he was, and the more so that *you* sent them him. He has a warm heart and feels very much for you, and takes warm interest in all my brothers and sisters.

I am glad you are going to see dear Fritz of Baden; he will be so pleased. We shall see Louise at Coblenz.

The plans for our house are come, and even the simplest is far above what we poor mortals can build.

November 6.

. . . Yesterday, Mrs. Combe, widow of George Combe and daughter of Mrs. Siddons, came to see me, and was some time with me. Such a clever, amiable old lady. It gave me such pleasure to see and talk with her. Will you tell Sir James Clark so, as she is an old friend of his?

1863

Dearest Mama, Marlborough House: May 14.

Our parting this morning was most painful to both of us—from you to whom we *owe* so much, and whom we love so dearly.

May God comfort and support you, beloved Mama, on your sad and weary pilgrimage!

Marlborough House: May 16.

I could not get your dear face and your sweet voice out of my mind for an instant, and everywhere I thought I must see you or dear Papa. It seemed so strange; I had the tears in my eyes all day. The worst was the Opera, for I had never been without you or Papa, and all was the same and yet so different! It was very trying to me; and so will the Drawing-room be to-day. . . . I saw Lady Jocelyn, Duchess of Manchester, Sir Charles Locock, and Lord Alfred Paget, to show them Baby, and all find her like what we all were. How much *we* have to thank for in her name. Your affection for her and all you have done for her have touched us more than I can say. It seemed to me quite wrong to take her from you.

On Wednesday, Alix [Princess of Wales] and myself go to the studios. This morning we drove in Battersea Park.

May 19.

. . . The Drawing-room was long, but Alix and I were not so tired, considering the length of time, for we stood, excepting twenty minutes, in the middle, when there was a block and the people could not come.

In to-day's letter you mention again your wish that we should soon be with you again. Out of the ten months of our married life five have been spent under your roof, so you see how ready we are to be with you. Before next year Louis does not think we shall be able to come; at any rate when we can we shall, and I hope we shall be able to see you for a day or two in Germany to divide the time.

Darmstadt: May 23.

. . . Baby[5] has been so much admired, and all the clothes you gave her.

[5] Princess Victoria of Hesse.

Darmstadt: May.

I shan't have time to write more than a few words, as we have just returned from church, and are going to Mayence till Wednesday. The Grand Duke came all the way to Kranichstein yesterday to go about with us, and see how to arrange it comfortably. He is most kind, and sat an hour with me.

We have received two deputations this morning, and my things, which ought to have been here before us, only arrived to-day.

Mayence: June 2.

Now when I return I shall have to unpack and pack again for Kranichstein, and arrange the house there, which has not been lived in for eighty years, so that for writing I have barely a moment.

I have good accounts of Baby, whom all the old gentlemen run out of their houses to look at when she walks in the garden, and try to tell Moffat [her nurse] what they think of her, but she of course understands nothing.

Darmstadt: June 3.

I write to you to-day, as Louis is going for all day to Worms to-morrow, and I am going to Jugenheim to Uncle Alexander. It is already warm here, and we are going in a day or two into the country.

The Queen of Prussia passes through here to-day, and I shall probably hear from her what her intentions are about England. I have received a splendid bracelet from the Empress of Russia—for Baby's picture. She is said to be far from well.

Darmstadt: June 6.

. . . Louis was away from four o'clock yesterday morning till eleven at night. He was at Worms with Uncle

Louis. Tuesday is his birthday, and we shall very likely go on Monday to Mayence, as Uncle Louis is always wishing for us.

I took a walk at Jugenheim yesterday with Uncle Alexander,[6] his wife and children, of more than two hours, and it was so beautiful, and numberless little birds singing. Uncle Alexander was so grateful for all your kindness, and was above all so charmed with you. It always makes me so happy to be able to talk about you, and to hear you appreciated as you ought to be, darling Mama.

June 8.

. . . Baby sits up quite strong, and looks about and laughs. She has got on wonderfully, and she is so good. She was an hour with us yesterday evening wide awake, and so good. She is as well and as strong as any child could be. To-day we go to Mainz, and to-morrow night from thence to Kranichstein. All our beds must be moved meanwhile, as there are none in the house.

Kranichstein: June 12.

Louis went at six this morning to Darmstadt for the inspection of his regiment by Uncle Louis. Princess Charles's birthday is on the 18th. The Grand Duke will be at Friedberg, and we are to go for the day, which will be rather tiring, as it is a good way by rail and back again, and we have to wait an hour at Frankfort.

Louis is going to take his seat in the Chamber on the 23rd. He was unable to do so last year, as we left for England two days before the time.

June 19.

. . . You ask me again if I occupy myself much and seriously? Not a moment of the day is wasted, and I

---

[6] Prince Alexander of Hesse, uncle of Prince Louis of Hesse.

have enough to read and to think about: what with the many and different papers, and interesting books. Dr. Becker comes daily, and I have a good deal to look after.

June 23.

... You will be amused to hear that I have taken a little black (a Malay) into my service. He is a dear good boy, was brought over two years ago by a gentleman, to whom he was given away by his own parents as a mark of gratitude for some service done. This man has had him here two years, but has never had him taught anything. He has no religion, and can neither read nor write. I am going to have him taught, and, later, christened. He is very intelligent, thirteen years old.

We shall remain here for the present; we go about a good deal seeing things near by, and then it is the first time we have our household and stable, so that on account of Haushaltung [housekeeping], &c., we are going to remain here for a little time. It is very pleasant besides, and constant moving is far too expensive for us. We give dinners here, which are also useful, as I know so few people. Some of the Standesherren are coming to-morrow, and later some of the Abgeordneten [Deputies] of the Second Chamber, which will give us an opportunity of making the acquaintance of some of the Liberals in the country.

I cannot get rid of my rheumatism, which is so unpleasant.

Louis is very busy; he reads to me sometimes out of Lord Macaulay's last volume of the English History, which I had not yet read. Twice a week Louis takes drill with his cavalry regiment, and he has to ride out at six in the morning, as it is some way off.

June 27.

... I bathe every morning and swim about; there is a nice little bathing-house.

I hear Baby shrieking out of doors; she does not cry very much, but she is very passionate. She was vaccinated two days ago by Dr. Weber, and I am going to be done next week; the small-pox is at Darmstadt, and a man died of it yesterday. Louis is very industrious and busy; he has all the papers of the Stände [State papers] to read and look through, and reads other useful books, besides papers and other things which he must read. He wrote to Lord Derby to express his thanks for having been made a Doctor at Oxford. He takes a great deal of exercise, riding, walking, rowing, swimming. We get up at six every morning, and go to bed after ten.

Louis has always a good deal to do at home, and a good many things which would never be expected of him in England. He knows the necessity and importance of working. I hope next month Uncle Ernest [7] will come to us for a day on his way back from Homburg. He has asked us for a few days to the Calenberg whilst you are in Germany, and then in the winter we hope to be for a few days at Gotha.

The Lützows,[8] and Miss Seymour dine with us to-day.

June 30.

To-morrow is our dear wedding-day. With what gratitude do I look back to that commencement of such happiness, and such real and true love, which even daily increases in my beloved husband. Oh! may we not be deprived of it too soon! I admire and respect him for his true-hearted,

---

[7] Duke of Saxe-Coburg-Gotha.

[8] Count Lützow was at this time the Austrian Minister and Plenipotentiary at the Court of Darmstadt.

generous, unselfish, and just nature! Oh, dear Mama, if you only knew how excellent he is! I wish I were good like him, for he is free from any selfish, small or uncharitable feelings. You should see how he is beloved by all his people; our servants adore him. I open my heart to you, who have so warm and sympathising a heart, that even in the midst of such deep grief and sorrow as yours will listen to what your children, who love you so dearly, long to say.

Our little one is grown so pretty; she has little pink cheeks, and is so fat and so good-humoured. I often think her like you when she smiles.

July 2.

You can fancy how much we thought of this day last year, and of you and all the love and kindness you showed us then. How truly we both love you, and, when we can, how willingly we shall come to your side, and be of the least use to you, you know, for I feel for you and with you, more than words can describe.

Our first large dinner yesterday went off very well. We make our arrangements, sitting, &c., all as you and dear Papa had it, which is new here, but, I am happy to say, approved of. We always dine at four. Baby appeared afterwards, and really never cries when she is shown, but smiles, and seems quite amused. She is immensely admired, particularly for her healthy appearance and fine large eyes. I really think her like you now; she is very much changed, and, when she sits up, looks so pretty and dear.

July 4.

Shortly we are going to pay Prince Solms-Lich, the President of the First Chamber, a visit. He is very liberal on the whole, rich, and a nice old gentleman. He knew

Grandpapa in the year 1820, also Uncle Charles, Uncle Hohenlohe, Aunt Feodore, and Eliza.[9] Lady Fife, Annie,[1] and Mr. Corbett from Frankfort are coming to us to-day.

The Grand Duke of Weimar was here yesterday for dinner at the Schloss.

What you say about Germany is so true; and Louis has the real good of his country near at heart. They always have to vote for or against what the Second Chamber brings forward, and the other day a vote was sent in from the Liberals for an alteration of a Press Law. Only one voice in the whole Chamber was for it, which was Louis', and this produced a very good effect among the Liberals. He is no coward, and will say what he thinks, if it is necessary, even if all are against him.

Kranichstein: July 15.

To-day is Uncle Alexander's birthday, and we have to drive for dinner to Seeheim. To-morrow morning we leave for Lich at five in the morning.

Two nights ago a horrid and *schauerliches* [appalling] event took place here. I went out about eight down to the pond, which is close to the house, to meet Louis. I met an odd-looking pale man, who neither bowed nor looked about, walking slowly along; and when I joined Louis he asked me if I had seen him, as he had been prowling about all the afternoon. We stopped a little longer, when at the end our grooms were running. We rowed on to see what was the matter, and on coming near, a body was floating in the water, the face already quite blue and lifeless. I recognised him at once. Louis and the others with trouble fished him out and laid him in our boat to bring him on shore. It was very horrid to see. We brought him on shore, tried

---

[9] Princess Hohenlohe's eldest daughter, who died at Venice.
[1] Lady Fife's eldest daughter, now Marchioness of Townsend.

all means to restore him to life, but of no avail. He was carried into the stable. He had committed suicide, and we heard afterwards that he was a very bad character. You can fancy that it was very unpleasant to me, to have that disfigured corpse next me in the boat: and it haunts me now—for a violent death leaves frightful traces, so unlike anything else. But half or quarter of an hour before, I had passed that man in life, and so shortly after to see him floating by quite lifeless! It brings death before one in its worst form, when one sees a *bad man* die by his own hand. The indifference with which the other people treated it, and dragged him along, was also revolting to one's feelings; but one must be manly, and not mind those things; yet I own it made me rather sick, and prevented my sleep that night.

I am glad we are going away for a few days; the change will be pleasant.

It was such a pleasure to me to have seen dear Lady Frances Baillie the other day, and she was looking well, though she is very thin.

You kindly gave me our dear Papa's Farm Book for the Farmers' Union here; the people are so touched and pleased. I send you the letter of thanks to read.

Lich: July 18.

. . . We leave to-morrow afternoon for Frankfort, and the next day we go to Homburg on the way home. The Prince and Princess are most kind and civil; they have a fine Schloss, and are rich. The latter is clever and amiable, and the young people—their nephews and nieces —are very nice and very kind. It is a fine rich country, and they seem very much beloved. The sister of the Princess, Princess Solms-Laubach, *née* Büdingen, is here also.

Her husband was in the Prussian service, and they lived at Bonn whilst dear Papa was there. He came to see them and to spend the evening there very often. She told me how handsome he then was, and how much praised and liked by all. She asked after Rath Florschütz,[2] after Eos,[3] and if dear Papa continued later on to be so sleepy of an evening, as he was even then.

Kranichstein: July 21.

Our visit at Lich went off very well. Everything is so 'vornehm' [in such good style] and so well arranged.

July 23.

We are going to give Heinrich[4] a rendezvous somewhere, perhaps at Kreuznach, which is not very far. On August 1 we are going to the north of the country—a part which I do not know—and on the way we stop at Giessen, where we have been invited to see an Agricultural Exhibition. On Monday we give a tea and a dance—between fifty and sixty people. The advantage of this place is its nearness to Darmstadt, and that there is room enough to receive people.

The Russian and French ambassadors, with their wives, and Mr. Corbett and Lord Robert S. Kerr, dine with us to-day.

July 27.

I have no news to give. To-night we give our first large party—seventy people.

August 1.

Yesterday we were all day at Rumpenheim: so kindly received! The Landgrave, his two brothers Frederic

---

[2] Tutor of the Prince Consort during his boyhood and early youth.

[3] A favourite greyhound of the Prince Consort's, which he brought to England at the time of his marriage.

[4] Prince Henry of Hesse, brother of Prince Louis.

and George, the Dowager Duchess of Mecklenburg-Strelitz, her daughter Duchess Caroline, Aunt Cambridge, Mary,[5] Augusta[6] and Adolphus;[7] Fritz[8] and Anna of Hesse and good Princess Louise,[9] kindness itself. Aunt Cambridge was very amiable, and spoke most tenderly of you. To-morrow morning Louis goes to Oberhessen, where I join him in two days. I go to see Uncle Alexander at Jugenheim; go on Monday to Friedberg, where there is an asylum for blind people, of which I am Protectorin [Patroness]. I go to see it, and sleep at the Castle. The next day I stop on my road to see Marburg, and shall be in the evening at Alsfeld, where I find Louis. The next day I go on to Herr von Riedesel at Altenburg, where I breakfast, and I dine and spend the night with another Riedesel family at Eisenbach. Louis joins me that evening. The next day we go on through the country, as the people are anxious to see us, and the country is very beautiful. On Thursday and Friday we shall be at Giessen, on Saturday at home.

Giessen: August 7.

I am very hot and tired; we have only just reached this place, and have to go out almost immediately to see the animals and machines.

Our journey has been most prosperous, but rather tiring, and the heat quite fearful. We were most kindly received everywhere. English, Hessian, German flags everywhere, and 'Gesangvereine' of an evening.

Last night we slept at Schotten, and posted from thence

---

[5] Princess Mary of Cambridge.
[6] Grand Duchess of Mecklenburg-Strelitz.
[7] Hereditary Grand Duke of Mecklenburg-Strelitz.
[8] Landgrave and Landgravin of Hesse.
[9] Princess Louise of Hesse, sister of the Duchess of Cambridge.

to-day through a lovely, rich, wooded and mountainous district, the Vogelsberg.

We have had but one room everywhere, and have remained only long enough at a place to see it, so that writing has been impossible. To-morrow evening we return to Kranichstein, and then I will write to you an account of everything. Here, with no time, and such heat and noise, it is impossible.

Kranichstein: August 9.

. . . We went, when I last wrote to you at Giessen, to see the different machines at work, in a crowd close round us and a smothering heat. It was interesting, though, in spite of all. The people cheered and were very civil. That day, at the meeting of the agriculturists, Count Laubach told me dear Papa's book lay on the table, and is of the greatest use and interest. I am so pleased to have been the first in Germany to make known something of Papa's knowledge in this science, one of the many in which dear Papa excelled. The people are so grateful to you for having sent it. In the evening the president and some other scientific gentlemen came to tea with us. I was so glad to see how pleased the people were at the interest Louis takes in these things. A procession was really very pretty; large carts, decorated with the different agricultural emblems, peasants in their different costumes—it was something quite new to me.

At Marburg, I saw in the beautiful church the grave of St. Elizabeth, the castle where she lived, and many other things which Kingsley mentions in his *Saint's Tragedy*.

This week the Emperor of Austria and other potentates came to Frankfort. The King of Prussia has refused, so that now, as it is not a universal meeting, it will not be what it might have been.

Buckingham Palace: October 28.

Thousand thanks for your dear lines! How sad that we should be reduced to writing again! It was such a happiness to speak to you, and in return to hear all you had to say—to try and soothe you, and try to make your burthen lighter. I always feel separation from you so much, for I feel for and with you, more, oh, far more, than I can ever express! I can only say again, trust, hope, and be courageous, and every day will bring something in the fulfilment of all your great duties—which will bring you peace, and make you feel that you are not forsaken, that God has heard your prayer, felt for you, as a loving Father would, and that dear Papa is not far from you.

Darmstadt: November 2.

Before going out (half-past six) I begin these lines. You will have heard what an awful passage we had. Christa and I had one of those cabins near the paddle-box, and good old May[1] was with us. Each wave that broke on the ship Christa and I groaned, and May exclaimed, 'Oh, goodness, gracious me! what an awful sea! Lord bless you, child, I hope it is all safe!' and so on. If we had not been so wretched, and had not looked so awful with those mountains of waves about us, I should have laughed. All the maids and Moffat were sick. Baby was sick all over her nice new shawl, which was a great grief.

Uncle Louis and Uncle Gustav received us at the station. My parents-in-law don't return till Wednesday. Yesterday Uncle Louis gave us a large dinner, and to-day he dines *en famille* in our house with Prince Adalbert of Bavaria, Uncle Gustav,[2] and ourselves.

[1] Mrs. Hull, a former nurse of the Princess and her brothers and sisters.
[2] Prince Gustav Wasa, first cousin to Prince Charles of Hesse.

I was quite done up by this journey. At four in the morning we changed carriages at Cologne, and did not get here till past twelve o'clock—twenty-nine hours under way.

November 5.

. . . Yesterday evening Louis and I were at a chemical lecture, which was very interesting, by young Hallwachs, the brother of the one Becker spoke to you about.

Our house is getting on very well, and we are often there.

Louis is very grateful and touched by your kind message, and kisses your hand. He is often away for those tiresome Jagden [shooting-parties] from five in the morning till eight at night, as it is some way off.

November 14.

It is not yet eight, and I have such cold fingers. The messenger leaves at nine—so I must write now. We are going to Mayence to-day, to see a house of our architect, Kraus, which is said to be very pretty and very English.

I paid Becker and his mother a visit yesterday. Their rooms are so nice, pictures and presents from you and dear Papa in all directions, remembrances of past, such happy, years!

Yesterday also I drove Baby out in my little carriage. She sat on Christa's knees and looked about her so much; she went to sleep at last.

November 17.

. . . Yesterday I was all the morning with Julie Battenberg buying Christmas presents. To-day also I am much occupied. We get up at seven, with candles, every morning, as this is the best time for doing all business, and breakfast at eight.

November 21.

... The Holstein question, I fear, will lead to war, Fritz's[3] rights are so clear. And I am sure all Germany will help him to maintain his rights, for the cause is a just one.

I am sure, dear Mama, you are worried to death about it, which is very hard, for you cannot undo what once exists. *Anything* only to *avoid* war! It would be a sad calamity for Germany, the end of which no one can foresee.

My Baby has this morning cut her first tooth, and makes such faces if one ventures to touch her little mouth.

To-day I am going to visit the hospital in the town, which is said not to be good or well looked after. I want to be able to do something for it and hope to succeed, for the people have plenty of money, only not the will. The Burgomaster and Gemeinderath [the Town Councillors], will meet me there.

I have just called into life what did not exist, that is, linen to be lent for the poor women in their confinements, and which I hope will be of use to them, for the dirt and discomfort is very great in those classes.

November 28.

... My visit to the hospital was very interesting, and the air was good, the place clean and fresh. There were few people dangerously ill there, and they looked well taken care of. Air and water are making their way into these places to the benefit of mankind.

I was so much distressed the other day; for the poor man who fell in our house has died. He was a soldier, and so respectable and industrious, not above twenty-four. This is already the second who has died in consequence of a fall.

[3] The late Duke Frederic of Augustenburg.

November 30.

A few words of love and affection from us both on this dear day—the third anniversary of the commencement of all our happiness, which dear Papa and you enabled us to form.

Those happy days at Windsor and those awful days the year after! I assure you the season, the days, *all* make me sad—for the impression of those two years can never be wiped out of my mind. I can write but a few lines, as to-morrow we leave for Amorbach, and to-day I go with Louis out shooting. It is cold and fine, as it was two years ago.

Darling Mama, again and again we thank you and beloved Papa for all your love to us at that time.

Amorbach: December 2.

. . . We arrived here at half-past four yesterday—after a bitter cold drive in an open carriage over hard roads, all being frozen, since ten in the morning. The country we came through was beautiful, though all white, up and down hill all the way, through many villages, through woods, &c. The house is large and comfortable, full of souvenirs of dear Grandmama [Duchess of Kent], of Uncle Charles.

I am so pleased to be with Ernest and Marie[4]—it is a bit of home again.

December 8.

. . . Think, only yesterday evening at a concert they played *Ruy Blas*, which I had not heard since Windsor. The room, the band, dear Papa, all came before me, and made my heart sink at the thought that *that* belonged to the bright recollections of the past! I cried all the way

[4] Prince and Princess of Leiningen.

home. Such trivial things sometimes awaken recollections more vividly, and hurt more keenly, than scenes of real distress. I am sure you know what I mean.

December 12.

... I must close—my tears fall fast, and I ought not to make you sadder, when you are sad enough already. Pray for me when you kneel at *his* grave—pray that my happiness may be allowed to last long; think of me when you kneel there where on that day my hand rested on your and Papa's dear hands, two years ago. That bond between us both is *so* strong, beloved Mama. I feel it as a legacy from him.

December 22.

A great pleasure I have had in arranging a tree for our good servants. I bought all the things myself at the market, and hung them on the tree: then I also got things for darling Louis.

December 26.

... We all had trees in one large room in the Palace, and our presents underneath it looked extremely pretty. Uncle Alexander's five children were there, and made such a noise with their playthings.

Baby had a little tree early at her Grandpapa and Grandmama's, with all her pretty things.

Many thanks for the turkey-pie; we give a dinner to-day in honour.

1864.

January 5.

... The cold here is awful. I skated yesterday, and to-day we are going to the pond at Kranichstein. (Very few people skate here—only one lady, and she very badly.) Baby only goes out for half an hour in the middle of the day, well wrapped up. It would not do to keep her quite at home, as she would become so sensitive when first taken out again. Of course when it is windy or too cold she stops in.

January 9.

I was aghast on receiving Bertie's telegram this morning announcing the birth of their little son. Oh, may dear Papa's blessing rest on the little one; may it turn out like dear Papa, and be a comfort and pride to you, and to its young parents! Your first English grandchild. Dear Mama, my heart is so full. May dear Alix and the Baby only go on well!

January 16.

. . . Baby says 'Papa,' 'Mama,' and yesterday several times 'Louis.' She imitates everything she hears, all noises and sounds; she gets on her feet alone by a chair, and is across the room before one can turn round. Her adoration for Louis is touching. She stops always, since the summer, alone in our room, so she never cries for Moffat [her nurse], and is very happy on the floor with her playthings. She is a very dear little thing and gets on very fast, but equally in all things, and is as fat as she was. It is so interesting to watch the progress and development of such a little being; and Baby is so expressive, she makes such a face when she is not pleased, and laughs so heartily when she is contented. She is more like a child of two years old a great deal.

January 30.

. . . These poor Schleswig-Holsteiners do what they can to liberate themselves from the Danish yoke, and to regain their lawful sovereign, Fritz. And why is England, who stands up for freedom of countries, who in Italy, where there was less cause, did what she could to liberate the country from her lawful sovereigns, to do what she can to prevent the Schleswig-Holsteiners from liberating themselves from a king who has no right over them, merely because they are unfortunate good-natured Germans, who allow themselves to be oppressed?

February 14.

... We have been in sledges to-day, and everybody drives about the town in them; it sounds so pretty, all the jingling bells.

... Shakespeare's words came home to one—

> Uneasy lies the head that wears a crown.

Thank God, my husband has none! I thank the Almighty daily for our peaceful homely life, in which sphere we can do a good deal of good to our fellow-creatures, without having to mix in those hateful politics.

Our life is a very very happy one. I have nothing on earth to wish for, and much as I loved my precious Louis when I married him, still more do I love him now and daily; for his character is worthy of love and respect, and a better husband or father, a more unselfish and kind one, there does not live. His love for you, you know; and on our return how glad we shall be to be near you once more.

February 16.

Louis is in the Chamber to-day from nine till one, long enough at a stretch, and immediately after breakfast. We always breakfast at eight; then Louis sees the three officers who come every morning on his military business, then Westerweller and all others who have business. We usually walk before luncheon, which is at twelve; and often drive at two or three. At five we dine; at half-past six, theatre, four times a week, till half-past nine; then we take tea together, Louis reads to me and I work. On other week-days there are concerts or parties. We are often in our new house, and in the garden, arranging things and watching the progress. We also go to lectures here, and are much occupied, which makes the day pass so quickly.

March 1.

I have learned much since I married, and, above all, not to be dependent on others in my existence. To be able to make a bright and comfortable home for my dear husband is my constant aim; but even in this one often fails, for self constantly turns up, like a bad sixpence. Oh, how dear Papa spoke about that! His whole noble life was that one bright example of sacrificing himself to his duty. Dear, adored Papa! such goodness, such love, when one thinks of it, must silence all complaints of petty troubles in the mouths of his children and servants. You, dear Mama, are the one who suffers the most, though this awful loss has touched all; and to soothe your grief and to help you lightens one's own.

March 5.

. . . Spring always makes me so *wehmüthig* [sad], I don't know why; one longs for everything and anything which is out of one's reach.

I will tell you of something I did the other day; but please tell no one, because not a soul but Louis and my ladies knows of it here. I am the patroness of the 'Heidenreich Stiftung,' to which you also gave a handsome present in the beginning. The ladies who belong to it go to bring linen to poor respectable *Wöchnerinnen* [lying-in women], who claim their assistance. They bring them food, and, in short, help them. All cases are reported to me. The other day I went to one incog. with Christa, in the old part of the town—and the trouble we had to find the house! At length, through a dirty courtyard, up a dark ladder into one little room, where lay in one bed the poor woman and her baby; in the room four other children, the husband, two other beds, and a stove. But it did not smell bad, nor was it dirty. I sent Christa down with the children, then with the husband cooked something for the woman; arranged her bed a little, took her baby for her, bathed its eyes—for they were so bad, poor little thing!—and did odds and ends for her. I went twice. The people did not know me, and were so nice, so good and touchingly attached to each other; it did one's heart good to see such good feelings in such poverty. The husband was out of work, the children too young to go to school, and they had only four kreuzers in the house when she was confined. Think of that misery and discomfort!

If one never sees any poverty, and always lives in that cold circle of Court people, one's good feelings dry up, and I felt the want of going about and doing the little good that is in my power. I am sure you will understand this.

March 14.

My own dear precious Mama,

These words are for the 16th, the first hard trial of our lives where I was allowed to be with you. Do you recollect when all was over [death of the Duchess of Kent], and dear Papa led you to the sofa in the colonnade, and then took me *to you*? I took that as a sacred request from him to love, cherish, and comfort my darling Mother to all the extent of my weak powers. Other things have taken me from being constantly with you; but nothing has lessened my intense love for you, and longing to quiet every pain which touches you, and to fulfil, even in the distance, his request.

Oh, darling Mama, were there words in which I could express to you how much I am bound up with you, how constantly my thoughts and prayers are yours, I would write them. The sympathies of our souls can only tell each other how tender my love and gratitude to you is, and how vividly I feel every new trial or new thing with you and for you. . . .

I was with another poor woman, even worse off, this morning, and on the third day she was walking in the room and nearly fainted from weakness. Those poor people!

March 26.

. . . Yesterday morning at nine we took the Sacrament— all the family and congregation together. The others then stopped for the rest of the service, till after eleven. I went home, and returned for the English service at twelve. At half-past six, in the Stadtkirche, Bach's 'Passion' was given.

April 5.

To-day is Victoria's birthday. What a day it was this time last year! Baby has her table in the room next to my sitting-room. Uncle Louis and the rest of the family expected to breakfast with us at twelve.

Munich: April 13.

. . . Between sight-seeing, and going to the Queen's room, and being with her, I have not a moment scarcely to rest or write. Yesterday we visited the whole Schloss full of frescoes, and the studios of all the famous painters—so interesting. How dear Papa would have enjoyed it! I was thinking the whole time what he would have thought of certain pictures, and how much he would have admired some. But at all times seeing things, and most of all pictures, is fatiguing.

Darmstadt: April 21.

. . . On Monday Louis goes into the country to shoot capercailzies [*Auerhähne*]. I accompany him part of the way, but stop at Schweinsberg with Christa's parents. The air is very good there, and we thought the country would do me good.

. . . We shall leave probably later [for England], after or just before your birthday. We have a great deal to do in London for our house, for which I should want a week; and from Windsor to leave you for a whole week I should not like, and to go up constantly is rather tiring.

We go from Mayence to Rotterdam by steamer, from thence by rail to Antwerp, and then wait for good weather to cross, so that we shall be long under way, but quite easily and comfortably.

April 25.

. . . We shall leave the week of your birthday. Louis wishes us to have a full fortnight in London.

Darmstadt: May 14.

Many thanks for your letter, and above all for your great kindness about the ships, for which I thank you many times.

Christa and Becker wrote an account of the wedding,[5] so I won't write any more about it save that it went off very well and was very *vornehm* and well-arranged. . . .

I have borne the fatigues well; but two days before, for two days and one night, I was very unwell. . . . Dr. Weber is a clever man, and is *vielseitig* [many-sided] in his views

---

[5] Of the Princess Anna of Hesse with the Grand Duke of Mecklenburg-Schwerin.

on medicine and treatment of illnesses. I think you will like him.

Baby runs alone through two rooms without falling now: she learnt it in a week. She will amuse you so much. Yesterday Louis drove me and his two brothers in a break, and Baby went with us much enchanted.

May 17.

. . . To-morrow afternoon Fritz and Anna leave. To-day the town gives a large ball, to which we all go, and before it there is a dinner at the Schloss.

May 21.

. . . It is excessively hot, which makes me so tired and weak. I am sure you suffered dreadfully from the heat.

The parting from Anna three days ago was dreadful; she so distressed, and her parents also. . . . They begin their old age alone, so to say, for there are no children in their house any more. It makes us both very sad to leave them, and seems so unfeeling; but we shall return to them soon. What a blessing that you have Beatrice and two brothers, still boys; and yet, for one alone what an anxiety!

Marlborough House: May 26.

Arrived here at half-past eleven, and quite rested. I at once write to you to thank you for your letter and for the great comfort of the ships. I feel so much better already from the air on the Rhine those two days, and the fresh sea air, that I have borne the journey this way with but little fatigue. I find Bertie and Alix both looking well, and the baby so pretty and dear.

I slept during the whole night passage, as I went to bed early. I had about twelve hours' sleep, which has completely set me up. Louis is paying visits. We have lunched, and in the afternoon Bertie and Alix have promised to call on Lady Augusta and Dean Stanley, and we join them. Aunt Cambridge and Mary we shall see afterwards.

[From May to August the Princess was in England on a visit to the Queen.]

Kranichstein: August 30.

. . . I have stood the journey well, though I am rather fatigued. It is very warm. Louis is off to Jugenheim. I am to go there to-morrow, and it takes my whole day, as it is so far. I have seen none of the family yet. I was so distressed to part from dear Ernest and Marie, they were so dear and good all along the journey. The weather was beautiful and the passage good.

September 2.

. . . I am so glad that, from all accounts, everything went off so very well at Perth;[6] it must have been most trying to you, and yet satisfactory. We read all the accounts you kindly sent us with much interest.

. . . The Emperor [of Russia] with his second and third sons arrived yesterday. We saw him at the station at Darmstadt, but did not join them as the rest of the family did. We go to Jugenheim to-day and Baby with us, as little Serge,[7] who is just Beatrice's age, has such a passion for her. The children are very nice, the two older sons very big. Uncle Gustav is here, which makes me think of you here this time last year.

September 13.

. . . Two days ago we had intense heat, and since great cold—the two extremes constantly, which is so unwholesome. The Emperor is very grateful for your message,

---

[6] The unveiling of a statue of the Prince Consort.
[7] Grand Duke Serge.

and sends his best remembrance. . . . There were seven young men to dinner yesterday, and your glass was used for the first time and looked so pretty.

September 20.

. . . What you say about the poor sisters, and indeed of all the younger ones, is true. The little brothers and Beatrice are those who have lost the most, poor little things! I can't bear to think of it, for dear Papa, more peculiarly than any other father, was wanted for his children; and he was the dear friend, and even playfellow, besides. Such a loss as ours is indeed unique. Time only increases its magnitude, and the knowledge of the want is felt more keenly.

. . . I was yesterday in our little house, arranging and clearing out the rooms. We shall have very close quarters, but it will not be uncomfortable.

Where people are unselfish, loving, good, and industrious, like my dear Louis, I always feel a certain likeness beginning to grow up with our dear angel Father! Don't you? Oh, may we all only become like him! I struggle so hard, dear Mama, in the many little trials I daily have, to become more like him. My trials melt away when I think of you, and I wish I were great and strong to be able to bear some of your great trials for you. Dear Mama, how I love you! how we both love you, and would shield you with our love from all new blows and trials, you know. God comfort you! My heart is often too full to say all that is in it; to tell you all my love and devotion, for your own precious sake, and for dear Papa's, who left you as a legacy to us all to love and to cherish for him.

September 23.

To-morrow Louis, I and my two ladies take the Sacrament in the little church here. I wished much to take it before my hour of trial comes. Dear Louis read to me yesterday evening Robertson's sermon on the 'Sympathy of Christ.'

We have fine autumn weather, and I am out as much as I can. . . . I sleep well and breakfast always at half-past eight; we dine at two, and take supper at eight, then my ladies read aloud, and I work or Christa plays, Louis reads his papers, &c. To myself I read Lord Malmesbury's Memoirs, which are very curious, and when Louis has time he reads Froude to me.

Darmstadt: October 14.

We are at length here, in great disorder, and I have been waiting half an hour only for a pen to be found. I am tired and not very well. . . . Augusta [Lady Augusta Stanley] being with you I am very glad of, and she must be such a comfort to you, for, besides being such a friend, she has that peculiar charm of manner which all the Bruces possess.

October 29.

. . . To-morrow we expect Vicky and Fritz [Crown Prince and Princess of Prussia] for two hours, and later Bertie and Alix on their way back from Amorbach, for a few hours. I shall be delighted to see them.

October 31.

. . . Yesterday we had the pleasure of having dear Vicky and Fritz and baby here for two hours, the former well and in such good looks, as I have not seen her for long. The baby is a love, and very pretty. We were very glad after a year's separation to meet again, and Vicky was so dear and loving. I always admire her understanding and brightness each time I see her again; and Fritz so good, so excellent. Bertie and Alix we expect in a day or two for a short visit. It is very cold, but not unpleasant. I go out twice a day.

Darmstadt: November 7.

... The little daughter [8] was but a momentary disappointment to us, which we have quite got over. We console ourselves with the idea that the little pair will look very pretty together.

November 20.

... We are both very much pleased at the arrangement about Brown and your pony, and I think it is so sensible. I am sure it will do you good, and relieve a little the monotony of your out-of-door existence, besides doing your nerves good. I had long wished you would do something of the kind; for, indeed, only driving is not wholesome. ... I have had two drives, which have done me good. ... My mother-in-law has been kindness itself all along—so attentive and yet so discreet. I can't be grateful enough. My good father-in-law also. ... Louis's mother is to be godmother, because it is customary here to ask someone of the name the child is to receive to stand on the occasion. We liked Elizabeth on account of St. Elizabeth being the ancestress of the Hessian as well as the Saxon House.

November 26.

... We probably go to Carlsruhe on Wednesday, the only place we can well go to near by; we can't take an inn at Baden or anything of that sort, and we only go for a week or ten days at most. ... I am very well and very careful; all people say I look better, and have more colour than I have had for long, and, indeed, I feel strong and well, and my fat Baby does perfectly, and is a great darling. Affie [9] and Louis and his brother are out shooting. The horrid weather has kept me in these three days.

[8] The Princess Elizabeth was born on the 1st of November, 1864.
[9] Duke of Edinburgh.

November 29.

... I ought to mention the christening. My mother-in-law held Baby all the time, and it screamed a good deal. Victoria stood with us and was very good, only kneeling down and tumbling over the footstool every two minutes, and she kept whispering to me, 'Go to Uncle's.' I thought so much of the christening last year, when Victoria behaved much better than her larger dark sister. Ella measured twenty-three and a half inches a fortnight ago, and she had not grown then. Victoria, I believe, was twenty inches.

Carlsruhe: December 5.

... Dear Dr. Macleod is coming with Affie to Darmstadt for the 14th. Vicky and Fritz will be with us also How kind of him to come, and it has made Affie so happy, for he is so devoted to him.

December 15.

I had not a moment to myself to write to you yesterday, and to thank you for the kind lines you sent me through dear Dr. Macleod. He gave us a most beautiful service, a sermon giving an outline of dear Papa's noble, great and good character, and there were most beautiful allusions to you in his prayer, in which we all prayed together most earnestly for you, precious Mama!

We talked long together afterwards about dear Papa, and about you, and though absent were very near you in thought and prayer.

Dear Vicky talked so lovingly and tenderly of you, and of how homesick she sometimes felt. She was not with us on that dreadful day three years ago, and that is so painful to her. Dear Affie was, as we all were, so much overcome by all Dr. Macleod said. Vicky, Affie, Louis and myself sat in the little dining-room; he read to us there. Fritz had left early in the morning. The day was passed quietly and peaceably together, and I was most grateful to have dear Vicky and Affie with me on that day. My dear Louis wishes me to express to you how tenderly he thought of you and with what sympathy on this sad anniversary. Never can we cease talking of home, of you and of all your trials. God bless and comfort you, my own dear Mama!

1865

January 1.

... Thousand thanks for your dear words, and for the wishes! I was thinking so much of you and of home, when your letter came in. It made me so happy! Darling Mama, I can feel so much with and for you during these days. I was all day on the verge of tears, for the very word *Neujahr* brought Papa and Grandmama, and all at Windsor as in former days, so vividly before me, it made my heart ache! That bright happy past, particularly those last years, when I was the eldest at home, and had the privilege of being so much with you both, my own dearly loved parents, is a remembrance deeply graven, and with letters of gold, upon my heart. All the morning I was telling Louis how it used to be at home, and how we all assembled outside your dressing-room door to scream in chorus '*Prosit Neujahr!*' and to give to you and Papa our drawings, writings, &c., the busy occupation of previous weeks. Then playing and reciting our pieces, where we often stuck fast, and dear Papa bit his lip so as not to laugh; our walk to the Riding-school [where the alms to the poor were distributed], and then to Frogmore. Those were happy days, and the very remembrance of them must bring a gleam of sunshine even to you, dear Mama. Those two dinners, when I was with you both, were such happy evenings. I am so grateful I remained at home, and lost not a day of those happy ones.

At eight this morning we two went to church; at half-past three there was a large dinner at the Schloss. I wore the bracelet with your pictures, as I always do on all particular days, for I like to be able to look at those dear faces.

January 2.

We mean to go out sledging. The cold, and all the ground being white this last month, has given me such bad eyes. I can do nothing of an evening at all, and reading even by daylight makes them so bad that they get quite red. The ladies read to me, instead, all sorts of instructive things. Louis has already found time to read through a whole volume of the *Lives of the Engineers*.[1] You could not have sent anything that would interest him more. He thanks you so much for the pretty New Year's wish also.

January 14.

Thousand thanks for your dear letter, for the nice enclosure from Dr. Macleod, and for the beautiful sermon by Dean Stanley. One remark struck me as singularly applicable to dear Papa, where he says: 'To die is gain; to be no longer vexed with the sight of evil, which they cannot control,' &c.—for dear Papa *suffered* when he saw others do wrong; it pained that good pure spirit: and though we long for him and want him, if we could call him back—even you who want him so much, I think, would pause before you gave vent to the wish that would recall him. . . .

[1] By Dr Samuel Smiles.

When trials come, what alone save faith and hope in a blessed future can sustain one!

... You can't think how much I am interested in every little detail of your daily life. Besides, you know it cannot be otherwise. Please say kindest things to Brown,[2] who must be a great convenience to you.

January 20.

... The more one studies and tries to understand those wonderful laws which rule the world, the more one wonders, worships, and admires that which to us is so incomprehensible; and I always wonder how there can be dissatisfied and grumbling people in this beautiful world, so far too good for our deserts, and where, after our duty is done, we hope to be everlastingly with those we love, where the joy will be so great and lasting that present sorrow and trouble must melt away before that sunshine.

January 23.

... We have rain and warm high wind, and leave at four o'clock this afternoon. Ella has her bath as a bed, and Victoria sleeps in the bassinet, which is done up with chintz for the occasion. I don't think they can catch cold. There is a stove in the centre compartment besides. You can fancy I feel shy going to Berlin into a perfectly new society; and I have been so little out on the whole since the year 1861. Marie Grancy[3] goes with us.

Berlin: January 29.

... The journey went off very well, and we are so happy to be here. Vicky and Fritz are kindness itself, and Vicky so dear, so loving! I feel it does me good, that

---

[2] John Brown, the Queen's faithful personal attendant.

[3] One of the Princess's ladies in waiting.

there is a reflection of Papa's great mind in her. He loved her so much, and was so proud of her. The King is, as always, very kind, and so pleased to see us here. Louis is very happy to meet his old comrades again, and they equally so to see him; and I am so glad that he can have this amusement at least, for he is so kind in not leaving me—and our life must be rather dull sometimes for a young man of spirit like him.

Berlin: February 4.

. . . I have not been sight-seeing anywhere, as it is too cold for that. We drive in a shut carriage, and then walk in the Thiergarten. We spend the whole day together, which is a great enjoyment to me, and of an evening we go out together. It is so pleasant to have a sister to go out with, and all the people are so kind and civil to us.

Sigismund [4] is the greatest darling I have ever seen— so wonderfully strong and advanced for his age—with such fine colour, always laughing, and so lively he nearly jumps out of our arms.

This house is very comfortable, and Vicky is surrounded with pictures of you and dear Papa—near her bed, on all her tables—and such endless souvenirs of our childhood: it made me quite *wehmüthig* [sad] to see all the things I had not seen for seven years, and since we lived together as children —souvenirs of Christmases and birthdays from you both, and from dear Grandmama, from Aunt Gloucester, &c. It awakened a thousand old remembrances of happy past times.

Berlin: February 7.

. . . How much do I think of you now, the happy Silver Wedding that would have been, where you could have been surrounded by so many of us! Poor Mama, I do

[4] Then the Crown Princess's youngest child.

feel so deeply for you. Oh, may I be long, if not altogether, spared so awful a calamity!

Morning, noon, and night do I thank the Almighty for *our* happiness, and pray that it may last.

These lines are for the dear 10th,[5] though they will reach you on the eve; and they are to tell you from Louis and myself how tenderly we think of you on that day, and of darling Papa, who made that day what it was. It will be a day of great trial to you, I fear. May the Almighty give you strength and courage to bear it! I am sure the dear sisters and brothers who are at home will try to cheer you with their different loving ways—above all, little Beatrice, the youngest of us all.

Louis goes to Schwerin to-morrow until Friday. They wanted us to go together, but one journey is enough at this time of the year.

Berlin: February 14.

... We leave next Saturday. I shall be so sorry to leave dear Vicky, for she is often so much alone. Fritz is really so excellent, it is a pleasure to look at his dear good face; and he is worked so hard—no health can stand it in the long run.

Berlin: February 17.

... This will be my last letter from here, and I only regret leaving here on account of parting with dear Vicky and Fritz, whom we see so rarely, and usually but for a short time. I have passed such pleasant hours with dear Vicky: that is what I shall look back to with so much pleasure and satisfaction.

Darmstadt: February 21.

I write once more from our dear little home, which I find very cold; snow and ice everywhere still—it seems

---

[5] The anniversary of the Queen's marriage.

as if winter would never end. We accomplished our journey very well. Poor Vicky will miss us very much, I fear, in the many hours when she is alone, and which we spent together. Writing does not make up for it.

We give a large masked ball in the Palace at Fastnacht [Shrove Tuesday], which is to-day week. It is the first thing we do for the society, and I hope it will go off well. I found so much to do since my return that I can write no more.

Before closing I must mention, though, that yesterday evening I heard *Elijah* beautifully given. How I thought of dear Papa! Nearly every note brought back to mind observations he made about it. I thought I could see him, and hear his dear sweet voice turning round to me with quite watery eyes, saying, ' Es ist doch gar zu schön ' [' It is really quite too lovely ! ']

Adored Papa! how he loved this fine music; the harmony in it seems like the harmony of souls, and Mendelssohn's music is so good, *fromm* [pious]—I mean, it makes one better to hear it. In the second part, in an air of Elijah towards the end, I found the part from which those beautiful responses are taken which Cusins[6] arranged, and which Papa liked so much.

March 4.

I have written to dear Tilla.[7] To think of home without her seems too sad, but I hope you will invite her sometimes. Everyone liked her in the house, she was so gentle and so kind. I shall never forget what I owe her, and I ever loved her most dearly. But she has never been the same again since 1861. It gave her a dreadful shock; she had such a veneration for darling Papa.

[6] Master of the Queen's private band.
[7] Miss Hildyard, the Princess's former English governess.

I hope this year we can show you our house, though it will not be far enough advanced for you to live in. For another year, I hope, we could make you so comfortable.

Darmstadt: March 6.

... I am reading at this moment a book by Herr von Arneth—the publication of letters from Maria Theresa to Marie Antoinette from 1770–80. I recommend it to you. The letters are short and interesting, and it would amuse you to take it up now and then, when you have a leisure moment. The advice the Empress gives her daughter is so good; she was a very wise mother.

I have read and studied a great deal about the human body; about children—their treatment, &c. It interests me immensely. Besides, it is always useful to know such things, so that one is not perfectly ignorant of the reasons why doctors wish one to do certain things, and why not. In any moment of illness, before there is time for a doctor to come, one can be able to help oneself a little. I know you don't like these things, and where one is surrounded by such as dear Sir James [Clark] and Dr. Jenner,[8] it is perfectly unnecessary and pleasanter *not* to know a good deal. Instead of finding it disgusting, it only fills me with admiration to see how wonderfully we are made.

March 18.

My poor children have been confined to the house with dreadful colds and coughs. Victoria looks the most pulled, though Ella's cough was much more violent. I am happy to say that they are really better to-day; but we have snow every day, and that makes their recovery slower.

[8] The Queen's own private physicians.

Yesterday night part of a large seed manufactory close by, near the artillery barracks, was burnt down. The flames were enormous, but the damage done was not great.

April 1.

... Since some days the snow is many feet deep; one can get about in sledges, and Louis drove me in one with four horses this morning. All intercourse by carriage is impossible, and this is very inconvenient to the people in the country when their 'Post' cannot drive.

April 4.

I must begin by telling you how much pleasure your telegram has given me. It is like my own dear Mama to have her arms open for those who want her kind support; and I can only repeat again, that with you, and under your care alone, should I like to leave my little ones so long! To them, indeed, it will in every way be an advantage, and I shall be quite easy in leaving them there, where I know they will have every care which can be given; and it would make us both so happy to feel that in this way we could give you some little pleasure.

Westerweller and Becker both wish very much we may take this winter, D.V., for a journey. As long as we have fewer servants and this small house, it is easy to break up the whole establishment—later, this will be less possible. Louis has never been able to travel, and the advantage of seeing other parts of the world would be so great for him. Without me he would not do it; he says, alone he should not enjoy it. I urge this journey principally for his sake, and I hope you will support me in this. Since our marriage we have seen nothing, and all who can try to enlarge their knowledge. From books alone it becomes tedious and less advantageous.

Victoria is going to have a party of thirty children to-morrow in Prince Charles's rooms. The snow is thawing at length, and the sun is much too hot. The sudden spring is not pleasant. We have been out riding, and this evening I shall accompany Louis to the Schnepfenstrich [woodcock-shooting [9]], which in a fine evening, when the birds sing, is lovely. . . .

April 8.

. . . We shall be delighted to receive you in Kranichstein, and if you will send your suite all to Darmstadt we shall be able to arrange, though we have not one spare room anywhere, and I feel you will be rather squeezed. How I look forward to meeting you again, after a year of separation, I can't say; and I am so glad that it will be under our roof that our joyful embrace will take place. As Uncle Louis is to have the Garter, may not Affie bring it to him *without* ceremony? He would like it so much better, if it can be so.

On the 17th Louis goes to Oberhessen to shoot capercailzies, and he deposits me and the children at Lich on his way, where he will join us again for my birthday.

Anna was safely delivered of a little girl this morning, and is doing well.

April 15.

. . . We have been very anxious about Anna [1] the last few days, for she has had fever since the 9th, and shivering still yesterday.

We have a great deal to do this morning, so I can write but shortly.

We have fine weather at length, and are out a great deal.

---

[9] This sport is practised in the evening twilight.

[1] Prince Louis's sister, the Grand Duchess of Mecklenburg-Schwerin. She died on the 16th of April, 1865.

Yesterday we took the Sacrament at nine, and numbers of people with us. The service lasted till past eleven, with a pause between.

April 18.

This is really a dreadfully sad death in our family, and will be a blow to my dear parents-in-law which will weigh them down for many a day. They who lived so retired, and to whom the family life was all—Anna the pet —'das Prinzesschen,' whom they gave up so unwillingly, and with whom they corresponded daily! It will be a blank in their existence, which I can't bear to think of! Such tender loving parents! My poor Louis was dreadfully distressed, though he feared the worst all along since we knew that Anna had fever. He left with Grolmann, having passed a dreadful morning. All the old servants, tutors, friends, came crying to us. Since he is gone I have passed sad lonely hours: and poor old Amelung[2] comes and sits in my room, sobbing that she should ever have lived to see this day.

Yesterday morning I went to the Rosenhöhe and picked flowers from Anna's garden, and wound a large wreath, which I have sent to Louis to place on her coffin. The three brothers feel it dreadfully—the first rent in the family circle is always hard to bear, and she so young, so good, so happy! I hear the poor little baby is nice.

Yesterday night Anna was taken into the Schlosskirche [Palace Chapel] upon Louis's arrival, after a journey of twenty-seven hours. I hope he won't be ill after all this *Gemüthsbewegung* [strain upon his feelings], and fatigue always upsets him and makes him sick, and he feels all so deeply and warmly. It is so shocking. I can think of

---

[2] Nurse of the Prince Louis and his brothers and sister.

nothing else; and I am very low and sad being so alone, and the warm weather makes one unwell.

The poor Cesarewitch has passed a tolerable night. I fear he is so reduced he can't get through it. The Empress doats on this son, and he is so like her. The poor Emperor has left for Nice.

April 21.

Oh, it is sad, very sad! Life indeed is but a short journey, on which we have our duty to do, and in which joy and sorrow alternately prevail. Anna was very good, very unselfish, and a true Christian, with her gentle, humble spirit, and as such she was loved and admired. What rare people my parents-in-law and their children are, I can't tell you—such childlike faith, such pure unselfish love to each other; I really feel unworthy to belong to them, and they are dear to me beyond description. As I have shared their joys, so with all my heart do I share their sorrow, and fervently pray for them! You will understand this, darling Mama. From you I have inherited an ardent and sympathising spirit, and feel the pain of those I love as though it were my own. To-morrow I have wished that there should be in the Palace Chapel a funeral service at the same time as the funeral at Schwerin, and all the people here seemed pleased at my wish. Bender, who taught her, confirmed her, and who married her not a year ago in that very church, will perform the service.

Poor Dagmar![3] what a journey for her, poor child! She begins her troubles early enough.

April 24.

... Many thanks for your kind letter, and for all the kind wishes for my birthday. It will be sad and quiet;

---

[3] Princess Dagmar of Denmark, now Empress of Russia, sister of the Princess of Wales.

but I hope my beloved Louis will arrive to-night, and be with me again—such cause for joy and thankfulness. When I have *him*, all sorrow is turned into peace and happiness. Could I but know you still had darling Papa at your side, how light would my heart be! Once when we have all fulfilled our allotted duties, and overcome that dark night, then, please God, we shall be together, never again to part!

The sympathy of all does my sorrowing family good, for it soothes so much! I had a few lines, so tender, so full of faith, from my dear mother-in-law to-day. Since Ella's birth I know to understand and love her most dearly. She suffered dreadfully, but no complaint passes her lips. She consoles her husband, her son-in-law, and this, with prayer, enables her to bear that which has almost broken her heart.

April 29.

I thank you so much for your kind sympathising letter. All my family are so grateful for all the kindness and sympathy you have shown them on this sad occasion.

To-day Uncle Louis arrives; on Monday the Emperor and Empress, and children. What a sad meeting! They go to Jugenheim direct, where last year they were so happy all together. I hear the Empress is worn out, mind and body; and she insists, instead of finishing her cure, on going in a fortnight to St. Petersburg to meet the remains of her child, and to do him the last honours. Louis fears that it will be more than her feeble frame can endure. In the Greek Church, too, the night Masses are long and exhausting, and she is sure to wish to do all.

We spent my birthday as every other day, and the weather was heavenly. I am painting in oil now, and that interests me much. I find it much easier than water-colours.

I hope Affie will come to pay his respects to the Russians. If you send them a kind message through him, it would please them much.

May 2.

. . . How well I understand your compassion being alike for mourners in all positions of life. It is but right and natural, and I can't imagine one's feeling otherwise.

Seeheim: May 21.

. . . Yesterday the Emperor and Empress and children left. So sorry to see them go! God knows when we shall all meet here again. We have been so much together, and so intimately, that I have grown very fond of them, and am very sad at the thought of the long and uncertain separation. Dear little Arthur was here, looking very well. The wooded hills here are so nice to ride about on, and the country is very beautiful.

May 31.

I read serious books a great deal, and of a Sunday together we read out of Robertson's sermons. In the second series there is one, 'The Irreparable Past,' for young people, so cheering, so encouraging, so useful. Louis read it to me on his return from Schwerin after poor Anna's death. A short life indeed, and it makes one feel the uncertainty of life, and the necessity of labour, self-denial, charity, and all those virtues which we ought to strive after. Oh, that I may die, having done my work and not sinned with *Unterlassung des Guten* [omission to do what is good], the fault into which it is easiest to fall.

Our life being so quiet gives one much time for earnest thought, and I own it is discouraging to find how much one fails—how small the step of improvement is.

I suffer still so much, and so often, from rheumatism.

I am taking warm soda-baths in the morning for it, and am rubbed afterwards with towels which have been dipped in cold water and then wrung out. It is not very pleasant.

June 7.

. . . You know how very Scotch we both are. Louis is devotedly attached to Scotland and his Scotch friends. Do tell them so always. But now I must tell you of yesterday. In the morning Affie, we, and our suite, drove into town for the investiture. At half-past three I drove with my ladies, a Kammerherr [Chamberlain], Becker, &c., to the Schloss, where Uncle Louis received us in *shorts*! Then Affie and Louis in their whole Garter dress arrived in a carriage with six horses and an escort. Uncle Louis, before the throne, and the family, Court, corps diplomatique, &c., received them. Affie read in English the address, to which Uncle Louis answered in German; then Affie buckled on the Garter; then Louis helped him to put on ribbon, cloak, &c., and fastened the sword on him, which was no easy task; but they acquitted themselves to perfection, and went out through the long Kaisersaal backwards, bowing.

There was a large dinner afterwards, at which your health was proposed by Uncle Louis, and in return Affie gave his. You have made a happy man, and he feels the honour—as he said to me in English—'utmostly'; and he wishes me to repeat once more how grateful he is to you. . . .

Affie did not return here last night; he slept at Darmstadt, and left this morning for Amorbach. To-day Uncle Ernest is coming to us, but only for one night. As we have again to go into town to fetch him, and it is very warm, I must close.

Seeheim : June 15.

. . . How it will amuse and please us to show the good excellent Scotchmen our home. It is a pleasure to hear of such devotion and attention to you as Brown's is, and indeed you are so kind to him, that his whole happiness must consist in serving so good a mistress.

I think you will be pleased to hear of a most kind and touching tribute which the Frauen [women] of Darmstadt have paid me. Two hundred and fifty have subscribed to have a splendid picture painted for me, by P. Weber, of Loch Katrine. I am to see it on Sunday. It is very much admired, and they sent the painter to Scotland to do it, thinking that something from my own country would please me most. Is it not kind of them? It has given me so much pleasure—but of all things the feeling which has prompted them to do it, as it shows me that, though I have been here so short a time, they have become attached to me, as I am with all my heart to my new home and country.

Ella crawls now, and is very strong; she has her first two teeth. Victoria is very wild, and speaks more German than English. I think her rather small, but other people say she is not. She goes out walking with her Papa before breakfast quite alone, with her hands in her pockets, and amuses him very much.

June 19.

Many thanks for your last letter from dear Balmoral. The parting from that lovely place must always be sad, and there is something in mountains which attaches one so much to that scenery.

Yesterday was a very trying day for my poor mother-in-law (her birthday), and she was very low, but, as all along, so resigned, so touching in the beautiful way she bears her grief; so unselfish with it, never wishing to make others sad, or to be less interested in their concerns than formerly.

Dear Mary Cambridge has been here, and we enjoyed her visit so much. We took her back to Frankfort to-day, where we gave her and Aunt Cambridge a luncheon in Uncle Louis's Palais.

June 21.

It is warm, but very windy and dusty here; we were nearly blinded out riding yesterday evening. I am reading that most interesting History of England by Pauli, in German, which commences with the Congress of Vienna in 1815, and is, I believe, very detailed and correct. It gives a sketch also of the reign of George III., and is so well written one can scarcely lay the book down. It is part of a work written by the best German professors on England, Russia, Italy, France, Spain, and Austria in those years, and I am reading them one after another. They are thick books, and eight volumes.

Kranichstein: July 2.

We are all to go for four weeks to Switzerland, beginning with Rigi Kaltbad. We go into the mountains at once for the bracing air. On Saturday until Tuesday we go to Baden for the christening of the baby. We both are god-parents.

Kranichstein: July 10.

. . . Ella already says, since some time, 'Papa' and 'Mama,' and calls herself, and crawls, and is very forward and merry—such a contrast to Victoria, who is so pale and fair, and *now* thin, for Ella's eyes are so dark blue, and her hair of such a rich brown, that you would never take the little things for sisters. They are very fond of each other, and so dear together, that they give us much pleasure. I would not change them for boys, if I could; this little pair of sisters is so nice, and they can be such friends to each other.

I hope you will be comfortable here, but we are much annoyed not to be able to be there to receive you. None of the family will be here, save perhaps my mother-in-law with poor Fritz Schwerin,[4] who is expected then.

We mean to start on the 25th, and we go as private people, on account of the expense. We are only going to the Oberland, and shan't go very far about.

Kranichstein: July 17.

... It was 95° in the shade yesterday at eight in the morning, and I think the heat increases. Dr. Lyon Playfair lunched with us yesterday; he is so charming. To-morrow morning at five we go to Bonn for the day, and shall be there before ten. The heat is too great to go at any other time. We start next Tuesday evening, and on Wednesday shall be on the Rigi.

This morning at six o'clock we rode to the exercising— I on a new horse, for two hours and a half over sand without any shade.

Mary [Duchess of Teck] has been so kind as to give us a boat, which we expect shortly. It is to be christened 'Mary Adelaide,' after her.

July 24.

Many thanks for your letter, and for the sad account of Victoria Brand's[5] death. It is quite shocking, and she

[4] Grand Duke of Schwerin, husband of Princess Louis' sister. He died 1882.

[5] Daughter of M. Van de Weyer, the Belgian Minister Plenipotentiary in England. She had been thrown out of her carriage, and died from the effect of the injuries received.

was my dearest friend of those contemporaries, and the one I saw the most of. 'In the midst of life we are in death;' and the uncertainty of all earthly things makes life a real earnest, and no dream. Our whole life should be a preparation and expectation for eternity. Merry as she was, she was yet very serious and thoughtful; but what a loss she will be to her poor parents and husband!

I have made all arrangements for your comfort here. I own I do not like your coming here when we and the whole family are away—it looks so *odd*! I forgot to tell you, in answer to your question about Ella's name, that she of course must be called 'Elizabeth,' *entre nous* only 'Ella,' for she bears my dear mama-in-law's name.

Rigi Kaltbad: August 1.

I am enchanted, delighted with this magnificent scenery. Oh, how you would admire it! When I am sketching, I keep telling Louis how much more like you would make the things; one can always recognise the places when you draw them.

We left Darmstadt at eight Wednesday morning, the 26th, slept at Basel that night, and we got there early enough to see the fine church in a thunderstorm. The next day we only went to Lucerne, as the weather was not fine enough to ascend the Rigi. It was a lovely afternoon, and the lake of a marvellous green colour. The Pilatus was quite clear for a few hours. The next morning we two, the children, Moffat, Harriet the nursery-maid, Logoz and wife, Jäger, and Beck, our whole party, started in a very crowded steamer for Wäggis. Splendid weather, though cloudy. We then, on horses and in chairs carried by three or six men, made our ascent along a winding, narrow, steep path, below rocks, past ravines, where little châlets are situated, and all over the green pasture cows and goats feeding with bells round their necks. Westerweller was here when we arrived; he acts courier, and when we make long expeditions remains with the children. This is a very roomy hotel, crammed full of people, among them some odd Austrian ladies whom we see below walking on the terrace—very smart, and smoking. We two have been on mules with a guide—such a funny man, who was a soldier at Naples, and was at the siege of Gaeta—on all the expeditions hereabout.

To-morrow we leave, and go till Monday to Buochs, on the other side of the lake; then to Engelberg, where Uncle Adalbert and his wife will be. The children are well; Victoria very troublesome, but Ella good and amiable as ever. As I am writing at the window, the clouds cover the lake and the lower mountains, and I can only see the quite high ones with glaciers, which are of such a splendid shape.

The colour of the Scotch mountains is, I think, finer; but here they are, first of all, so enormously high, and then such fine shapes, and the mountains are studded with trees and rocks down below, and of a green colour.

The air is very light and cold, but the sun intense. We are going off for the day again on our mules, so I must close. Of course many funny incidents take place, which I reserve to tell you when we meet.

I do hope the heat will be over for your journey, and that it will be fine when you are at our dear Kranichstein. Marie Grancy will be there to receive you, and do anything which is required.

Engelberg, Hôtel Titlis: August 8.

These lines I send by Becker, and hope you will receive them at Kranichstein. . . . I hope you found all you wanted in the rooms, and that the meals were as you like them. I ordered all, and wrote all down before leaving, as I know what you like.

We were for some days at Buochs, a very pretty village; and we lived in three detachments in different common Swiss houses, very comfortable on the whole, but not smelling very nice, so that I could scarcely eat while we were there.

Yesterday morning, in a very funny two-seated carriage with one horse, we left, the children and servants following in a bigger carriage. A nearly four hours' drive through the most beautiful scenery, up a narrow valley through which the Aa runs, brought us here. The last two hours are a steep ascent on the side of a precipice; beautiful vegetation through the wood all the way upwards; view on the high mountains with snow and glaciers close by. On coming to the top, there is a narrow and lovely green valley studded with peasants' cottages, and in the centre a Benedictine Abbey, near which our hotel is situated. The valley is of very green grass; the tops of the mountains quite rocky, with snow. Lower down, and skirting the valley, which is quite shut in by the hills, fine trees; several very high waterfalls, in the style of the Glassalt (near Balmoral), only much higher. This Alpine valley is said to give the most perfect idea of a Swiss valley up in the mountains. One can ascend the Titlis; but it is said to be dangerous, so we shan't attempt it. We are very careful, and Louis won't undertake anything risky. The scenery seen from the carriage merely is so splendid that one may well be content with that. Unfortunately, to-day it pours, and it is very cold. The children are very well. The journey has really done Victoria good, and she begins to have an appetite, which with her is a very rare thing.

The next place we go to is Meyringen. We mean to

ride there over the Joch Pass, but the children must go back the same way to get round, as there is no other way out of this valley. We will leave them then with Westerweller, and go to the Grindelwald, Interlaken, &c.; and then return home by the 29th, probably. The children are living in a cottage here also.

Pension Belle Vue, Tracht bei Brienz: August 14.

. . . Our ride from Engelberg over the Joch Pass to Meyringen was quite beautiful; but a worse way than any we have ever been out on in Scotland. We were eleven hours on the road, and the sun was very hot, and the walking on these steep bad paths made one still hotter; but we enjoyed it very much, and I never saw anything grander or more magnificent. . . . I have made little scribbles on the way. . . . To-day we two with two horses were to have walked and ridden to the Grindelwald, over the Rosenlaui glacier, and to have gone on the next day to Interlaken, but the weather is so bad that it is impossible, and, not being satisfied with the prices, &c., at the hotel of Meyringen, we came on here, an hour's drive, near to the beautiful falls of the Giessbach, which we saw on Sunday. . . . The weather will determine whether we can make an expedition to-morrow.

We shall be home on Friday by Thun and Basel, where we sleep. What day are we to be at Coburg, and for how long exactly? I believe only two or three days.

The white heather is from above Engelberg, near Brienz.

Pension Belle Vue: August 15.

I have this instant received your dear letter from Kranichstein, and, though only just returned from an expedition to the Rosenlaui glacier, I sit down at once to thank you with all my heart for such dear lines. How glad I am all was comfortable, and that you were pleased with your day in our nice Kranichstein! I am glad you missed us a little. . . . But I must tell you of to-day. We drove to Reichenbach, close to the falls, took a guide and horses, and in two hours by a steep stony path got to Rosenlaui. The view on the Wetterhorn, covered with snow, and on the Wellhorn, which is a rugged rock on the other side of it, the white sparkling glacier, is quite beautiful. The shapes and immense height of the mountains are so imposing. I look, admire, wonder; one can't find words to express what one feels. How you would admire the scenery! Papa was so fond of it all.

Kranichstein: August 21.

These will be my last lines until we meet. We returned here well, having unfortunately, though, much rain from Interlaken to Basel. At Thun we were in the same hotel as Blanche [6] and Mademoiselle Bernard,[7] and to-morrow we expect Uncle Nemours, Marguerite,[8] and Alençon,[9] whom we asked to dinner on their way to Frankfort. I am mostly at the Rosenhöhe with my mama-in-law, as she is quite alone. I was in town with her, and read to her this morning; she is ever so dear and kind. I do love her *so much*. Ever since Ella's birth we have been drawn so closely to each other, and I admire her also now that I know and understand her. There is so much beneath, so much *Gemüth*, tenderness, and delicacy of feeling. It is indeed a blessing to have such people as they are for parents-in-law.

[6] Youngest daughter of Duc de Nemours.
[7] Governess of Princess Blanche.
[8] Eldest daughter of Duc de Nemours.
[9] Second son of the same.

September 1.

Uncle George was here yesterday. Vicky remains with us till the 5th, and it gives me so much pleasure to be able to repay her for her hospitality this winter.

Kranichstein: September 8.

... After having missed the train they intended to come by, Bertie and Alix arrived at three o'clock. They dined with us. Louis then took him to the theatre, and I drove her about.

My poor father-in-law's throat is very bad, and gives him much pain. I am really very anxious about him.

We leave to-morrow afternoon at four, and shall spend the following day at Ostend, embarking in the evening. Till the end of the week we intend stopping in town, and if Bertie and Alix remain longer we shall leave by the limited mail (for Balmoral).

Inverness: October 8.

This is a very fine town, and the country is very beautiful. We took a walk this morning, and shall drive this afternoon. It was thought better not to go to a kirk, as the people seemed to look out for us.

Again a thousand thanks for having arranged this nice journey for us, which we enjoy so much. I thought so much of you and dear Papa yesterday during our ride.[1]

Sandringham: November 16.

... I am pleased that the children are well under your roof. I know they have all they can want. Bertie had such bad toothache yesterday: Louis also a little; the cold air must be the cause, for it is so sharp here.

---

[1] See *Leaves from a Journal*—Grantown, 1860.

Alix and I practise together for an hour of an evening. ... Alix drove me down to the sea the other day, and a most alarming drive it was, for the horses pulled, and, to our astonishment, the coachman suddenly alighted between us, with his feet in the air, from the back seat, and caught hold of the reins—it was too funny. I hope to be near you again on Saturday.

Darmstadt: November 28.

... I find my father-in-law looking better, I am happy to say, though far from strong; and alas! one of his lungs is affected. Though, with care, one can guard him from evil consequences, still of course it is an anxious thing. All the family are very grateful for your kind messages, and send their respects to you.

... The children are very well, and Victoria said to my mother, 'Meine Grossmama, die Königinn, has got a little vatch with a birdie,' and she is always speaking of all at Windsor, but principally of the things in your room. I am so glad that you are pleased with the children's picture. I admire it so much.

Darmstadt: December 5.

Many thanks for your letter received yesterday, with the account of Lenchen's *Verlobung* [betrothal]. I am so glad she is happy, and I hope every blessing will rest on them both that one can possibly desire.

I had a letter from Marie Brabant[2] two days ago, where she says dear Uncle's [King Leopold's] state is hopeless; but yesterday she telegraphed that he was rather better. What a loss it would be if he were to be taken from us, for his very name and existence, though he takes no active part in politics, are of weight and value.

Yesterday I was painting in oils, and I copied my sketch

---

[2] Duchess of Brabant.

of the Sluggan, and, if it be in any way at all presentable and fit to give, I will send it to you. I hope it won't be very Chinese, for our sketches had a certain likeness to works of art of that country. Louis is very busy here. He has begun his military duties; he has the command and *Verwaltung* [administration] of the Cavalry Brigade. To-day he has to go to the Chamber, and he is going to attend the different offices—home department, finances, justice, &c. —so as to get a knowledge of the routine of business. . . .

Darmstadt: December 8.

We are so grieved and distressed at dear Uncle Leopold's[3] alarming state, and have given up all hope, the accounts are so bad. Oh, were there but a chance for you, or for any of us who love him so dearly, to be near him during his last hours!

December 11.

Many thanks for your letter. Alas, alas! beloved Uncle Leopold is no more! How much for you, for us, for all, goes with him to the grave! One tie more of those dear old times is rent!

I do feel for you so much, for dear Uncle was indeed a father to you. Now you are head of all the family— it seems incredible, and that dear Papa should not be by your side.

The regret for dear Uncle Leopold is universal—he stood so high in the eyes of all parties; his life was a history in itself—and now that book is closed. Oh, it is so sad, and he is such a loss! I am almost glad this sorrow has fallen into those days already so hallowed by melancholy and precious recollections. How I recollect every hour, every minute of those days. In thinking of them

---

[3] King of the Belgians.

one feels over again the hope, the anxiety, and lastly the despair and grief of that irretrievable loss. The Almighty stood by you and us, and enabled us to bear it, for I always wonder that we lived through that awful time.

The future world seems so like a real home, for there are so many dear ones to meet again. There is something peculiarly sad in the death of the last one of a large family — to feel that none is left to tell of each other, and of their earlier life, which the younger ones could know only through their lips.

December 15.

Many thanks for your letter. I was so anxious to hear something of our beloved Uncle's end; it seems to have been most peaceful.

There will be many Princes at Brussels, I believe.

How much I thought of you and of dear Papa on the 14th! Dear Louis leaves me this afternoon. He will reach Brussels at five to-morrow morning, and remain over the Sunday.

The accession of a new King and the honours that have at once to be paid are so painful, following so closely on the death of one we have loved and known in that position. As the French say: 'Le Roi est mort. Vive le Roi!'

December 20.

. . . I was sitting up for Louis till half-past eleven with Countess Blücher—who leaves to-day, and has spent a few days with me—when he and, to my astonishment, Bertie also, came into the room. The next day, alas! he had to leave again at four; but still, short as his stay was, it was a token of his constant love for me, and it touched me very much, for I ever loved him so dearly.

Everything went off well at Brussels, as you will have

heard. The more I realise that we shall never see beloved Uncle Leopold again, the sadder I grow. He had, apart from all his excellent qualities, such a charm as I believe we shall seldom find again.

The dear Countess is well. We made the dining-room into a bedroom for her, and we dined downstairs. I was so afraid of her getting cold, if she lived out of the house.

Darmstadt: December 24.

... How I wish beloved Uncle were brought to Windsor to rest there as he had wished! I wondered so much that everything had taken place at Laeken, knowing that dear Uncle had wished it otherwise.

Uncle Louis wishes me to thank you once more for the Christmas eatables, and my mother-in-law likewise for the lovely little frame and photograph. They are both much touched by this kind attention on your part.

Christmas Day.

... To me Christmas is always sad now, and for Louis and his family it was so likewise this year; my parents-in-law felt it very much. We went to the Military Church at eight this morning. It is the service we like best; but it was bitterly cold, everything snow white.

I hope my little picture, though very imperfect, found favour in your eyes. It gave me such pleasure doing it for you, thinking of you and our expedition the whole time I was doing it.

December 30.

This is my last letter this year. In many ways a happy one has it been, though it has deprived us of many dear and near ones. Each year brings us nearer to the *Wiedersehen* [reunion with the dead], though it is sad to think how one's glass is running out, and how little good goes with it, compared to the numberless blessings we receive. Time goes incredibly fast.

Every earnest and tender wish from us both is yours, dear Mama, for this coming year with its expected events. May God's blessing rest on this new union which is to be formed in our family, and may dear Lenchen be as happy as all those who loved her can wish! I am so sorry to think that I shall probably not see her again until she is married; but I am glad for her sake that the *Brautstand* [the betrothal period] is not to be long.

I send you a locket with Ella's miniature, which I hope will please you.

1866

January 2.

I am at the head of a committee of ladies out of the different classes of society to make a large bazaar, in which all the country is to take part, for the Idiot Asylum. It is very difficult—all the more as I have never had anything to do with such things in my life. . . . I wanted, for the first public thing I undertake, to take in all principles, and my mother-in-law has given her name to it. I have chosen the committee out of different sets—half *adelig* [people of rank], half *bürgerlich* [of the citizen class], and all these ladies, half of whom I did not know before, come and sit in my small room and discuss—and, as yet, do not disagree.

January 6.

. . . The people here are so much pleased that my Louis takes such active part in all his duties—military and civil—for he attends the different offices, and as General,

I hear, he keeps great order where there was until now disorder and great abuse of power. Of course, I see him much less, and some days scarcely at all.

On the 14th we go to Gotha for about a fortnight, without the children.

Gotha: January 19.

Dear Uncle and Aunt are well, and we are very happy here, for they are always kindness itself to us. Uncle looks very well, but he grows very stout, I think. We saw the *Braut von Messina* [Schiller's] so well given two nights ago. I thought so much of dear Papa, who admired it greatly; and Uncle Ernest told me he had it given for you, when you first came here.

Gotha: January 22.

Our Quaker acquaintances have sent me a great deal for the bazaar, and an old gentleman who heard of it, 100*l*.! I could not believe my eyes. They are always so generous: and, hearing of my undertaking a work of this sort, they sent me this spontaneously. Is it not kind?

Darmstadt: February 1.

It is spring weather here altogether—quite warm when one comes out of the house. It is so unnatural. The children enjoy it, and are out a great deal, looking so well and strong: I wish you could see them. The little one is growing up to her sister very fast, and actually wears the frocks Victoria wore last year. I wish you could hear all the extraordinary things Victoria says. Ella is civil to all strangers—excepting to my mother-in-law, or to old ladies. It is too tiresome. There is a large ball given by the officers at their Casino to-night, to which we must go. It will be crowded and hot. Our house gets on tolerably. The housekeeper, a Berlinerinn, comes on the 20th, and we are told that we can go into the house next month. I can't help doubting it, and I regret leaving this nice little house, where our first happy years have been spent. I am so glad that you have at least been in the new house, so that I can always think that you are no stranger to it, which makes me like it much better.

February 10.

... I am happy to think you are quiet at Osborne after all you had to go through. The emotion and all other feelings recalled by such an event must have been very powerful and have tried you much.[4] It was noble of you, my darling Mama, and the great effort will bring compensation. Think of the pride and pleasure it would have given darling Papa—the brave example to others not to shrink from their duty; and it has shown that you felt the intense sympathy which the English people evinced, and still evince, in your great misfortune.

How to-day recalls those bright and happy former years! There is no cloud without a silver lining, and the lining to the black cloud which overshadows your existence is the bright recollection of the past blending into the bright hope of a happy future; a small part of it also is the intense love of your children and nation, which casts a light around you which many live to enjoy and admire, and which few—if any—possess like you. I wish I could have sent a fine nosegay of orange blossoms for to-day, but they could not have arrived fresh, so I gave it up.

Louis sends his tenderest love, and wishes me to say how much his thoughts with mine are to-day constantly with you. He is very industrious, and has a great deal to do now, and, I hear, does all very well.

---

[4] The opening of Parliament by the Queen for the first time after the death of the Prince Consort.

Darmstadt: February 15.

How dear of you to have written to me on the 10th—a day of such recollections! That last happy wedding-day at Buckingham Palace, how well I remember it, and all the previous ones at Windsor, when we all stood before your door, waiting for you and dear Papa to come out. You both looked so young, bright, and handsome. As I grew older, it made me so proud to have two such dear parents! And that my children should never know you both together—that will remain a sorrow to me as long as I live.

March 16.

How trying the visit to Aldershot must have been, but it is so wise and kind of you to go. I cannot think of it without tears in my eyes. Formerly that was one of the greatest pleasures of my girlhood, and you and darling Papa looked so handsome together. I so enjoyed following you on those occasions. Such moments I should like to call back for an instant.

Our house here is quite empty, and the *déménagement* creates such work. To-morrow night we sleep for the first time in the new house.

March 17.

I write from our dear little old house. May dear Papa's and your blessing rest on our new home, as I am sure it will! It is full of souvenirs of you both—all your pictures, photographs of dear brothers and sisters and home. It reminds me a little of Osborne, of Buckingham Palace, a little even of Balmoral. Could I but show it to darling Papa! If I have any taste, I owe it all to him, and I learned so much by seeing him arrange pictures, rooms, &c.

At half-past seven we go into our house to-night.

Bender is to say a prayer and pronounce a blessing, when we with all our household are assembled in hall; only Louis's parents and William besides ourselves. Yours and dear Papa's I pray to rest on us.

March 20.

That [the death of the Duchess of Kent] was the commencement of all the grief; but with darling Papa, so full of tenderness, sympathy and delicate feeling for you, how comparatively easy to bear, compared to all that followed!

. . . We are very comfortably established here, and I can't fancy that I am in Germany, the house and all its arrangements being so English. When can we hope once to have you here? Of course *that* is the summit of our wishes. Your rooms are on the east side and very cool—as you always go abroad when it is hot, and suffer so much from the heat. I shall die of it this year, as my rooms are to the west.

March 24.

. . . Our Grand-Uncle of Homburg has just died, so that Homburg falls to Uncle Louis now. But all the things of the Landgravine Elizabeth go to Princess Reuss, and her [Aunt Elizabeth's[5]] rooms are full of beautiful miniatures, oil-paintings, and ornaments *en masse*, like Gloucester House.

I shall be so glad to see dear Affie. His rooms are to be ready by this evening. The house is very comfortable, but the weather is awful—wind, rain, and sleet. In spite of it the house is so cheerful.

Dear Lady Frances Baillie was with me on Thursday, so dear and charming.

---

[5] Princess Elizabeth of Great Britain and Ireland, Princess Alice's grand-aunt.

April 2.

... We are living in such a state of anxiety and alarm. War[6] would be too fearful a thing to contemplate—brother against brother, friend against friend, as it will be in this case! May the Almighty avert so fearful a calamity! Here, at Mayence and Frankfort, it will begin, if anything happens, as there are mixed garrisons; and we must side with one against the other. For Henry,[7] who is still here, it is dreadful. He can't desert at such a moment, and yet if he should have to draw his sword against his country, his brothers fighting on the other side! Fancy the complications and horrors of such a war!

For Vicky and Fritz it is really dreadful; please let me hear by messenger what you hear from them. I am sure you think of us in these troubled times. What would dear Papa have said to all this? I long to hear from you, to know that your warm heart is acting for Germany.

March 26.

... The dear old Queen Marie Amélie[8] is gone to her rest at last, after a long and so stormy a life! Claremont is now also altered. How sad those constant changes are! It reminds one again and again that we are on a journey, and that the *real home* is elsewhere. All those who work hard and love their fellow-creatures meet again, and the thorny path will be forgotten which leads to the happy meeting. I sincerely mourn for the dear Queen, and she was so kind to me always. I am glad she was one of Victoria's godmothers.

---

[6] War between Prussia and Austria was now imminent.
[7] Prince Henry of Hesse, Prince Louis' second brother.
[8] Widow of King Louis Philippe.

April 7.

... Our Bazaar goes off wonderfully: 7,000 florins the first day, and to-day again a great deal. Affie was invaluable in arranging, selling, and assisting in every way. There have been crowds these two days, as in England: something quite unusual for the quiet inhabitants of this place. They have shown so much zeal and devotion that I am quite touched by it, as I am more or less a stranger to them.

April 25.

Thousand thanks for your dear lines, and for the money and charming bas-relief of you, which I think very good. I thought so much of former birthdays at home in Buckingham Palace. They were so happy. We did nothing in particular; merely dined at Kranichstein with Uncle Louis in the afternoon. It was warm and fine.

May 3.

... The prospect of war seems to be nearing realisation. It will be so dreadful if it does. God be with us, if such a misfortune befall poor Germany! These prospects have already done much harm to trade. The large manufactories send away their superfluous workmen, and they sell next to nothing. Most unpopular amongst high and low, and amongst people of all opinions, this civil war will be. . . .

I have made all the summer out-walking dresses, seven in number, with paletots for the girls—not embroidered, but entirely made from beginning to end; likewise the new necessary flannel shawls for the expected. I manage all the nursery accounts, and everything myself, which gives me plenty to do, as everything increases, and, on account of the house, we must live *very* economically for these next years.

If there is a war then, and Louis is away, what shall I do? This is my constant dread and apprehension. As long as he comes home safe again—that is all I shall think of. Please God to spare me that fearful anxiety, which weighs on me now already; for he, having only a brigade, could not keep out of danger, like Fritz [9] in Schleswig.

I put my trust wholly in the Almighty, who has watched over and blessed our life so richly thus far—so *much, much* more than I ever deserved, or can deserve; and He will not forsake us in the hour of need, I am sure.

These dangerous times make one very serious and anxious; the comfort of faith and trust in God, who does all well and for the best, is the only support. Life is but a pilgrimage—a little more or a little less sorrow falls to one's lot; but the anticipation of evil is almost as great a suffering as the evil itself, and mine always was an anxious nature, so I cannot banish the thoughts which all the dreadful chances of war force upon one.

May 7.

. . . I am so sorry for poor Louise and Beatrice, and whooping cough is a nasty thing, though I wish we could complain of that as our sufferings here. Anxiety, worry without end!

Uncle Alexander returned from Vienna two days ago. The Emperor, Uncle Alexander Mensdorff, all frantic at being forced into war, but fearing now no more being able to prevent it. Cannot the other three Powers interfere and step between at this dangerous crisis—proposing a Congress, or anything, so as to avert this calamity?

Henry, who was here on six weeks' leave, as he and Uncle Louis were to have gone to Russia (which now, of course, they won't do), had suddenly to return to Bonn, as

---

[9] Crown Prince of Prussia.

his regiment is made *mobil*. Uncle Alexander receives the command of the 8th Armeecorps, which I suppose and hope will be stationed somewhere near here, as Louis is in that, and *is to go*. He means to go to Berlin this afternoon for a day to see Fritz, and tell him how circumstances now force him to draw his sword against the Prussians in the service of his own country. The whole thing is dreadful, and the prospect of being left alone here at such a moment (for all our people, nearly, will accompany Louis) is dreadful! If I were only over my troubles I should not be so anxious, so nervous and unhappy, as I must say the anticipation of all these dreadful things makes me. Could I follow in the distance! But now that is impossible, and I have not a single older married person near me. When dear Louis goes, of course Westerweller goes too. I still pray and hope against hope that there may be no war; even if all the troops are assembled, I hope that the other Powers will interfere, and not look on whilst these brothers cut each other's throats. It is such an unnatural, monstrous war!

May 18.

. . . How glad I am to hear that Lord Clarendon is still hopeful! Here as yet, though there is no distinct reason for it, save the repugnance of all to this civil war, all still hope to avoid the war. Every day we have occasion to hear how the Prussians detest this war—army and all—and there are constant rows, with the Landwehr in particular. Men of forty, who have families and homes to look after, are taken away with their sons; and those who have horses are also taken, with their horses: so that the wife and children sit at home, unable to do anything for their land. It is ruining numbers, and murmurs get louder and louder. A revolution must break out if this continues.

... I do pray *most fervently* that the King will listen to the just advice, in no way derogatory to his dignity, of placing the hated question of the Duchies before the Confederation; but I fear he won't. If he would only listen to that advice and disarm, all Germany would do it at once—only too gladly—forgetting all the losses in the happiness of peace restored. Forgive my stupid letter, but we live really so in the midst of these affairs, on which our existence will turn, that I can think of nothing else.

Austria can't hold out much longer, and the country is getting very violent against the King and Bismarck. The Emperor is less able to concede and keep peace.

Now good-bye, dearest Mama. We are so grateful to you for taking the children, if anything comes to pass.

May 22.

... Anything you hear of Vicky and Fritz, will you write it to me? ... The cloud grows blacker every day, and the anxiety we all live in is very great. But I ought not to write to you to-day of such gloomy things, which, thank God, you only see and hear of from the other side of the water.

May 25.

... The Duke and Duchess of Nassau were here yesterday. They, like me, are in such an unpleasant position, should it come to blows, which I still hope may be averted — for why should we harmless mortals be attacked?

... We shall be beggars very soon, if all goes on as it promises to do; it is quite dreadful, and the want of other people (and dissatisfaction) increases. ... I have ordered a good travelling-bag for Louis, for much the same reason that some people take out an umbrella in fine weather to keep off the rain, and this is to be against a war. . . . I have a sort of *Ahnung* [presentiment] that it won't come to the worst—for us at least—and here we shall keep so quiet, only on the defensive, if attacked.

May 28.

. . . There seems a little chance of the dreadful prospects being bettered. How I do pray it may be the commencement of a better time; and that, if peace be established, it may be so *firmly*, so that one may not live in the daily dread of new quarrels re-opening between the two countries. . . .

June 8.

. . . How precious are your words of love and sympathy and the hope you still hold to, that war may somehow be averted! It does me good to hear it; and I know how much, and how lovingly, your thoughts dwell with dear Vicky and with me during this time of trial. . . .

June 13.

. . . I fear if the Bund orders the mobilisation, and goes against Prussia, our troops will be the first to go, and then Louis may get orders to be off any day. It is too dreadful! I live in such dread that he may have to go just before, or at the very moment of, my confinement. . . .

I hope Scotland will do you good. Please God, when you return matters may be better. If Austria and Prussia would only fight out their quarrel together; but the latter has taken refuge with the Bund now, because she wanted it.

Darmstadt: June 15.

. . . The serious illness of poor little Sigismund[1] in the midst of all these troubles is really dreadful for poor

[1] Son of the Crown Prince and Princess of Prussia. See *ante*, p. 101.

Vicky and Fritz, and they are so fond of that merry little child.

We have just received the news that the Prussians have crossed our frontier and established themselves at Giessen. The excitement here is dreadful, and it is very difficult to keep people back from doing stupid things—wanting to attack, and so on, which with our force alone would be madness.

Louis—as always—remains quiet; but we live in a perpetual fever, alarms being sent, being *gehetzt* [stirred up] from Vienna, as they want the Bund to go with them at once. It is a dreadful time. I anticipate it will be the close of the existence of the little countries. God stand by us! Without the civil list Uncle Louis and the family are beggars, as all the private property belongs to the country.

It is so kind of dear Lady Ely to offer to come. I shall be very glad of it, for from one day to another I don't know what Louis' duties may be; and, when I am laid up, it is so pleasant to have someone who can write to you.

June 18.

These lines I send by our children, whom you so kindly will take charge of—alas, that the times should be such as to make this necessary! In your dear hands they will be so safe; and if we can give you a little pleasure in sending them, it would be a real consolation in parting from them, which we both feel very much.

The state of excitement here is beyond description. Troops arriving, being billeted about—all will be concentrated from here to Frankfort. Two days ago the Bund telegraphed for Uncle Alexander to come, as the Prussians were advancing; we, of course, were all unprepared, and the confusion and fright were dreadful; but, thank God, they retreated again, when they got wind that troops were assembling. . . .

June 24.

. . . The state of affairs is awful; perpetual frights and false news arrive. The Prussians are coming from Wetzlar or Bingen; all the bustle and alarm for necessary defence; it is really dreadful. Louis' chief has his staff at Frankfort. Louis' cavalry brigade is there likewise, so he has his adjutant, &c., there, and does his work early in the morning at Frankfort, returning here in the afternoon, which has been kindly allowed on account of me. I remain here, of course, as near dear Louis as I can; and now that the children are gone, I have only myself to look after. . . . I have not the least fear, but my anxiety about Louis will be very great, as you can imagine. . . . Collections are already being made for the hospitals in the field, and the necessary things to be got for the soldiers. Illness and wounds will be dreadful in this heat. Coarse linen and rags are the things of which one can't have enough, and I am working, collecting shirts, sheets, &c.; and now I come to ask, if you could send me some old linen for rags. In your numerous households it is collected twice a year and sent to hospitals. Could I beg for some this time? It would be such a blessing for the poor Germans; and here they are not so rich, and that is a thing of which in every war there has been too little. Lint I have ordered from England by wish of the doctors; and bandages also they wished for. If you could, through Dr. Jenner, procure me some of these things, I should be so grateful. . . . Four dozen shirts we are making in the house. Every contribution of linen, or of patterns of good cushions, or any good bed which in the English hospitals has been found useful, we should be delighted to have. . . . For the moment the people beg most for *rags*; our house being new, we have none. I am tolerably well, and cannot be too thankful for good nerves. Louis is very low at times, nervous at leaving me; and for him I keep up, though at times not without a struggle. May the Almighty watch over us, and not separate us, is my hourly prayer!

In your hands we feel the children so safe, though we miss them much. It is so kind of you to have taken them, and they are strong and healthy. . . .

June 25.

Two words by Lady Ely's courier. I am so glad she is here. She performed the journey in a day and night without difficulty; and Christa, who merely came from Cassel, took three days coming by road.

Alas! to-morrow Louis' division moves on into the country to make room for other troops, and he must go. It will be too far for him to return—save with special permission for a few hours—so we shall have to part. My courage is beginning to fail me, but I bear up as best I can. God knows what a bitter trial it is! He is just in front, so the first exposed. William is to go in Uncle Alex's staff, and my poor mama-in-law is beginning to break down now. We try to cheer each other. The whole thing is so hard: against her countrymen—there where Louis has served. The whole thing is so *contre-cœur*, and the Prussian soldiers dislike it as much as we do.

I am going to Frankfort with ever so many poor wives to take leave of their husbands, who march to-day.

The heat is awful. I have no time to think of myself, or I dare say I should have heat, &c., to complain of. Being still off and on with Louis, and having things to do, keeps me up; but when he is gone, and I have no man here to reassure me, it will be dreadful.

I must close. . . . Letters from home *now* are such a pleasure; do let anyone write to me sometimes to give me news of you all.

Your own child,
ALICE.

Darmstadt: July 1.

. . . The parting *now* was *so* hard! and he feels it so dreadfully. I can scarcely manage to write. The heat, besides, is overpowering. Our dear wedding-day four years ago! Four years of undisturbed, real, and increasing happiness. How I thank and bless the Almighty for them, and how fervently I pray that we may live over this most bitter trial!

. . . Whether Henry is engaged or not we don't know, and can get no news of him. At any rate he is cut off from news of us and the rest of Germany; and, as our army is moving, and he is on the extreme wing, at any moment he may find himself opposite to his own brothers and countrymen. It is most painful, and has been to my poor father-in-law a great shock, as we all hoped he had got away. Please let my brothers know this. They will feel for this unheard-of position for three brothers to be in. . . .

Dear Lady Ely is a comfort and support to me, and it was quite a relief to Louis to leave her with me. We are both so grateful that she came. Christa is quite out of sorts about her country, and sees everything black. Marie is low about her brother; and we are so in the middle of it all, that an English person who has no one concerned in it all is really a relief.

I am so glad that you are pleased with the little ones. You will be sure, I know, not to let them get in the way of infection, if there is still any.

July 3.

... Poor Vicky! She bears her trial [the death of her son, Prince Sigismund] bravely, and it is a heavy one indeed. This dreadful war is enough to break one's heart. Those lives sacrificed for nothing—and what will be the end of it all? All our troops are gone now, too, and, what is so unpleasant, of course we here don't know where they go to—where they are. Letters are fetched by the Feldpost, and as they are chiefly not near the railroads— at least not Louis—we cannot telegraph. At such a moment I know dear Louis fidgets dreadfully for news, and I not less. Since he has gone I have heard nothing.

I am so very uncomfortable, and it wants courage and patience and hope, under such circumstances, to bear all. Of course anxiety about beloved Louis is the chief thing, and longing for news. The Prussians are collecting a large army near Thüringen, in which direction ours are marching. Probably Uncle Ernest against ours! He might so well have remained quiet, and sent his troops to Mayence, as was settled.

For dear Lenchen's wedding-day receive every warm and affectionate wish. May God's blessing rest on their union! I am so glad you are pleased with the dear children. I have already found that likeness in Ella to Affie's picture by Thorburn, but she is so like dear Louis.

July 6.

... There seems a chance of an armistice.[2] I trust it is so, and that peace will ensue. The enormous bloodshed on both sides this fortnight is too awful to think of.[3]

---

[2] An armistice of five days was agreed upon on July 22.

[3] On June 27, the Austrians had been defeated after a stubborn fight at Nachod, with a loss of over six thousand men killed. Other battles took

Poor Austria! it is hard for her. But as she is said to be ready to cede Venice, then at least the Italian war will be at an end.

Surely the neutral Powers will try and prevent Austria and Prussia beginning again; it is too horrid!

The rest of Germany now must knock under; but that is better than again shedding so much blood on the chance of getting the upper hand.

I have had some lines from dear Louis from the north of Hesse. He is well; how I do hope now that they won't come to blows.

How kind of you to give the children frocks for the wedding! Will you kiss the dear little ones from me? I miss them very much.

Beloved Mama,   Darmstadt: July 19.

What a time I have passed during these eight days since Baby's birth![4] Firstly, I have to thank the Almighty for having preserved my own sweet and adored husband, and for the blessing of having had him by me, so dear, so precious, during my confinement. After three days he had to go, and when he got near Aschaffenburg found fighting going on.[5] We could hear the guns here. The Prussians shot from the roofs of the houses; they fought in the streets; it must have been horrid. Our troops retreated (as had always been intended) in perfect order. The wounded were brought in here the following day. The 13th and 14th they fought. Louis was there on the 14th; since then I have not seen him—God knows when I shall again.

place within a few days at Podoll, Münchengratz, and Trautenau. On July 3 was fought the decisive battle of Sadowa, in which the Austrians are said to have lost nearly forty thousand men.

[4] Irène, born July 12, 1866.

[5] On July 14 the German Federal troops were defeated at Aschaffenburg.

The Prussians have taken Frankfort, and they are at home here. No communications allowed; get no papers or letters; may send none! An existence of monstrous anxiety and worry, which it is impossible for those to imagine who have not lived through it.

I had a letter from Louis from the Odenwald this morning, written yesterday. They expected to pass Amorbach to-day. They are trying to meet the Bavarians, who are never to be found.

I long for a letter from you. We have none at all, and I have had none from you since Baby's birth. The people, who are such cowards and so silly, fly from here in all available droschkies.

How I pray some end may soon come to this horrid bloodshed! Ah! the misery around us you can't imagine. Henry has never received his discharge, and has gone unscathed, in spite of being so exposed through all these battles.

I myself am very well, and I don't give way, though the anxiety about Louis leaves me no peace.

Baby is well and very pretty. The time she came at prevented a thought of disappointment at her being a girl. Only gratitude to the Almighty filled our hearts, that I and the child were well, and that dear Louis and I were together at the time. The times are hard; it wants all a Christian's courage and patience to carry one through them; but there is *one Friend* who in the time of need does not forsake one, and He is my comfort and support. God bless you, my own Mama, and pray for your child,

ALICE.

Friday, July 27, 9 o'clock P.M.

At this moment the messenger has arrived, to leave again at five to-morrow morning. A thousand thanks for your dear letter, the first I have received since Baby's birth!

To-night (since Sunday no news of Louis) at length I have heard that dear Louis is well. These last four days they have been fighting again. I had a few lines from him. These last two nights he slept in a field, and the country is so poor that they had nothing but a little bread during two days to eat. Now the Prussians, having made peace with Austria, and having refused it to us, are advancing on our troops from three sides.

I can scarcely write; this anxiety is killing me, and my love has been so exposed! All are in admiration of his personal bravery and tender attention to the suffering and want of all around. He never thinks of himself, and shares all the dangers and privations with the others.

Louis says they long for peace. He disapproves the different Governments for not now giving way to Prussia, and begs me to use my influence with Uncle Louis to accept Prussian conditions to spare further bloodshed.

From all parts of the country the people beg me to do what I can.

The confusion here is awful, the want of money alarming; right and left one must help. As the Prussians pillaged here, I have many people's things hidden in the house. Even whilst in bed I had to see gentlemen in my room, as there were things to be done and asked which had to come straight to me. Then our poor wounded—the wives and mothers begging I should inquire for their husbands and children. It is a state of affairs too dreadful to describe.

The new anxiety to-night of knowing a dreadful battle is expected, perhaps going on, in which dear Louis again must be! I can scarcely bear up any longer; I feel it is getting too much. God Almighty stand by us! My courage is beginning to sink. I see no light anywhere; and my own beloved husband still in danger, and we cannot hear, for the Prussians are between us and them. Anything may have happened to him, and I can't hear it or know it! I could not go to him were he wounded.

What I have suffered and do suffer no words can describe—the sleepless nights of anxiety, the long days without news—*how* I pray it may soon end, and dear darling Louis be spared me!

In these days I have so longed to hear from you. It would have been such a comfort, and I longed for it much.

If we live, and peace is restored, the country and everything will be in such a mess, and both of us in such want of change, that we must go somewhere; but we shall then, I fear, be next to ruined. You can't think what war in one's own country—in a little one like this—is! The want is fearful. I must go to bed, as it is late. I am well, so is the little one; but I can't sleep or eat well all along; and the worry of mind and much to do keep me weak.

Oh, that we were together again! Good-bye, beloved Mama. These next days I fear will be dreadful. May the Almighty watch over dear Louis! You will pray for him, won't you?

P.S.—The standard of Louis' cavalry regiment, which they did not take with them, and which is usually kept at the Schloss, is in my room for safety.

Forgive the shocking writing, but I am so upset to-night, since my messenger of Tuesday returned with Louis' letter.

Darmstadt: August 4.

... The linen, &c., for the wounded has arrived, and been so useful; a thousand thanks for it! Matters here change from one day to another, and I hope Louis may soon be able to return with the troops. Uncle Louis I do hope and pray will then return, and I hope he will regain the favour which he had lost, for any change now would be dreadful.

My father-in-law is really in such a state since these events, and his nerves so shattered, that my mother-in-law trembles for him, and tries to keep him out of all. He is so angry, so heartbroken at the loss of Oberhessen, which is probable, that he wishes not to outlive it. My poor mama-in-law burst into tears this morning in my room, where this scene took place.

I have just returned from having been to enquire after the wounded at the different hospitals and houses, which are filling fast, as they can be brought from Aschaffenburg, Laufach, &c. As soon as I am better, I will go to them myself; but the close and crowded wards turn one easily faint.

Becker saw Louis three days ago, and accompanied him to Munich for a day. I hear he is well, though for six nights he had slept out of doors, and the last three nights it had poured incessantly; and all that time—on account of ours not having a truce, and expecting to be attacked—they were, being such a mass together, without provisions, barely a morsel of bread. I am so distressed about poor Anton Hohenzollern[6] and Obernitz; so many acquaintances and friends have fallen on both sides, it is dreadful!

The town is full of Prussians. I hope they will not remain too long, for they pay for nothing, and the poor inhabitants suffer so much. There is cholera in the Prussian army, and one soldier lies here ill of it. I hope it won't spread.

---

[6] Prince Anton Hohenzollern, son of Prince Hohenzollern. He died from diphtheria in a hospital, the result of a wound received during the war.

August 13.

... It is fearful. Those who have seen the misery war brings with it, near by—the sufferings, the horror—know well what a scourge it is. May the Almighty spare our poor Germany this new evil! I forgot to thank you in Louis' name, as he had told me, for your letter, which he found here on his return. He is to-day still at Berlin, and we are so grateful for your having written to good Fritz. What he can do I know he will.

Uncle Louis is still at Munich, and I don't think he will abdicate; besides, he is at this moment doing what his country wishes.

I received a letter from Julie Battenberg,[7] saying what Uncle Alexander had written to her about Louis: 'Le Prince Alexandre m'écrit qu'il a obtenu du Grand Duc la démission de Perglas' (who commanded the troops so badly), 'et la nomination du Prince Louis en commandement de nos troupes; il me dit à cette occasion que votre Mari pendant cette triste campagne s'est fait aimer et apprécier de tout le monde, qu'il s'est fait une excellente réputation, et qu'il sera reçu à bras ouverts par la troupe.' ... It is a large command for one so young, and with so little experience—all the more so, as we don't know how long peace may last. He is sent to Berlin, as the country all look to Louis to prevent new evil; and all this without poor Louis having any direct position of heir to be able to enforce his opinion. He has no easy life of it.

The horse you gave Louis he rode in the different engagements, and praised him very much. He stood the fire quite well, but not the bursting of the shells close by.

About the children, the 23rd is quite soon enough for their departure.

[7] Princess Battenberg, wife of Prince Alexander of Hesse.

We shall not call baby 'Irène,' unless all seems really peaceful, and at this moment it does not look promising. I am very sad and dismayed at the whole look-out. My mother-in-law was so pleased with your letter, and thanks you warmly for it.

Nierstein, Gelbes Haus: August 17.

This dear day makes me think so much of you, of home, and of those two dear ones whose memories are so precious, and who live on with us, and make me often think that we had parted only yesterday.

We are so pleased at your saying that you claim Louis as *your* son. He always considers *himself* in particular your child, and if anything helps to stimulate him in doing his duty well, it is the sincere wish of being worthy to claim and deserve that title. Darling Papa would be proud of him, and pleased to see how earnestly he takes his duties, and how conscientiously and unselfishly he fulfils them, for he has had and still has many trials—things I can tell you of when we meet again.

Life is such a pilgrimage, and so uncertain is its duration, that all minor troubles are forgotten and easily borne, when one thinks what one must live for.

Before leaving Darmstadt yesterday to come here, we went to see some of the wounded again. One poor man had died since I was last there: he had been so patient, and had suffered so much. Another had had an operation performed and was very low—he was crying like a child. I could scarcely comfort him; he held my hand and always moaned out 'Es brennt so' [It burns so]. Such nice people most of those young men are—very young, and for that class so well educated. All who are well enough are reading.

I must praise the ventilation and cleanliness in the

different hospitals; in these things they have made wonderful progress here.

We are here in Rheinhessen, as Louis has to take his command. This place, Nierstein, lies between Worms and Mayence, and all our troops are quartered about here. Louis' staff is at Worms, where he himself is to-day, and was already last night.

He was more hopeful about the prospects for Oberhessen on his return from Berlin, and had been so kindly received by dear Vicky and Fritz.

When Louis wrote his Farewell to his cavalry brigade (who are so sorry to lose him), as a remembrance that he and they had stood in the field together for their first campaign, he asked these two regiments, officers and men, to stand sponsors to Baby, as she was born during that time, and they are delighted, but wish the child to have one of their names! We wait till the troops can come home to christen Baby, on that account. . . . I don't think we shall be here very long. Whenever the Prussians leave Darmstadt, we can return.

Nierstein, Gelbes Haus: August 21.

. . . We are here still, and all our troops, and Louis has a great deal to do. To-morrow the armistice is over, and at present we have no news as to its prolongation or the settlement of peace; but it must be one or other. A little private war of Prussia against us would be absurd and impossible, so the troops remain quartered in the different villages about here. The country here is so rich and fertile, the villages so clean, with such good houses; but the people are blessed with children to an extraordinary extent! It is the most richly populated part of all Germany, and there are more people on the square mile than in England.

The change of air—though it is but two hours from Darmstadt—has done me good, and if later, through your great kindness, a little journey should be possible to us, it would be very beneficial to both of us.

This house is quite close to the Rhine, and this instant our pioneers have come by from Worms on their pontoon bridge singing a quartett, about twenty or thirty men. It looks so pretty, and they sing so beautifully. On their marches the soldiers always sing, and they have so many beautiful songs, such as: 'Der gute Kamerad.' The Germans are such a *gemüthlich* [simple, kindly, sociable] people. The more one lives with them, the more one learns to appreciate them. It is a fine nation. God grant this war, which has produced so many heroes, and cost so many gallant lives, may not have been in vain, and that at length Germany may become a mighty, powerful Power! It will then be the first in the world, where the great ideas and thoughts come from, free from narrow-minded prejudice, and when once the Germans have attained political freedom, they will be lastingly happy and united.

But the present state of things is sad, though one should not despair of some good resulting from it.

My letter is quite confused. I beg a thousand pardons for it, but I have been interrupted so often.

Gelbes Haus: August 29.

. . . The children arrived well and safe, and in such good looks. It was a great pleasure to see them again; and I tried to make Victoria tell me as much as possible of dear Grandma and uncles and aunts, and when she is not absent-minded she is very communicative. How much we thank you, darling Mama, for having kept them and been so good to them, I can't tell you. This change has been so good for them; for now there are both cholera and small-pox at Darmstadt, which is still full of Prussian soldiers. More have come, and our peace is not yet concluded. I hope it is no bad sign, and that the hopes of losing less will not disappear.

We were only in Darmstadt for the day when the children arrived, and we go there for a few hours to-morrow on business. Louis has a great deal to do, and all the military things are in his hands.

I am not feeling very well. The air here after a few days is relaxing, and I begin to feel more what a strain there has been on my nerves during this time. I have such a pain in my side again. Mountain air Weber wants me to have, and quiet, away from all bothers; but I fear that is impossible *now*, on account of Louis not being able to leave—and then financially.

I have some *Heimweh* [home-sickness] after dear England, Balmoral, and all at home, I own, though the joy of being near dear Louis again is *so* great! But life is meant for work, and not for pleasure, and I learn more and more to be grateful and content with that which the Almighty sends me, and to find the sunshine in spite of the clouds; for when one has one's beloved, adored husband by one's side, what is there in the world that is too heavy to bear? My own darling Mama, when I think of darling Papa and of you, and that he is not *visible* at your side now, I long to clasp you to my heart, in some way to cheer the loneliness which is a poor widow's lot. Oh, none in the world is harder than that!

Darmstadt: August 31.

. . . Thank you for telling me how you spent that dear day; it must have been peaceful and solemn, the beautiful country harmonising well with the thoughts of that great and beautiful soul which ever lives on with us. He remains nearer and nearer to me, and the recollection of many things dear Papa told me is a help and a stay in my actions, particularly of late. The separation seems so short. I can see him and hear him speak so plainly. Alas! my children have never seen him. Through you, darling Mama, and in your rooms, and at your side, they must learn to know him, that they may become worthy of their descent.

Yesterday we saw the children. Victoria is not quite well, but Ella is well, and won't leave me when I come into the room; she keeps kissing me and putting her fat arms round my neck. There is each time a scene when I go away. She is so affectionate: so is dear Victoria. I send you a photograph of our smallest, who is such a pretty child, and very good.

The peace is not concluded yet; more Prussians have been quartered in and around Darmstadt. The people are very angry at this lasting so long. . . . They believe it is *Strafeinquartierung* [done to punish us]. Nothing is settled as to what we keep or lose, and we know and hear nothing. Waiting here, uncomfortably lodged, the troops impatient to go home, as they have nothing to do, gets very irksome.

Gelbes Haus: September 8.

. . . At last the peace is concluded, though not yet ratified. The terms are not so bad. We lose the Hinterland and the Domains there, as also the whole of Hesse-Homburg—in all sixty-four thousand souls—pay three millions contribution, besides having kept a large part of the Prussian army six weeks for nothing, which cost the country twenty-five thousand florins daily. For Oberhessen we go into the North-German Bund, and half the army is under Prussian command, which will make a dreadful confusion.

Louis would prefer having it for the whole, particularly in anticipation, alas! of a coming war.

The railroads, posts, and telegraphs also become Prussian; and they demand, besides, some fine old pictures, books, and manuscripts, which had once belonged to the Kölner Dom, and were made a present of to this country years ago; and for our Domains no *Entschädigung* [compensation]. In exchange for Homburg we get some small places—amongst others, Rumpenheim.

When the peace is ratified and the money paid, the Prussians leave the country, which must now be very shortly. Until then Louis must stop here, and as he can only get leave now and then to go to Darmstadt, and that always uncertain, Baby's christening is still impossible, as Louis must be there. She will be called 'Irène Louise Marie Anna.'

Gelbes Haus: September 11.

. . . Tired of constantly putting off and waiting, we settled yesterday to have Baby christened to-morrow, as it is Louis' birthday, and to go for the day to Darmstadt. Though the Prussians are still there, some of the godfathers are coming over, otherwise it will be quite quiet.

. . . How true and sad is what you say, dear Mama, about life and its trials! Alas! that it should be you, dear loving kind Mama, who have had to drink so deeply of that cup of bitterness! Those who possess all they love, as I do, can, however, feel all the more keenly, and sympathise more truly with you for what you have lost, though it is a grief we do not know. How I do long always to alleviate this grief for you, dearest Mama; but that is the world's trial. None can bear the burden for you. One must carry it oneself; and it wants patience and courage to bear such as yours, dear Mama. I feel for you now more than ever since during that month I feared from day to day my happy life might be brought to a violent close, and anticipated all the misery that *might* come, but which the Almighty graciously averted.

Darmstadt: September 16.

The name Irène,[8] through other associations, is one my parents-in-law and we like; it stands, besides, as a sort of recollection of the peace so longed for, and which I so gladly welcomed. It will always remind us of the time, and of how much we have to be grateful for.

Darmstadt: September 24.

. . . We are settled here again; our troops have returned and Uncle Louis likewise. The former were received most warmly by the inhabitants and showered with nosegays—Louis also, who rode at their head. We saw them all in front of the Schloss, and it was sad to see the thinned ranks and to miss the absent faces we knew so well. On the 13th and 14th of July at Frohnhofen, Laufach, and Aschaffenburg, out of 8,000 we lost 800 men and 11 officers, and of the officers just those who were very intimate with the Prussians, and who wished Germany to be united under Prussia.

This afternoon we are going to see after the poor wounded, some of whom are still very ill with such horrible wounds. So much suffering and pain and grief to those poor people, who are innocent in this unhappy war!

If only now the other sovereigns will forget their antipathies and the wrongs they have suffered from Prussia, and think of the real welfare of their people and the universal fatherland, and make those sacrifices which will be necessary to prevent the recurrence of these misfortunes!

---

[8] The Princess Charles had a sister, who died when a child, who had borne that name.

The poor Homburgers marched by with our troops, and their tears and ours fell as we saw them (who had fought so bravely under Uncle Louis) for the last time before they become Prussians, and return to their homes as such.

October 1.

. . . I can but write a few lines, as we are going with the children to Uncle Alexander to Jugenheim for a few days. The change of air is wanted for Ella, who is still pale; and Irène has never had any change yet, and is also rather pale.

We were at Frohnhofen and Laufach a few days ago to see where the unfortunate engagement was, and visited the graves of our soldiers. In the middle of a field there is a mound, below which some eighty men and some officers lie, and so on. It makes a very sad impression, for as our troops retreated, and they were buried by the people, none know which of the common soldiers or even which of the officers lie in the different places. We found some balls, and things the soldiers had thrown off during the fight. In one grave in the churchyard, the wounded who died afterwards are buried. I asked who lay there, and the gravedigger answered, 'Ein Preuss' und ein Hess' liegen dort beisammen' ['A Prussian and a Hessian lie there together'], united in death, and fallen by each other's hand, perhaps. Some of the officers who accompanied us, and had not been there since the engagement, were much overcome on seeing the graves of their comrades. I put wreaths and flowers on them, and ordered crosses where we knew who lay there.

The wounded here are recovering, and I go often to see after them.

As you say, this large Prussia is by no means an united Germany; but, nevertheless, I think the duty of the other

German sovereigns, in spite of all, is to unite with Prussia and place themselves under her, so as to make her unite with Germany. Otherwise, the next opportunity, they will be annexed.

Darmstadt: October 22.

On Thursday we are going to Waldleiningen for a fortnight and take Victoria with us. The two little girls knew your photograph at once, and began, of course, to talk of you and of England.

Waldleiningen: October 31.

. . . It is quite beautiful here. We found dear Ernest, Marie [9] and children well; the former so kind and dear, as they always are. Victoria and Alberta [1] get on tolerably together. The little boy is splendid, so strong and fat.

The Castle is so fine and lies just in the midst of mountains and woods, and there are walks without end—many of them reminding me so much of Scotland.

The Nichels came to see us, and Marie and I played with Nichel; [2] it reminded me so much of the good old times to see him.

Ella's birthday is to be kept when we return. She is too small to know the difference of the day. I thank you beforehand for the locket for her with dear Papa's picture. The children always speak of their two Grandpapas—dear Grandpapa in Heaven, and dear Grandpapa in Darmstadt. Victoria, hearing Papa so often mentioned, and seeing his pictures about everywhere, asks no end of questions about him.

---

[9] Prince and Princess Leiningen. [1] Princess Alberta of Leiningen.

[2] Formerly one of the Royal Band in England. Madame Nichel had been a dresser of the Duchess of Kent's.

Darmstadt: November 14.

I am better, thank you, but I am so weak without the least reason, and dreadfully chilly. Still, I go out regularly in all weathers and take exercise, but of an evening I am quite knocked up.

We always breakfast at half-past eight, as Louis gets up early and prefers it; so that I lead a very healthy life, and in spite of that am not well. A change quite into another climate for a few months was what I really required; but it was impossible. On that account, dear Mama, I shall hope to have a full three months in England when we come, and perhaps part of the time with Bertie, if he can have us. I went through a great deal this summer during my confinement. The excitement and the will to keep well kept me so at the time, but I feel it now, alas! and show it, too, for I am getting so thin again.

November 22.

A thousand thanks for the precious book,[3] and for your dear lines. The former I have nearly finished. I got it yesterday morning, and you can well imagine that every spare moment was devoted to its study.

I think it very well done, and I am only sorry that General Grey cannot continue it, as the other persons, I believe, did not know dear Papa. The longer I live, the more I see and know of the world, the deeper my tender admiration grows for such a father. It makes me feel myself so small, so imperfect, when I think that I am his child, and am still so unworthy of being it. How many people here who like to hear of dear Papa ask me about him, and you can understand with what pride and love I talk of him, and tell them things which make them all share our sorrow at not having him here any more! But

---

[3] *The Early Years of the Prince Consort*, by the late General Grey.

if ever a life has outlived a man, dear Papa's has done so. In my thoughts and aims he ever remains the centre and the guiding star. Dear beloved Papa, he never half knew how much, even when a foolish child, I loved and adored him. His great life will be a model for many and many for generations to come, and his great thoughts and aims can leave none idle who knew them.

You kindly ask how I am. Better, thank you, since I have begun some bark—quinine I can't take, or else I should have been well sooner.

Victoria I am teaching to read—in playing with cards with different letters on them.

November 30.

To-day it is six whole years since we were engaged to each other in the Red Drawing-room at Windsor, when we in dear Papa's little room afterwards received your and dear Papa's sanction to it. And the following year—how sad that already was, for darling Papa was beginning to be unwell! How constantly do I think of you, beloved Mama, during that fortnight of anxiety and sorrow! God mercifully spared you to us, though for yourself it was the commencement of the sad and lonely existence you lead without dear Papa.

I am sure it is good for little Henry[4] to be this winter with you in England: the Berlin climate is very unwholesome. Health is such a blessing. If one has children, the first wish is they should be healthy, for ill health influences all, and nothing more than temper.

We intend, if possible, going for a day or two to Carlsruhe. Poor Louise and Fritz went through so much that is painful this summer. . . .

I read an immense deal now of serious, and what some

---

[4] Son of the Crown Prince and Princess of Prussia.

call dry, books; but it is a great resource to me, and the thought of standing still, if one does not study, urges me on. The long winter evenings we always spend together, and twice in the week receive in the evening, when I play on the piano duets with such as play on the violin, and pass the evenings very pleasantly.

Carlsruhe: December 6.

Thousand thanks for your dear letter! I congratulate you on all having gone off so well at Wolverhampton,[5] and am very grateful for the account. Dear Bertie's visit is over, and it has been a very great pleasure to us to have seen him again, and to have him under our own roof—where we at length had an opportunity, in a small way, to return his hospitality and constant kindness to us. God bless him, dear brother! he is the one who has from my childhood been so dear to me.

We have come here, and I think it has pleased good Fritz. Louis seems very well. I saw Lady Fanny Baillie yesterday, looking dear and pretty as ever. It is a pleasure to look at her sweet face.

Carlsruhe: December 11.

As every year during *these days* my thoughts are with you, and as each year brings round again the anniversary of that dreadful misfortune, it seems more and more impossible that five years should already have elapsed, since He whom we all loved so tenderly was taken from our sight. How I thank the Almighty again and again, as this season returns, that He spared you to us, when at such a moment we trembled for your precious life, fearing that two so united in life even in death could not be parted! What should we poor children, what would the country have done, had that second misfortune come over us! Yet it seemed

---

[5] The uncovering of the monument to the Prince Consort.

selfish and unkind to wish for your loving wife's heart the solitary widow's existence. How bravely and nobly you have borne it!

Now I must end, beloved Mama. God bless you and comfort you, and in these days let sometimes the thought of your absent child, who was at your side during that dreadful time, mingle with the recollection of the past!

Beloved, precious Mama,   Darmstadt: December 14.

On awaking this morning, my first thoughts were of you and of dear darling Papa! Oh, how it reopens the wounds scarcely healed, when this day of pain and anguish returns! This season of the year, the leafless trees, the cold light, everything reminds me of that time!

Thousand thanks for your dear letter received yesterday. *Well*, only *too well*, do I remember every hour, almost every minute, of those days, and I have such an inexpressible longing to throw my arms round your neck, and to let my tears flow with yours, while kneeling at that beautiful grave.

The tender love and the deep sorrow caused by His loss remain ever with me, and will accompany me through life. At the age I then was, with its sensitive feelings, it made an impression which, I think, nothing can efface— above all, the witnessing your grief. Happily married as I am, and with such a good, excellent and loving husband, how far more can I understand *now* the depth of that grief, which tore your lives asunder! I played our dear Papa's organ under his beloved picture this morning, and my heart and my thoughts were in dear England with you all.

We found our children well on our return, and Irène prospers perfectly on her donkey's milk.

My mother-in-law is so much pleased with the book,[6] and it has interested her very much. She came to see me early this morning on account of its being the 14th. She is always so kind and full of attentions.

Darmstadt: December 21.

. . . I hope by this time that you are quite recovered, though this mild damp weather is not made to give one strength. I feel it so much also, and am really only kept alive by steel, for off and on I am so weak, that I nearly faint if I have to stand any time, and this is so unpleasant.

. . . I am trying to found what is no small undertaking: a 'Frauenverein,' to be spread all over the land in different committees, the central one being here under my direction, for the purpose of assisting the International Convention for nursing and supporting the troops in time of war, which was founded at Geneva, and to which this country also belongs. The duty in time of peace will be to have nurses brought up and educated for the task, who can then assist in other hospitals or amongst the poor, or to nurse the rich, wherever they may be required. In time of war this committee of women has to collect all the necessary things for the wounded and for the marching troops, has to see to their being sent to right places, &c.

All these things were done by private people in this war, and, though quantities of things were sent, the whole plan was not organised, so that there was want and surplus at the same time.

In time of peace these things should be organised, so that, when war comes, people know where to send their things to, and that no volunteer nurses go out who have not first learnt their business.

[6] General Grey's *Early Years of the Prince Consort.*

The same thing exists in Baden, in Bavaria, and in Prussia, and here it is much wanted. But all these undertakings are difficult, particularly in the choice of persons to assist one. Still I hope I shall be able to do it. My mother-in-law helps me, and I hope before long to be able to begin.

The Elector is coming here on a visit to-day, and Uncle Alexander returned from Petersburg last night.

Darmstadt: December 30.

... May the Almighty give you every blessing of peace and comfort which the world can still give you, till you gain that greater blessing and reward above all others, which is reserved for such as my own sweet mother! May every blessing fall on my old dear home, with all its dear ones! May peace, and the glory which peace and order bring with it, with its many blessings, protect my native land; and may, in the new year, your wise and glorious reign, so overshadowed by dear Papa's spirit, continue to prosper and be a model and an ornament to the world!

This year of pain and anxiety, and yet for us so rich in blessings, draws to a close. It moves me more than ever as its last day approaches. For how much have we not to thank the Almighty—for my life, which is so unworthy compared to many others, the new life of this little one, and above all the preservation of my own dear husband, who is my all in this life!

The trials of this year must have brought some good with all the evil: good to the individual and good to the multitude. God grant we may all profit by what we have learnt, and gain more and more that trust in God's justice and love, which is our guide and support in trouble and in joy! Oh, more than ever have I felt in this year, that God's goodness and love are indeed beyond comprehension!

... I am really glad to hear that you can listen to a little music. Music is such a heavenly thing, and dear Papa loved it so much, that I can't but think that now it must be soothing, and bring you near to him. ...

1867

Gotha: January 15.

I am delighted to hear of dear Arthur having passed so good an examination. How proud you must be of him! And the good Major,[7] who has spared no pains, I know—how pleased he must be! Arthur has a uniform now, I suppose.

Berlin: January 26.

... We remain here a little longer, probably until the following Saturday, as the King, owing to his cold, could not see us often, and begged us to remain longer.

I saw Amalie Lauchert[8] here two days ago, looking so well and charming as ever.

Little Vicky is such a darling, very like her poor little brother—so merry, so good, one never hears her cry—and it is really a comfort to Vicky to have that dear little thing. Poor Vicky is very sad and low at times.

After intense cold it is quite warm, like spring, which is very unwholesome and tiring.

Darmstadt: February 16.

... I think I can understand what you must feel. I know well what those first three years were—what fearful

---

[7] Major Elphinstone, Prince Arthur's Governor from 1859, now Sir Howard Elphinstone, K.C.B.

[8] Princess Amalie of Hohenlohe-Schillingsfürst, niece of Queen Victoria's late brother-in-law, Prince of Hohenlohe-Langenburg, married to an artist, Herr Lauchert.

suffering, tearing and uprooting those feelings which had been centred in beloved Papa's existence! It is indeed, as you say, 'in mercy,' that after the long storm a lull and calm ensues, though the violent pain, which is but the reverse side of the violent love, seems only to die out with it, and that is likewise bitter. Yet, beloved Mama, could it be otherwise? There would be no justice or mercy, were the first stage of sorrow to be the perpetual one; and God grant, that time may still soothe and alleviate that which it cannot change! I can only imagine what the loss must be, if I measure it by the possession of that one adored being, who is the centre and essence of my existence.

Darmstadt: February 28.

. . . Yesterday we had a very interesting lecture in our house about Art in Venice, by a young Swede [Herr von Molin], who has been studying three years in Italy. We had the room full of people, artists and professors, who liked to listen.

. . . All the natural cleverness and sharpness in the world won't serve nowadays, unless one has learnt something. I feel this so much; and just in our position it is more and more required and expected, particularly in a small place, where so much depends on the personal knowledge and exertions of the Princes.

Darmstadt: April 1.

. . . I could not write the other day, as I had a good deal to do with two committees for charities, which had to be got into order, and which took up a great deal of my time.

Cold, hail, snow, and rain have returned; and Irène has got a cold, which most people here have. The weather is so unpleasant.

We shall stop here in town until we go to England, as

we have nowhere to go to before. It is a pity for the children to have no country air, and they miss the flowers in their walks. I can't praise Orchard [9] enough. Such order she keeps, and is so industrious and tidy, besides understanding so much about the management of the children's health and characters.

Darmstadt: April 5.

Thousand thanks for your dear letter, and for the kind wishes for Victoria's birthday! I pray she may be a worthy granddaughter and goddaughter of my darling Mama! I shall never forget that day—your kindness to us, and the tender nurse you were. . . .

Victoria means to dictate a letter to you; she is so much pleased with her presents. Irène has not a tooth yet, and is not very fat, poor little thing! but she is fresh and rosy, and, I think, strong.

This last week the excitement here has been dreadful, as all anticipated a war with France on account of Luxemburg. I fear sooner or later it will come. May the Almighty avert such a calamity!

The Moriers were quite in ecstasies about your handsome present. The christening [1] went off very well.

April 8.

. . . We have just returned from church, and tomorrow morning we all take the Sacrament at nine o'clock in the Schlosskirche. Professor Jowett is here on a visit to the Moriers, and is going to read the service on Sunday. I have not had an opportunity to attend our English service since we were at Windsor, excepting one Sunday at Berlin with Vicky and Fritz.

People think now, the evil of war is put off for a few

---

[9] Their nurse, who is still with the youngest child, Princess Alix.

[1] Of their child, to whom Queen Victoria stood sponsor.

weeks, but that is all. Henry is here for Easter, and says the same from all he heard at Berlin.

April 21.

... How I wish you may be right in *not* believing in war! I always fear it is not Luxemburg, but the intense jealousy of the French nation, that they should not be the first on the Continent, and that Germany is becoming independent and powerful against their will. Then, again, the Germans feel their new position, and assert their rights with more force because unanimous, and neither nation will choose to give in to the other.

The war would be totally useless, and sow no end of dissension and hatred between the two neighbour countries, who, for their own good as for that of mankind, ought to live in peace and harmony with each other.

We seem drifting back to the Middle Ages, as each question is pushed to the point of the sword. It is most sad. How dear Papa would have disapproved of much that has happened since 1862!

Is the Catalogue which Mr. Ruland sent some time ago to Mr. Woodward for dear Papa's Raphael Collection in print now?[2] So many people know of its coming out, and are anxious to see it, as, indeed, I am likewise, for it is the only complete collection in the world, and the world of art is anxious to know all about it. Will you, perhaps, let me know through Mr. Sahl,[3] as I believe it is already a good while since you approved of its being published, and gave the orders for its being printed?

May 2.

As yet none dare to be sure of the peace, but all live again since there are more chances for its being main-

---

[2] This Catalogue was not completed and made public till 1876.
[3] Her Majesty's private librarian.

tained. But then, I trust it will be a permanent peace, not merely a putting off till next year!

The French press was so very warlike, and it always talks of the French honour not being able to allow such a mighty empire as the German is becoming to gain the upper hand; and then rectification of her frontiers, always wishing for the Rhine.

May 29.

. . . I presided at my committee of seven ladies and four gentlemen a long while yesterday, and to-morrow I have my other one, which is more numerous. It is an easy task, but I hope we shall have good results from our endeavours.

Paris: June 9.

I really am half killed from sight-seeing and fêtes, but all has interested me so much, and the Emperor and Empress [of the French] have been most kind. Yesterday was the ball at the Hôtel de Ville, quite the same as it had been for you and dear Papa, and there were more than 8,000 people there. It was the finest sight I have ever seen, and it interested me all the more, as I knew it was the same as in the year when you were at Paris.

Every morning we went to the Exhibition, and every evening there was a dinner or ball. It was most fatiguing. To-morrow morning we leave, and had really great trouble to get away, for the Emperor and Empress and others begged us so much to remain for the ball at the Tuileries to-morrow night; but we really could not, on account of Wednesday's concert,[4] as we should barely arrive in time.

The *attentat* on the Emperor of Russia was dreadful, and we were close by at the time. The Empress can't get over it, and she does not leave Uncle Sache's[5]

---

[4] At Buckingham Palace.   [5] The Emperor of Russia.

side for an instant now, and takes him everywhere in her carriage.

To-day we are going with the whole Court to Versailles. Dear Vicky is gone. She was so low the last days, and dislikes going to parties so much just now, that she was longing to get home. The King [of Prussia] wished them both to stop, but only Fritz remained. How sad these days will be for her, poor love! She was in such good looks; everyone here is charmed with her.

Darmstadt: August 4.

We arrived here at midnight on Friday, and I was so knocked up . . . that I was incapable of doing anything yesterday.

. . . My poor Willem was buried yesterday. Everyone regrets the poor child, for he was very dear. I miss him so much here, for he did everything for me, and liked being about me and the children. All our servants went to the burial. It quite upset me here not to find him, for I was really attached to him, and he learnt so well, and was in many ways so nice, though of course troublesome too at times. How short life is, and the instant one is gone, he is so wiped away for others, and one knows *so absolutely nothing* about the person any more! Were it not for a strong faith in a future, it would indeed be cruel to bear. No one of the family is here. We leave to-morrow for Zürich, where we shall be at ten at night; the next day to Chur and the next day to St. Moritz.

St. Moritz: August 8.

With perfect weather we accomplished our journey perfectly, and were enchanted with the beautiful scenery from Zürich hither, not to speak of this place.

The first day—5th—we left Darmstadt at 11 A.M., and did not reach Zürich till eleven at night. We got two little rooms in the Hôtel Baur, but the whole place was full. The next morning after breakfast we went to look at the lovely lake, which is green and quite transparent. It was a beautiful warm morning. We left by rail at ten, partly along the lake of Zürich and then along the Wallenstädter See, which is long and narrow, with high perpendicular mountains down to the water—very wild and picturesque. This lake likewise is of that marvellous green colour. We reached Chur at three that afternoon—a pretty small town, situated close up against a mountain. We visited a beautiful old church there, which contains fine old pictures and relics; it was built in the time of the Romans, and is still the chief church of the bishopric.

The next morning we two, with Sarah, Logoz and our footman, left at six o'clock in a diligence (we both sitting in the coupé in front) with four horses, for here the road is the grandest one can imagine, perpetually ascending for two hours, and then descending again, always along precipices, and the horses at a quick trot turning sharp round the corners—which, I assure you, is a trial to the best nerves. We drove over the Julier Pass, which was a road already used by the Romans, and which is almost the highest in Switzerland. One passes close to the top of the mountains, which have snow on them, and are wild and rugged like the top of Lochnagar. Lower down, the mountains are covered with bright green grass and fir trees, but rocks look out everywhere, and there are constantly lovely waterfalls.

After crossing the Pass, we drove down—very steep, of course nothing on the edge of the road, always zigzag, and at a sharp trot—for some distance down to Silva Plana, where the view over the valley and lakes of the Engadine, where St. Moritz lies, is beyond description beautiful.

We reached this in the evening at six o'clock, the weather being most beautiful. The Curhaus is below the town, and looks like a large asylum. It is overfilled with people. We have two rooms, but our people as yet none, though they hope for some to-morrow.

I saw Dr. Berry, a little Swiss man, and he recommended me to take the baths twice a week, besides drinking the waters; which I have begun this morning at seven o'clock, the usual hour, as one has to walk up and down a quarter of an hour between the glasses. The bath I took at ten. It is tepid and also iron water, which bubbles like soda water, and makes one feel as if insects were crawling over one.

Lina Aumale is here, the Parises and Nemours. Fritz and Louise [of Baden] leave to-morrow. This afternoon we drove with them, in two funny little 'Wägeli' with one horse, to Samaden, where Louise went into the hotel to see Mme. d'Usedom, who was lately upset with her carriage off the road, as there is no barrier, and hurt herself severely. We saw her brother likewise.

I have sent you a nosegay of Edelweiss and other Alp flowers. I hope it won't arrive quite dead. You must fancy them alive, and, if they could speak, they would tell you how much I love you, and how constantly I think of you, and of my dear, dear home!

St. Moritz: August 11.

. . . All the Orleans' left this place suddenly yesterday, as there are three cases of scarlatina in the house. We consulted the doctor immediately, whether he thought it safe for Louis to remain, he never having had it, and he said 'Perfectly, as we are at the other end of the house, and out nearly all day.'

Victor and Lolo [Count and Countess Gleichen] are

here, and we went out drawing together yesterday; but it is too difficult here. I think constantly how much you would admire this place: it is indeed exquisitely beautiful —much the finest scenery I have ever seen. It is very wild, and reminds me in parts of dear Scotland.

You say that our home in England is dull now for those who like to amuse themselves. It is *never* dull, darling Mama, when one can be with you, for I have indeed never met a more agreeable charming companion. Time always flies by, when one is with you. I hope it is not impertinent my saying so.

St. Moritz: August 13.

. . . . I knew you would feel for me at the loss of my poor Willem. Of course one must feel that sort of loss more than that of many a relation, if one knew the latter but little. I said to Louis at the time, that Willem's death distressed me more than would that of several relations who were not intimate with me. . . .

Yesterday we and the Gleichens went to the Rosegg Glacier, and to get there had to go from Pontresina in little *Bergwagen*, which are strong miniature *Leiterwagen* without springs, and we went over a horrid path with quantities of stones, so the shaking was beyond description.

Victor and Lolo go mostly with us, and we always dine together.

I take three glasses beginning at seven in the morning, and a bath at eight. One lies in a wooden thing, covered over up to one's chin with boards, and remains so twenty minutes.

We lunch at twelve, and dine at half-past six, and go to bed early. We are out nearly all day long. It is very warm, the sun scorching; my face is quite red-brown, in spite of veils and parasols. I feel already very much better, and Louis says my face is quite fat. I wish we could remain longer than the end of the month, but Louis must be home.

St. Moritz: August 16.

Yesterday we made a beautiful expedition, which it may amuse you to hear of, as in an exaggerated way it reminded me of our nice Scotch ones. The evening before, we left with Victor and Lolo (without servants) about eight o'clock for Pontresina. The country looked more beautiful than ever in the brightest moonlight. We found two very small but clean rooms in an hotel outside the village.

The next morning we got up at half-past four, dressed, and breakfasted, then got on four horses with most uncomfortable saddles, with our guide, Adam Engler, an amusing man, most active and helpful. We saw the sun rising over the snow-covered mountains, and the valleys gradually coming out clearer.

We were to ascend the Piz Languard, a mountain 1,200 feet high. We rode for two hours by a worse and much steeper road than up the Glassalt, then walked over rocks, sand, and slippery grass, so steep that one could not look up to see where one was going to, quite precipitous on each side, leaving snow and glacier below us. The last bit has a sort of immensely high steps hewn in the rock. After an hour and a half's hard labour we reached the summit, which is rocky and small—enormous precipices all round. Poor Lolo was giddy for some time, which was very unpleasant. The view from the top is most extensive. The Italian, Swiss, and Tyrolese Alps are all to be seen, but the view was not very clear. We rested and ate something, and drank some Lochnagar whisky. The sun was getting intense. We commenced our descent at eleven o'clock, and had to walk the whole way back, for one can't ride down. We did not reach Pontresina till nearly four, as we had to rest several times, our limbs ached so, for there is no level ground the whole way, and the stones slip, and it was very hot. I had quite sore feet with blisters all over, so that the last hours were really agonising. But it is a thing to have done, and the view amply repaid one, though one does not feel tempted to do it a second time. I feel very well, excepting my face (which is still burning and quite red), and my unfortunate feet.

St. Moritz: August 21.

. . . Now I will tell you of our expedition. Louis and I, Victor and Lolo, and a guide, with each a small bag, left this early on the morning of the 17th (dear Grandmama's birthday) in a carriage for Pontresina; from thence, in two of those shaky *Bergwagen*, over part of the Bernina Pass, past the magnificent Morteratsch Glacier, which we saw perfectly. The guide told us he had been there with Professor Tyndall, and that the latter had observed, that the glacier advanced a foot a day in the warm weather, and old people recollect it having been a mile higher up. We soon left the high-road, and all vegetation, save grass, for a bad path into the Val da Fain. The heat was again intense. We lunched and rested, and then took the horses out of the carts for us ladies to ride. The scenery was wild and severe, until we began again to descend, and came down upon the lovely Livigno Valley, which is Italian, and covered with brown châlets. We reached the village of Livigno, with only wooden huts, by six o'clock, and turned into a funny little dark inn, in which we four found one small but clean room for us— most primitive. As the inhabitants speak a sort of Italian, we had the greatest difficulty to make ourselves understood. Victor cooked part of the dinner, and it was quite good.

We all slept—I resting *on* a bed, the other three on the floor—in this little room, with the small window wide open.

The next morning we left at nine, and drove on no road in such a small carriage—of course, no springs—our husbands at first getting a lift on the horses, without saddles; then on foot up a steep and dangerous ascent. Splendid weather, but too hot. We went over the Pass of the Stretta: a more difficult and rough ground I never crossed in my life, but splendid scenery. We came on a view which was glorious—such enormous snow-covered mountains and glaciers, with the green valleys deep below looking on Italy and the Tyrol.

We reached Bormio by seven, and took up our residence at a bathing-place, quite magnificently situated, very high up—also Italian. The next morning we started early in carriages, and went over the Stelvio Pass. There, nearly at the risk of my neck, I picked for the first time some Edelweiss, which I am very proud of, as it is always difficult and rare to get.

We got down to St. Maria, which is at the upper end of the Münsterthal and belongs to Switzerland. In the afternoon, dreadfully hot, I was very thirsty and drank off a glass of milk; but how it tasted! It was goat's milk; the people keep the cow's milk for butter and cheese. We remained the night there, and left the next morning for here, by Zernetz and Ofen. To get from one valley into another, one has always to ascend and descend enormous heights, and always by narrow paths at the edge of precipices. We enjoyed our tour immensely, and got on perfectly without servants. Packing up my things, though, every morning was a great trouble, and the bag would usually not shut at first. The trees growing here are splendid larches and arven;[6] the latter grow only in these very high regions and in Siberia. Victor and his wife are most amiable and pleasant travelling-companions, and pleased with everything; not minding to rough it, which we had to do.

Schloss Mainau: August 30.

... We left St. Moritz at seven, and reached Chur at seven in the evening. The next day we came on here to Louise of Baden. Fritz is at Carlsruhe. This place is very lovely, though, alas! the fine mountains are gone, which one always misses so much.

I thought of you more than I can say on the dear 26th, and I felt low and sad all day. Dear Papa! Time has not yet accustomed us to see each anniversary come round again, and he still remain away. It is so inexpressibly hard for you, and you must feel such intense longing for the dear past. There remains a future! that is the only consolation.

To-day we went with Louise by carriage, and then across part of the lake to the property of the Emperor Napoleon, Arenenberg, which the Empress gave him eight years ago, and which was his home with his mother, and where she died. Every picture and bit of furniture is replaced as it was when the Emperor lived there, and he was there himself and replaced everything. It is quite a page in history to see all the things that surrounded the Emperor in the days of his misfortune.

Darmstadt: September 8.

... I spent three days and two nights with dear Alix at Wiesbaden, and I find her leg decidedly better.

---

[6] A kind of dwarf tree—half pine, half juniper—which grows in the highest regions of the Alps, and supplies most of the soft wood used by the Swiss wood-carvers.

... It is a little less hot to-day, but much hotter even now than we ever have it in England. Stallmeister Meyer [7] came to see us yesterday, and we took him out riding, which made him quite happy. Anyone who reminds me of the good old times before the 14th of December does me good; it is a pleasure to speak about those past so happy days! When they came to a close, I lost the greater part of my joyousness, which, though I am so happy, has never returned. A certain melancholy and sadness sometimes overcome me, which I can't shake off; then I have *Heimweh* after adored Papa to such an extent that tears are my only relief.

Darmstadt: October 3.

Yesterday evening I returned from Wiesbaden, leaving Alix well, but having caught a bad cold myself. The children have equally heavy ones.

Darmstadt: October 8.

Many thanks for your letter just received, and for the review of dear Papa's Life, which is excellent, and which I sent on to Aunt Feodore, as you desired. I have been laid up for a week with influenza, and am only about again since yesterday, though not out of the house. I am quite weak from it. The whole house is laid up with bad colds, and Baby can't shake hers off at all. The cough is so tiring, and she whoops whenever she coughs. Poor Jäger, who is, alas! we fear, consumptive, broke a blood-vessel two days ago, and is dangerously ill, to the great grief of all in the house. He is our best servant, and so devoted; he never would take care of himself, as he could not bear letting anyone but himself attend on Louis. We have just got a *Diakonissin* [Deaconess] to nurse him; on account of his great weakness he can't be left alone one instant.

[7] Riding-master to the Prince Consort and the Queen from 1840 to 1871.

Sir William, Lady and Charlotte Knollys have been on a visit to us; also Lady Geraldine Somerset for two nights. They are all interested to see our house.

Uncle George has made me a present of one of the horses the Sultan sent him.

Darmstadt: October 10.

I can't find words to say how sorry I am that dear sweet Arthur should have the small-pox! and that you should have this great anxiety and worry. God grant, that the dear boy may get well over it, and that his dear handsome face be not marked! Where in the world could he have caught it? The Major kindly telegraphs daily, and you can fancy, far away, how anxious one is. I shall be very anxious to get a letter with accounts, for I think constantly of him, and of you. My parents-in-law wish me to tell you how they share your anxiety, and how they wish soon to hear of dear Arthur's convalescence; of course my Louis likewise, for he shares all my feelings, being a real brother towards my *Geschwister* [brothers and sisters].

Darmstadt: October 14.

How glad I am to see by your letter that darling Arthur is going on so very well! One can't be too thankful; and it is a good thing over, and will spare one's being anxious about him on other occasions.

Bertie and Alix have been here since Saturday afternoon, and leave to-morrow. They go straight to Antwerp, and Bertie is going back to Brussels to see the cousins.

The visit of the King went off very well, and Alix was pleased with the kindness and civility of the King. I hear that the meeting was satisfactory to both parties, which I am heartily glad of. Bearing ill will is always a mistake, besides its not being right.

Dear Alix walked up our staircase with two sticks, of course very slowly, but she is improving wonderfully, though her knee is quite stiff.

Poor Jäger is a little better, and the momentary danger is past, though I fear he cannot ultimately recover. How hard for poor Katrinchen! There is much sorrow in the world, and how often such a share falls to the best and gentlest! I of course go to see him daily, but it always goes to my very heart to see that attached and faithful creature dying slowly away. How is Brown's sister?

We hope that Countess Blücher will return here with Vicky and me from Baden for a few days, as it is an age since Vicky has seen her.

Dear Alix is writing in my room at this moment, and is so dear and sweet. She is a most loveable creature.

Darmstadt: October 23.

The accounts of poor dear Aunt Feodore are so sad, and I hear she does not look well, and is so low about her eyes.

Schweinsberg: October 24.

Dear Vicky and Fritz left us yesterday morning. It is such a pleasure to me to think that they, like Bertie and Alix, know my house, and that they have lodged under our roof. When will you, darling Mama? If ever again you go abroad and wish to rest on your way, all in the world we have is at your disposal. How happy that would make us!

We ourselves left at four yesterday afternoon, remaining the night at Marburg, and leaving at a quarter to five in the morning, so that Louis could reach Alsfeld in time to join the shooting-party. We parted at Kirchhain, and I came here with Christa to her mother's house—so sad and changed since three years ago. It is most kind of them to have taken me up here, and the bracing air will do me good. They know that I can understand what a house of mourning is, and that I don't want to amuse myself.

Ella cried on parting with us yesterday, and wanted to get into the train with us.

Victoria is going to have a little lesson every other day, when I go back, from Mr. Geyer, who taught poor Willem, and who teaches little girls particularly well. She must begin in my room, as it is better not to have lessons in the nursery, I think. Vicky and I spoke much together about education and taking a governess. I thought to wait a year (for financial reasons), and I think it time enough then—do not you?

November 15.

. . . It is so good and wholesome not always to be one's own master, and to have to suit oneself to the wish of others, and, above all, to that of one's mother and sovereign. —— feels it as such, and often told me so, regretting how seldom such was the case.

The Moriers are often with us, and we value them much; they are such pleasant companions, and such excellent, clever people.

Darmstadt: December 6.

. . . The visit to Claremont must have been quite peculiar for you; and I can fancy it bringing back to your mind the recollections of your childhood. In spring it must be a lovely place, and, with gayer papers on the walls, and a little modern comfort, the house must likewise be very pleasant. Ella, who was breakfasting with me just now, saw me dip my *Bretzel* in my coffee, and said: 'Oh, Mama, you must not! Do you allow yourself to do that?' because I don't allow her to do it. She is too funny, and by no means quite easy to manage—a great contrast to Victoria, who is a very tractable child. Ella has a wonderful talent for sewing, and, when she keeps quiet a little while, sews quite alone and without mistakes. She is making something for you for Christmas, which she is quite excited about. Victoria's little afternoon lesson answers admirably, and is the happiest time of the day for her. She can read words already.

We have snow and ice, and no sunshine since some time, and it is not inviting to take the dull walks in the town. But I make a rule to go out twice a day, and keep nearly the same hours as at home.

The account of your visit to Lady Palmerston and to her daughter is most touching. It is so inexpressibly sad for grandmother and mother, for it is unnatural for parents to survive their children, and that makes the grief a so peculiar one, and very hard to bear.

December 9.

. . . During the long winter days, when Louis is away sometimes four times in the week from six in the morning till six in the evening, and then when he returns from his shooting has his work to do, I feel lonely. I am often for several hours consecutively quite by myself; and for my meals and walks only a lady, as she is the only person in the house besides ourselves. It is during these hours, when one cannot always be reading or at work, that I should wish to have some one to go to, or to come to me to sit and speak with; but such is not the case, and it is this I regret—accustomed as I was to a house full of people, with brothers and sisters, and, above all, the chance of being near you. I always feel how willingly I would spend some of those hours with or near you—and the sea ever lies between us! When Louis is at home and free—for in the morning I don't see him—then I have *all* that this world can give me, for I am indeed never happier than at his dear side; and time only increases our affection, and binds us closer to each other.

We have deep snow now and sledging the last two days.

December 12.

Before going to rest, I take up my pen to write a few loving words, that they may reach you on the morning of the 14th. The sound of that date brings with it that sad and dreary recollection which, for you, my poor dear Mama, and for us, time cannot alter. As long as our lives last, this time of year must fill us with sad and earnest feelings, and revive the pain of that bitter parting.

I ought not to dwell on those hours now, for it is wrong to open those wounds afresh, which God in His mercy finds little ways and means to heal and soothe the pain of.

Dear darling Papa is, and ever will be, *immortal*. The good he has done; the great ideas he has promulgated in the world; the noble and unselfish example he has given, will live on, as I am sure he must ever do, as one of the best, purest, most Godlike men that have come down into this world. His example will, and does, stimulate others to higher and purer aims; and I am convinced that darling Papa did not live in vain. His great mission was done; and what has remained undone he has placed in your dear hands, who will know best how to achieve his great works of love and justice. I shall think much, very much, of you on the 14th, and you will be more in my prayers than ever. Think also a little of your most devoted child!

Darmstadt: Christmas Day.

We missed poor Willem so much in arranging all the things; and poor Jäger's illness was also sad. We gave him a tree in his room. He looks like a shadow, and his voice is quite hoarse.

To two hospitals, the military and the town one, I took presents yesterday, and saw many a scene of suffering and grief. My children are going to give a certain number of poor children a *Bescheerung* on New Year's Day. It is so good to teach them early to be generous and kind to the poor. They even wish to give some of their own things, and such as are *not* broken.

Your many generous presents will find their use at once, and the Christmas pie, &c., be shared by all the family. The remembrances of those bright happy Christmases at Windsor are constantly before me. None will ever be again what those were, without you, dear Papa, and dear kind Grandmama.

Darmstadt: December 27.

... I am sure you will have felt under many a circumstance in life, that if any momentary feeling was upon you, and you were writing to some one near and dear, it did you good to put down those feelings on paper, and that, even in the act of doing so, when the words were barely written, the feeling had begun to die away, and the intercourse had done you good.

1868

Darmstadt: January 24.

... To-night I am going to act with two other persons in our dining-room a pretty little piece called *Am Klavier*, but I fear I shall be very nervous, and consequently act badly, which would be too tiresome.

I have never tried to act in anything since *Rothkäppchen*.

February 1.

What a fright the news of dear Leopold's dangerous attack has given us! Mr. Sahl's letter to Becker arrived yesterday afternoon containing the bad news, and he spoke of so *little* hope, that I was so upset and so dreadfully distressed for the dear darling, for you, poor Mama, and for us all, that I am quite unwell still to-day.

When your telegram came to-day, and Louise's letter, I was so relieved and only pray and hope that the improvement may continue. May God spare that young bright and gifted life, to be a comfort and support to you for many a year to come!

Had I only had a telegram! for, the letter being two days old, until your telegram came I passed six such agonising hours! Away from home, every news of illness or sorrow there is so difficult to bear—when one can share all the anxiety and trouble only *in thought*.

The day passes so slowly without news, and I am always looking towards the door to see if a telegram is coming. Please let me hear regularly till he is quite safe; I do love the dear boy, as I do all my brothers and sisters, so tenderly!

How I wish you had been spared this new anxiety! Those two days must have been dreadful!

Darling Mama, how I wish I were with you! God grant that in future you may send us only good news!

Louis and my parents-in-law send their respectful love and the expression of their warmest sympathy, in which the other members of the family join.

February 2.

How glad and truly thankful I am, that the Almighty has saved our darling Leopold and spared him to you and to us all! For the second or even third time that life has been given again, when all feared that it must leave us! A mother's heart must feel this so much more than any other one's, and dear Leopold, through having caused you all his life so much anxiety, must be inexpressibly dear to you, and such an object to watch over and take care of. Indeed from the depth of my heart I thank God with you for having so mercifully spared dear Leo, and watched over him when death seemed so near!

You will feel deeply now the great joy of seeing a convalescence after the great danger, and I know, through a thousand little things, how your loving and considerate heart will find pleasure and consolation in cheering your patient.

That for the future you must ever be so anxious is a dreadful trial, but it is to be hoped that Leo will yet outgrow this strange illness. I am sure good Archie [8] takes great care of him, and by this time he will have gathered plenty of experience to be a good nurse.

Darmstadt: February 13.

... First let me wish you joy for the birth of this new grandson,[9] born on your dear wedding-day. I thought of you on the morning of the 10th, and meant to telegraph, but those dreadful neuralgic pains came on before I had time to look about me, and really laid me prostrate for the whole day, as they lasted so very long. I have never felt so unwell, or suffered so much in my life, and this moment, sitting up in Louis' room, I feel more weak than I ever felt on first getting up after my confinements. Quinine has kept me free from pain to-day, and I hope will do so to-morrow. I have been in bed a week and touched absolutely nothing all the time. Yesterday evening, as throughout

---

[8] Archibald Brown, his valet, younger brother of the Queen's personal attendant.

[9] Prince Waldemar of Prussia, fourth son of the Crown Prince and Princess. He died of diphtheria on the 27th of March, 1879.

the day, I had had (but much more slightly) a return of these agonising attacks, which seized my left eye, ear, and the whole left side of my head and nose. I got up and sat in Louis' room; I could only bear it for two hours, and all but fainted before I reached my bed. If I can get strength, and have no return of pain, I hope to go out after to-morrow. I could not see the children or anyone during this week, and always had my eyes closed, first from pain, and then from exhaustion when the pain left me. I really thought I should go out of my mind, and you know I can stand a tolerable amount of pain.

Darmstadt: February 24.

To my and, I fear, dear Vicky's great disappointment, Dr. Weber won't let me go to Berlin, and wants me to go to Wiesbaden for a cold-water cure instead. The latter will be intensely dull, as I shall be there for four weeks all alone; but I believe it will be very beneficial, as with every year I seem to get more rheumatic, which at my age is of course not good.

We shall hope to be able to come to Windsor, middle of June, as you desire. The exact time you will kindly let us know later.

Darmstadt: March 14.

I send you a few lines to-day for the 16th, the anniversary of the first great sorrow which broke in upon your happy life. How well do I recollect how I accompanied you and dear Papa down to Frogmore that night, our dinner in the flower room, the dreadful watching in the corridor, and then the so painful end! Darling Papa looked so pale, so deeply distressed, and was so full of tender sympathy for you. He told me to go to you and comfort you, and was so full of love and commiseration as I have never seen any man before or after. Dear, sweet Papa! that in that same year we should live together through such another heartrending scene again, and he not there to comfort or support you, poor Mama!

It sometimes, even at this distance of time, seems nearly impossible that we should have lived through such times, and yet be alive and resigned.

God's mercy is indeed great; for He sends a balm to soothe and heal the bruised and faithful heart, and to teach one to accommodate oneself to one's sorrow, so as to know how to bear it!

Darmstadt: April 5.

Only two words to-day, as my heart is so full of love and gratitude to you who took such care of me this day five years ago, who heard Victoria's first cry, and were such a comfort and help to us both. All these recollections make Victoria doubly dear to us, and, as in this world one never knows what will happen, I hope that you will always watch over our dear child, and let her be as dear to you as though she had been one of us.

April 3.

I am so distressed at dear, good Sir James [Clark's] illness. I hope and trust that this precious old friend will still be spared for a few years at least.

Gotha: April 25.

. . . It is now eleven years since I spent my birthday with dear Vicky, and she has been so dear and kind, and dear Aunt and Uncle likewise. We spend the day quite quietly together, and the bad weather prevents any expeditions.

After to-morrow we go home.

Darmstadt: May 4.

Accept my best thanks for your last letter written on dear Arthur's birthday. The playing of the band I am sure gave him pleasure; but it would be too painful for *all* ever to have it again on the terrace as formerly. There are certain tunes, which that Marine Band used to play, which, when I have chanced to hear them elsewhere, have quite upset me, so powerful does the recollection of those so very happy birthdays at Osborne remain upon me! Those happy, happy days touch me even to tears when I think of them. What a joyous childhood we had, and how greatly it was enhanced by dear, sweet Papa, and by all your great kindness to us!

I try to copy as much as lies in my power all these things for our children, that they may have an idea, when I speak to them of it, of what a happy home ours was.

I do feel so much for dear Beatrice and the other younger ones, who had so much less of it than we had!

Darmstadt: May 11.

For your sake I am sorry that my condition should cause you anxiety, for you have enough of that, God knows. But I am so well this time that I hope and trust all may go well, though one is never sure. It is this conviction which I always have, and which makes me serious and thoughtful, as who can know whether with the termination of this time my life may not also terminate?

This is also one of the reasons why I long so very much to see you, my own precious Mama, this summer, for I cling to you with a love and gratitude, the depth of which I know I can never find words or means to express. After a year's absence I wish so intensely to behold your dear, sweet, loving face again, and to press my lips on your dear hands. The older I grow the more I value and appreciate that mother's love which is unique in the world; and having, since darling Papa's death, only you, the love to my parents and to adored Papa's memory is all centred in *you*.

Louis has leave from the 11th of June to the 11th of August.

Uncle Ernest is coming here to-day for the day from Frankfort, where he has been to a cattle-show. Uncle Adalbert is here, so much pleased with having seen you again, singing the praise of both Lenchen and Louise, which of course I joined in, as it is such a pleasure to hear others admire and appreciate my dear sisters.

Darmstadt : May 14.

I know you will be grieved to hear that we all have had the grief of losing good, excellent Jäger.[1] He was, on the whole, better and was out daily, and he went to bed as usual, when in the middle of the night he called one of the men, and before they could come to his assistance he expired, having broken a blood-vessel. Poor Katrinchen's despair and grief were quite heartrending, when we went together to see our true and valued servant for the last time. I was so upset by the whole, that it was some days before I got over it. We made wreaths to put on his coffin, which was covered with flowers sent from all sides, and we both were at the door with our servants when he was carried out, and tried to console the poor unfortunate *Braut* [Bride], who remained at home.

He was the best servant one could find; never, since he has been in our service, had he been found fault with by anyone. He was good, pious, and gentle, and very intelligent. The death of a good man, who has fulfilled his allotted duty in this world as a good Christian ought, touches one deeply, and we have really mourned for him as

---

[1] A footman, much valued by the Prince and Princess.

for a friend, for he was one in the true sense of the word. Jäger rests alongside my poor Willem, in the pretty little cemetery here; a bit of my heart went with them.

Fritz, on his way back from Italy, spent a few hours with us, and told us much of his journey. He heard the strangest rumours of France intending to break out in sudden hostilities with Germany, and asked me what you thought of a probability of a war for this summer. I hope to God, that nothing horrid of that sort will happen! Do you think it likely, dear Mama?

Darmstadt: May 19.

My own darling and most precious Mama,

The warmest and tenderest wishes that grateful children can form for a beloved parent we both form for you, and these lines but weakly express all I would like to say. May God bless and watch over a life so precious and so dear to many! It is now six years since I spent that dear day near you, but I hope that some time or other we shall be allowed to do so. Our joint present is a medal for you with our heads. We had it made large in oxidised silver on purpose for you. I myself have braided and embroidered with Christa's help (who begged to be allowed to do something for you), a trimming for a dress, which I hope you will like and wear. It took a deal of my time, and my thoughts were so much with you while I was doing it, that I quite regretted its completion.

We are having a bracelet with our miniatures and the three children's in it made for you, but unfortunately it is not finished, so we shall bring it and give it to you ourselves.

Osborne: August 6.

I was just sitting down to write to you when Ernest came in with your dear letter. Thousand thanks for it!

These parting lines will be such a dear companion to me on our journey. I can't tell you how much I felt taking leave of you this time, dear Mama; it always is such a wrench to tear myself away from you and my home again. Where I have so, oh, so much to be thankful and grateful to you for, I always fear that I can never express my thanks as warmly as I feel them, which I do indeed from the bottom of my heart. God bless you, darling Mama, for all your love and kindness; and from the depth of my heart do I pray that nothing may cause you such anxiety and sorrow again as you have had to bear of late. . . .

When I left you at the pier the return to the empty house was so sad! It felt quite strange, and by no means pleasant, to be here without you and all the others. We lunched alone with Victoria, and dined in the hot dining-room with the ladies and gentlemen, sitting on the terrace afterwards.

It has rained all the morning, and is most oppressive. As it is so foggy, we have to leave at two; but there is no wind, and I hope the sea will be quite smooth. I am sure you must feel lonely and depressed on this journey, poor Mama; but the change of scene and beautiful nature enjoyed in rest and quiet must surely do you good.

Kranichstein: August 10.

. . . We left Osborne at two on Thursday in rain and wind. The children and I were dreadfully sick an hour after starting, but the passage got smoother later; and, though I was very wretched in every way, I was not sick again. The same sort of weather on the *Alberta* next morning, but it cleared up later. The Rhine steamer was very comfortable, and Doctor Minter accompanied us to Dordrecht. The last afternoon and night on board I suffered dreadfully. Since I arrived here, I am better, but not right yet. Had it not been for your great kindness in giving us the ship, I am sure I should not have got home right. This awful heat adds to my feelings of fatigue and discomfort.

Kranichstein: August 11.

I have just received your letter from Lucerne, and hasten to thank you for it.

How glad I am that you admire the beautiful scenery, and that I know it, and can share your admiration and enjoyment of it in thought with you! It is most lovely. The splendid forms, and the colour of the lake, are two things that we don't know in dear Scotland, and which are so peculiar to Swiss scenery.

Louis is in town from eight till our two o'clock dinner, and has a great deal to do.

For your sake as for my own I long for a respite from this unbearable heat, which is so weakening and trying.

Kranichstein: August 16.

... How satisfactory the accounts of dear good Arthur are! From the depth of my heart do I congratulate you on all that Colonel Elphinstone says about his character, for with a real moral foundation, and a strict sense of duty and of what is right and wrong, he will have a power to combat the temptations of the world and those within himself. I am sure that he will grow up to be a pride and pleasure to you, and an honour to his country.

Brown must have been glad to be allowed to continue wearing his kilt, and, as it is a national dress, it is far more natural that he should give it up nowhere. I am sure that he and Annie [2] must admire the place.

[2] Mrs. McDonald, the Queen's first wardrobe-maid.

Kranichstein: August 26.

I have just received your dear letter, and am so pleased to hear that you enjoyed your excursion, and that you have now seen the sort of wild scenery high up in the mountains, which I think so beautiful and grand in Switzerland. For all admirers of that style of scenery there is nothing to be compared to Switzerland.

Since it became cool again, I have had neuralgia in my head, and I have had a dreadful sty, which had to be cut open, and made me quite faint and sick for the whole day. In spite of it I went to the station here, with a thick veil on, to see the Russian relations pass two days ago. The Emperor looks even more altered and worn since last year, and is suddenly grown so old.

Kranichstein: September 4.

. . . How too delightful your expeditions must have been! I do rejoice that, through the change of weather, you should have been able to see and enjoy all that glorious scenery. Without your good ponies and Brown, &c., you would have felt how difficult such ascents are for common mortals, particularly when the horses slip, and finally sit down. I am sure all this will have done you good; seeing such totally new beautiful scenery does refresh so immensely, and the air and exertion—both of which you seem to bear so well now—will do your health good.

Yesterday we both were two hours at Jugenheim. To-day the two little cousins are coming to see my children.

Louis' business is increasing daily, and until the 19th, manœuvres, inspections, &c., won't be over. He will even have to be away on his birthday, which is a great bore. There is a great review for the Emperor on Saturday.

September 15.

... Like a foolish frightened creature as I am, I have worried myself so much about this sudden talk of war and threatening in all the French papers, saying that October, November, or thereabouts would be a good time to begin. Do tell me, if you think there is the least reasonable apprehension for anything of that sort this year. I have such confidence in your opinion, and you can imagine how in my present condition I must tremble before a recurrence of all I went through in 1866!

I am so grieved that you should have been so unwell on the journey home. Dear beautiful Scotland will do you good. I envy your going there, and wish I could be with you, for I am so fond of it. Remember me to all the good people.

Darmstadt: October 28.

... The Queen of Prussia is coming to lunch with us on Saturday on her way to Coblenz.

I have a cold these last days, and Victoria is still confined to the house with her swelled neck. She had quite lost her appetite, and I tried some porridge for her, which she enjoys, and I hope it will fatten her up a little, for she is so thin and pale. Would you please order a small barrel of oatmeal to be sent to me? Dr. Weber thinks it would be very good for Victoria, and one cannot get it here.

Darmstadt: November 20.

It is with the greatest interest that I read about the Mausoleum,[3] as I was very anxious to know whether all would be finished. Having been present before at all the important steps in the progress of this undertaking, I feel

---

[3] The Royal Mausoleum at Frogmore.

very sorry to be absent at the last, and I shall be very impatient to see it all again.

Winter has quite set in now here, and when there is no wind the cold is very pleasant.

Darmstadt: December 4.

Thousand thanks for all your dear kind wishes, for your first letter to me, for the one to Louis, and finally for the eatables! I can't tell you how touched, how pleased we both are at the kind interest all at home have shown us on this occasion. It has really enhanced our pleasure at the birth of our little son,[4] to receive so many marks of sympathy and attachment from those in my dear native home, and in my present one. My heart is indeed overflowing with gratitude for all God's blessings.

The time itself was very severe, but my recovery is up to now the best I have ever made, and I feel comparatively strong and well.

The girls are delighted with their brother, though Victoria was sorry it was not a sister. Darling Louis was too overcome and taken up with me at first to be half pleased enough. Baby is to be called, by Louis' Uncle Louis' wish, *Ernst Ludwig*, after a former Landgrave[5]; then we would like you to give the name of *Albert*; *Charles*, after my father-in-law; and *William*, after the King of Prussia, whom we mean to ask to be godfather. The christening is most likely to be on the 28th or thereabout.

I am on my sofa in my sitting-room with all your dear photos, &c., around me, and your pretty quilt over me.

December 12.

. . . Every new event in my life renews the grief for dear Papa's loss, and the deep regret that he was not

---

[4] Hereditary Grand Duke Ernst Ludwig, born on the 28th November, 1868.   [5] Who died on the 8th of November, 1825.

here to know of all, to ask advice from, to share joy and grief with, for he was such a tender father, and would have been such a loving grandfather.

You, darling Mama, fill his place with your own, and may God's support never leave you and ever enable you to continue fulfilling the many duties towards State and family! The love of your children and people encircles you.

Darmstadt: December 18.

. . . The presents you intend giving Baby will delight us, and in later years I can tell him all about his Grandpapa, and how I wish and pray he may turn out in any way like him, and try and aim to become so.

I think it would be best, perhaps, if you asked my mother-in-law to represent you and hold Baby. I think it would pain her, should anyone else do it, and I will ask her in your name, if you will kindly telegraph to me your approval.

I am sorry Arthur cannot come; it would have given us such pleasure had it been possible.

The greater part of Baby's monthly gowns have been put away, as from the beginning they were too small. He is so very big.

Christmas Day.

. . . Louis thanks you a thousand times, as we do for the charming presents for the children. They showed them to everyone, shouting, 'This is from my dear English Grandmama;' and Ella, who is always sentimental, added: 'She is so very good, my Grandmama.' Irène could not be parted from the doll you gave her, nor Victoria from hers. Baby was brought down, and was wide awake the whole time, looking about with his little bright eyes like a much older child.

We spent a very happy Christmas eve, surrounded by the dear children and our kind relations.

Darmstadt: December 29.

. . . Prince Hohenzollern with three gentlemen was sent by the King, and the former dined with us after the ceremony. All went off so well, and Baby, who is in every way like a child of two months, looked about him quite wisely, and was much admired by all who saw him.

I am so sorry that you have never seen my babies since Victoria, for I know you would admire them, they look so mottled and healthy. Weather permitting, Baby is to be photographed to-morrow.

1869

Darmstadt: January 8.

. . . Dear charming Lady Frances [Baillie] is on a visit with us, and I enjoy having her so much. We talk of old times at Frogmore, and so many pleasant recollections.

I am glad that you like Baby's photograph, though it does not do him justice. He is a pretty baby on the whole, and has a beautiful skin, very large eyes, and pretty mouth and chin; but his nose is not very pretty, as it is so short at present. He is a dear good child, and, though immensely lively, does not give much trouble. He is a great source of happiness to us, and I trust will continue so.

Darmstadt: January 13.

. . . Is not the death of Leopold's son shocking?[6] Such suffering, such a struggle for months between life

---

[6] The only son and heir of the King of the Belgians.

and death; and for the poor parents to have in the end to relinquish their child, their only son! I think it heart-rending. May the Almighty continue to support them even now, as he did these many months! I cannot say how much and truly I feel for them both. This world is full of trials, and some seem to be called upon to suffer and give up so much. Faith and resignation alone can save those hearts from breaking, when the burden must be so heavy.

A few days ago at two o'clock we had another shock [of earthquake], and it seemed as if the house rocked; at the same time the unearthly noise. I think it uncommonly unpleasant, particularly this repetition.

January 30.

Our thoughts and prayers are so much with you and dear Leopold on this day [his Confirmation]. May the Almighty bless and protect that precious boy, and give him health and strength to continue a life so well begun and so full of promise!

It seems to me quite incredible, the eighth of us should already be old enough to take this step in life, and to have his childhood in fact behind him. Dear Papa's blessing surely rests on him, and his spirit is near you as you stand there alone by the side of his child, about whom he always was so anxious.

Darmstadt: March 8.

. . . We shall go to Potsdam the first week in May, and from there go for a week or ten days to Fischbach. My mother-in-law, Tante Mariechen,[7] and Uncle Adalbert[8] are all going to spend my mother-in-law's birthday there.

The Moriers are going to England in the first days of

---

[7] Queen of Bavaria, sister of Princess Charles of Hesse.

[8] Prince Adalbert of Prussia, brother of Princess Charles of Hesse.

April, and I hope that you will see them. We see a good deal of them, and like them both much. He is wonderfully clever and learned, and takes interest in everything; and she is very agreeable, and a most satisfied, amiable disposition—always contented and amused.

March 19.

I thought of you so much on the 16th. From that day dated the commencement of so much grief and sorrow; yet in those days you had *one*, darling Mama, whose first and deepest thought was to comfort and help you, and I saw and understood only then *how* he watched over you, and how and everywhere he sought to ward off all that was painful and strange from you, and took all that pain alone for himself, for your sake! I see his dear face—so pale, and so full of tears, when he led me to you early that morning after all was over, and said, 'Comfort Mama,' as if those words were a *Vorbedeutung* [presage] of what was to come. In those days, I think he knew how deep my love was for you, and that, as long as I was left in my home, my first and only thought should be you and you alone! This I held as my holiest and dearest duty, until I had to leave you, my beloved Mother, to form a home and family for myself, and new ties which were to take up much of my heart and strength.

But that bond of love, though I can no more be near you, is as strong as ever.

Darmstadt: March 23.

. . . Yesterday it was very warm, and to-day it snows; the weather continues so changeable, and many people are ill. Ella has again had one of her bad attacks in her throat, but, thank God, it passed away very soon. Two nights ago she could not speak—barely breathe—and was so uncomfortable, poor child! It makes one so anxious each time; but I hope she will outgrow it, when she is six or seven years old.

Victoria is already now composing a letter for your birthday. I won't have her helped, because I should like you to see her own ideas and style—it is much more amusing.

March 26.

... We had such an unexpected pleasure the other day in the visit of good General Seymour, and I was so pleased to see some one who had seen you lately, and who could give me news of my home. He had not been here since he came with us after our marriage, and was of course interested in seeing everything.

April 2.

... The constant anxiety about the children is dreadful; and it is not physical ill one dreads for them, it is moral: the responsibility for these little lent souls is great, and, indeed, none can take it lightly who feel how great and important a parent's duty is.

Darmstadt: April 5.

... Thousand thanks for your dear letter, and for all the tender wishes for our dear child's birthday! The child born under your roof and your care is of course your particular one, and later, if you wish to keep her at any time when we have been paying you a visit, we shall gladly leave her.

Victoria is so delighted with what you sent her, and sends her very warmest thanks and her tenderest love. She is in great beauty just at present, as she is grown stouter; and I look with pleasure on those two girls when they go out together. They possess, indeed, all we could wish, and are full of promise. May the Almighty protect them and give them a long life, to be of use and a joy to their fellow-creatures!

April 16.

... Rain and wind have at length cooled the air, for this heat without any shade was too unpleasant. Louis left at five this morning to inspect the garrison at Friedberg and Giessen, and then to go to Alsfeld to shoot *Auerhähne* [capercailzies]. He will return on the 21st or 22nd probably.

We shall indeed be so pleased, if later you wish to have any of the granddaughters with you, to comply with any such wish, for I often think so sadly for your dear sake, how lonely it must be when one child after another grows up and leaves home; and even if they remain, to have no children in the house is most dreary. Surely you can never lack to have some from amongst the many grandchildren; and there are none of us, who would not gladly have our children live under the same roof where we passed such a happy childhood, with such a loving Grandmama to take care of them.

April 25.

... May I only know the way to give my children as much pleasure and happiness as you have ever known to give me!

The dinner of family and suite is here in the house to-day—or rather I should call it a luncheon, as it is at two o'clock.

The Irish Church question, I quite feel with you, will neither be solved nor settled in this way; and instead of doing something which would bring the Catholics more under the authority of the State, they will, I fear, be the more powerful. It seems to me that one injustice (with regard to the Protestants) is to be put in the place of a former one, instead of doing justice to both, which would not have been an impossibility through some well-considered settlement and giving in on both sides. Such a *changement* requires so much thought and wisdom, and, above all, impartiality.

May 3.

... My children are, on the whole, very well behaved and obedient, and, save by fits and starts, which don't last long, very manageable. I try to be very just and consistent in all things towards them, but it is sometimes a great trial of patience, I own. They are so forward, clever, and spirited, that the least spoiling would do them great harm.

How glad I am that the dear Countess [Blücher] is with you again! She is the pleasantest companion possible, and so dear and loving, and she is devoted to you and dear Papa's memory as never anyone was.

Potsdam: May 25.

How much we thought of you yesterday, I can't say. Lord Augustus Loftus lunched with us three and the elder children; and we drank your health, the band playing 'God save the Queen!' All our girls had wreaths of natural flowers in honour of the day.

Potsdam: June 1.

... To-day is regular March weather, and the palace is cold and draughty.

We were in Berlin yesterday, to visit the Gewerbe-Museum [Industrial Museum]; then luncheon at Lord Augustus Loftus's, and from thence to the Victoria bazaar and Victoria Stift, and then home.

It is always so tiring to see things at Berlin; an hour's rail there and the same back takes so much time. Before returning, we paid a short visit to Baron Stockmar and his wife, who is very pleasing, and seems to suit him perfectly. They look as if they had always belonged to each other.

Potsdam: June 13.

Our time here is soon drawing to a close, much to my regret; for the life with dear Vicky—so quiet and pleasant—reminds me in many things of our life in England in former happy days, and so much that we had Vicky has copied for her children. Yet we both always say to each other, no children were so happy, and so spoiled with all the enjoyments and comforts children can wish for, as we were; and that we can never (of course, still less I) give our children all that we had. I am sure dear Papa and you, if you could ever hear how often, how tenderly, Vicky and I talk of our most beloved parents, and how grateful we are for what they did for us, would in some measure feel repaid for all the trouble we gave, and all the anxiety we caused. I ever look back to my childhood and girlhood as the happiest time of my life. The responsibilities, and often the want of many a thing, in married life can never give unalloyed happiness.

We are looking for a governess for the two elder girls for next year, and a lady with the necessary knowledge and character, and yet of a certain rank, is so difficult to find.

Potsdam: June 19.

Louis went two days ago to Fischbach for his mother's birthday, and returns to-morrow morning. Vicky was very low yesterday; she has been so for the last week, and she told me much of what an awful time she went through in 1866, when dear Siggie [Sigismund] died. The little chapel is very peaceful and cheerful, and full of flowers. We go there *en passant* nearly daily, and it seems to give dear Vicky pleasure to go there.

Vicky goes on the 7th of July to Norderney.

Fischbach, Schlesien: July 2.

We arrived here in this exquisitely lovely country two days ago, and were received by our parents-in-law and Aunt Mariechen, whose guests we are in the pretty old Castle of Fischbach, surrounded by fine old trees, with a view on the beautiful Riesengebirge, which reminds me a little of Scotland, and also of Switzerland. The valleys are most lovely, and the numberless wooded hills, before one reaches the high mountains, are quite beautiful. The trees are splendid, and the country looks very rich and green.

All the people of the village and the neighbourhood came out to see us and our children, and old servants of Louis' grandparents, who were so delighted and pleased that I and my children should be here, and that they should have lived to see the younger generation.

We are out seeing the beautiful spots nearly all day long. The weather is fine, and not very warm, so that one can go about comfortably. Yesterday we went over for tea to Erdmannsdorf. If only dear Vicky and Fritz were there now! We must hope for another year to be there together. The parting from them, who had made our *séjour* under their hospitable roof such a very happy one, was very sad, and the pouring rain was in accordance with our feelings. We left them and dear lovely Potsdam and the pleasant life there with much regret, and many a blessing do I send back in thought to its dear inmates.

Yesterday afternoon we were at Schmiedeberg. We went to see a very interesting carpet-manufactory, worked by hand, and all by girls, and a very simple process, much like making fringe, which you used to do and then make footstools of after Beatrice's birth.

Yesterday our wedding-day—already seven years ago—made me think so much of Osborne, and of you, darling Mama, and of all that passed during that time. It was a quiet wedding in a time of much sorrow, and I often think how trying it must have been for you.

Kranichstein: July 21.

Yesterday, after eighteen hours' very hot railway journey, we arrived here all well. Many thanks for your letter, which I received at Dresden. It was impossible to write, as I had to pay visits and to see things, during those two days.

I went to see the picture-gallery, which has some exquisite pictures, though the Sistine Madonna surpasses all others, and the famous Holbein, of which the Dresden gallery has been for long so proud, is now recognised as a copy, and the one that belongs to my mother-in-law as the original. We visited the Grüne Gewölbe [the Green Vaults], where the magnificent jewels and other treasures are preserved, and the King was kind enough to lead us over the rest of the castle himself, including his own rooms, in one of which the life-size pictures of his last four daughters (all dead) stand, of whom he cannot speak without tears. How dreadfully he and the poor Queen must have suffered these last years!

Kranichstein: July 25.

Thousand thanks for your kind letter which I received yesterday, at the same time that the beautiful christening present for Ernest arrived! Thousand thanks for this most beautiful and precious gift for our boy, from Louis and from myself! We are so pleased with it! It is to be exhibited here, and it will interest and delight all who see it, I am sure.

I have just received a letter from Bertie, announcing his arrival here for the 28th. We shall be greatly pleased to see them all; but we have so little room, and our house in town is all shut up and under repair, so that we shall have some trouble to make them comfortable and shall be quite unable to do it as we should wish. But I trust they will be lenient and put up with what we can offer.

The heat is very great, though this place is comparatively cool.

Kranichstein: August 11.

. . . Victoria has often ridden on Dred, and also the other girls, on a Spanish saddle, and he goes very well. They delight in him. Baby rolls about the room anywhere now, and tries to crawl properly. He calls Papa, and tries no end of things; he is very forward, and is now cutting his fifth tooth, which is all but through.

Friedberg: August 26.

On this dear day I must send you a few words. The weather is so beautiful, and the sun so bright, as it used to be at Osborne in former years. I don't care for the sun to shine on this day now, as it can't shine on Him whose day it was. It makes one too *wehmüthig* to think of darling Papa on those happy birthdays, and it must be more so for you than for any of us, poor Mama.

Yesterday was Ludwigstag; all the town decorated with flags, illuminations, &c., and English flags and arms with the Hessian everywhere.

We started on horseback along the high road at half-past seven this morning, and did not get off till one. A lovely country and very interesting to see. To-morrow we shall have a very long march, and the night Alice Morier,[9]

---

[9] Mrs. now Lady Morier, daughter of General Peel.

I and William (Louis is undecided) will spend at Prince Ysenburg's at Büdingen. The next morning we have to ride off at half-past five, and a long day back here.

Kranichstein: September 11.

... What charming expeditions you must have made in that lovely country![10] What I saw of it some years ago I admired so intensely. You can well be proud of all the beauties of the Highlands, which have so entirely their own stamp, that no Alpine scenery, however grand, can lessen one's appreciation for that of Scotland.

The day before yesterday we went to Mayence to see a 'Gewerbe-Ausstellung' [Industrial Exhibition] of the town, which was very good and tastefully arranged. From there we went to Frankfort to our palace, for a rendezvous with Aunt Cambridge, Uncle George, Augusta and Fritz Strelitz. I showed them the children, and afterwards, when our relations left, we took our children to the Zoological Garden, which delighted them.

Many thanks for the grouse, which has just arrived, the first since two years ago!

Darmstadt: October 3.

... I am very glad that you also approve of Louis' journey, which I know will be so useful and interesting for him, though it was not possible to attain this without parting from each other, which is, of course, no small trial for us, who are so unaccustomed to being separated. But we never thought of that when we considered the plan of Louis joining Fritz, which was my idea, as travelling in new countries is so good for a man, and Louis may never find

---

[10] This refers to the Queen's stay at Invertrossachs, and the excursions to the neighbourhood. These are described in *More Leaves from a Journal of a Life in the Highlands*, pp. 116-147 (London, 1884).

so good a chance again. I am looking forward very much to seeing Geneva—where we spend a day—and the south of France, and, above all, seeing the sea again. Fritz passes through here to-morrow. Louis starts Saturday morning, *viâ* Munich, for Venice, where he will join Fritz next Sunday afternoon, and spend the following Monday there before they go to Brindisi. Vicky comes here with her children on the 12th or 13th, and a suite of twenty-five people. She goes on with the big boys to Baden, and I follow with the other children on the following day. I don't like separating Victoria and Ella, who like being together; the three girls will be so well taken care of at their grandparents'. I have written down rules for meals, going out, to bed, to lessons, &c.; and my mother-in-law, who never interferes, will see that all is carried out as I wish. I shall miss them so much, but having one child at least is a comfort; and Baby is beginning to talk, and is so funny and dear, and so fond of me, that he will be company to me when I am alone. I take no one but Orchard, Eliza, Beck, and my Haushofmeister [steward], who used to be with Lord Granville.

Darmstadt: October 11.

Yesterday morning at eleven we had the hard separation from each other, which we both felt very much. My own dear, tender-hearted Louis was quite in the state he was in when we parted at Windsor in 1860 after our engagement. He does not like leaving his children, his home, and me, and really there are but few such husbands and fathers as he. To possess a heart like his, and to call it my *own*, I am ever prouder of and more grateful for from year to year. Nowadays young men like Louis are rare enough, for it is considered fine to neglect one's wife, and for the wife also to have amusements in which her husband does not share. We sisters are singularly blessed in our husbands.

Dear kind Countess Blücher has been here the last two days—such a happiness to me just now, for the house feels far too lonely.

Grand Hôtel, Cannes: November 5.

... I have this instant received another letter from dear Louis from Constantinople, giving the accounts of what they did and saw there until the 29th ult., when they left for Jaffa. He seems delighted, and very greatly interested with all he has seen. Louis thought so much of the Sultan's English visit in 1867, on seeing him again. He found him more talkative than then. He saw also several of the suite who were in England. They went to Scutari, into the Black Sea, and visited all in and near Constantinople, and on the last day they visited the Emperor of Austria, who had just arrived. There is something very funny in hearing of these Royalties, one after another, all running to the same places. They must bore the Sultan considerably.

This journey will be of great advantage to dear Louis, who has never had an opportunity (through marrying so young) of travelling like others.

This afternoon we went to see poor Princess Waldeck.[1] She is still in great grief at the loss of her eldest daughter, who suffered so long, and knew she was dying, and bore her lot with such resignation and such goodness. She was only fifteen-and-a-half, I think.

I was very much pleased to see Lord and Lady Russell again the other day. We hope to be able to pay them a visit at San Remo, though one can't go and return in the same day.

[1] Mother of the Duchess of Albany.

The country has looked too lovely to-day; the sunset is always most beautiful, for it sets behind the Esterel mountains, which lie to the right from this bay, and have a very lovely jagged form.

I am reading to Vicky a new Life of Napoleon, by Lanfrey, which is very well and impartially written.

Cannes: December 14.

. . . The heavenly blue sea, stretching so far and wide, is in accordance with one's feelings, and the beauties of nature have always something comforting and soothing. . . .

The Duke of Argyll's sister, with his pretty daughter Victoria, are here, and we have been twice to see them, and are distressed that they should be so anxious about the dear Duchess, of whom the news to-day is worse. How dreadful, should anything happen to her, for her husband and for the many children!

The Eburys and Lord Dalhousie have likewise arrived here, but we have not seen them yet.

To-morrow we had intended leaving this, but during the night poor Vicky had the dreadful fright of Waldie's being taken ill with the croup. Thank God, he is better this morning, but our journey will have to be put off for a few days, so that Vicky cannot now reach Berlin in time for Christmas. As we don't wish to spend that day *en route*, we have telegraphed to our husbands, who reach Naples to-day, to ask whether they will not join us here, that we may all spend Christmas together before leaving.

This is all unsettled, and I will telegraph as soon as anything is definitively arranged. Rollet [2] is here to-day, and spends this day in quiet with us.

---

[2] Madame Rollande, formerly the Princess's French governess.

Cannes: December 20.

We both had the happiness yesterday of receiving our dear husbands safe and well here after so long a separation.

They had been to Naples and Pompeii, and Louis went for a day to Rome, so that he has seen an enormous deal, which is very instructive for him, and will be such a pleasure for him to look back upon in later years.

I am so glad that Louis has had the opportunity of making this journey; and it seems to have done his health good also, for he looks very well.

The journey back is so long and difficult for me to manage alone with Louis—as Vicky's people, particularly in the nursery, have helped mine—that I am obliged to wait until the 26th, and to go with Vicky and Fritz, for they travel slower than I would do if I went with Louis, who goes back direct day and night. The doctor would not consent to my travelling with Ernie from this warm climate into the great cold so fast, and during the night, for he is cutting four back teeth at this moment.

The day before yesterday we visited Lord Dalhousie and Lady Christian, and found him very gouty, but in good spirits. Lady Ebury and Oggie[3] came to see us this afternoon. Prince and Princess Frederic of the Netherlands and their daughter have arrived here. The poor Princess is so weak, and looks like a shadow.

Hôtel du Jura, Dijon: December 28.

Just as we were leaving Cannes your last letter reached me, for which many thanks. It was cold the morning we left Cannes, very cold at Avignon, where we spent the night, and still colder, and snow and frost, on

[3] Miss Grosvenor, Lady Ebury's daughter.

reaching this place yesterday evening. We and the children are all well, and the poor little ones are very good on the journey, considering all things. In an hour we leave for Paris, rest there to-morrow, and then go to Cologne, where I shall take leave of dear Vicky and Fritz, and go straight home. I have been so much with dear Vicky this year, that the thought of parting from her costs me a great pang, the more so as I do not think it likely that I shall meet her in this new year.

On New Year's eve I arrange a Christmas-tree for all my children, and in advance I thank you for all the presents you have been kind enough to send us, and which we shall find at Darmstadt. . . .

1870

January 8.

. . . My three girls have had fearful colds—Ella bronchitis, which Ernie also took from her, and during twelve hours we were in the very greatest anxiety about him: the difficulty of breathing and his whole state caused great alarm. Thank God, he is now quite convalescent; but those were hours of intense suffering for me, as you can imagine. Weber is most attentive and most kind on such occasions, and in such moments one is so dependent on the doctor.

. . . Some very good lectures have been given here lately, undertaken by a committee, which we are at the head of, and of which Mr. Morier is a member. They have been a great success hitherto, and we are going to one to-night by Kinkel, who in 1848 was a refugee in England, and is now a professor at Zürich.

Beloved Mama, January 16.

We are very grateful for your kind inquiries, and for your letter received this morning. The violence of the fever and the great pain in the throat have abated, and dear Louis is going on favourably.[4] The nights are not good as yet, and his head pains him.

I am cut off from all intercourse with anyone in the house, on account of the dear children; and I trust they may escape, for they still cough, particularly Ella and Ernie. I see Christa when I am out walking, not otherwise, as she comes in contact with the part of the house where the children live. I read to Louis, and play to him, as my sitting-room opens into the bedroom. I keep the rooms well aired, and not hot, and at night I sleep on a sofa near his bed. The first two nights were anxious ones, and I was up all night alone with him; but now, thank God, all seems to be going well. . . .

January 20.

I am happy to say that all is going on well. Louis has no more fever, but his throat is still far from well; it has still the character of diphtheria, though in a mild form —a sort of skin and bits of blood come away when he coughs. He is a very good patient, and I leave him very little alone save when I take my walks, which in this high cold wind are very unpleasant. I hear Ella is still so hoarse and coughs, and Victoria is not quite well. Orchard writes to me every evening, and Dr. Weber[5] sees them in the morning before he comes downstairs.

This instant Weber tells me that Victoria has the scarlet fever, and I have just been up to see her. She suffers very

---

[4] Prince Louis was ill with an attack of scarlet fever.
[5] Prince and Princess Louis' own physician.

much, poor child; the fever is very high and the rash much out. It is too late now to separate the others, and those who are not predisposed will escape; but those who are inclined to take it have it in them by this time.

It is a source of great anxiety. Orchard and Emma have never had it. . . .

January 23.

I was very glad to get your dear lines of the 22nd, full of sympathy for me during this anxious time. Victoria's fever has been very high; and so much discomfort and pain, with a dreadful cough, which she has had for the last six weeks. She is very low, and cries every now and then from weakness, &c., but is a very good patient, poor little one! Amelung comes every afternoon and sits with her, and she is a great favourite with the children, as she knows countless pretty stories.

Louis is not out of bed yet, on account of his throat, &c.; but he is much better, though in this treacherous climate, which is proverbially bad for throats and lungs, I fear that even with the greatest care there is a risk.

The other children are as yet well, though I don't think Ella looking well; she has still a cold, and is as hoarse as when I came home. Ernie is all right again, and looks the best of them all. I doubt their escaping, though it is quite possible, as they did not take it when Victoria did. I keep the rooms fresh, and continually aired.

All the balls and parties are going on here now. Of course, I can neither go anywhere nor receive anyone, on account of the infection. It is a wearisome time indeed, and being so much in sick rooms and so little out begins to tell upon me. How kind of you to send the books! Louis will be delighted. I have just read to him Russell's book of Bertie and Alix's journey, and am now reading to him a new Life of Napoleon, by Lanfrey, which is very well written—more against than for Napoleon. Of course, newspapers and the *Revue des Deux-Mondes* I read to him besides. . . .

January 31.

. . . Though dear Baby has had two bad, restless nights, yet I am happy to say that he has the illness so slightly, with so little fever or sore throat, that we are in great hopes it will get no worse. He is cutting his back teeth just now, which is the worst moment possible to be ill in.

Victoria looks very hollow-eyed, pale and wretched, poor darling, but is in good spirits now. The other two are as yet free. The weather is most beautiful—frosty and clear—and I have been skating daily for the last six days, which does me much good, and enables me to see people again. This afternoon I have a large party on the ice at Kranichstein, and this is always a great amusement to the young people. . . .

Mayence: April 10.

. . . Yesterday evening we had to give a large party here, half to the military, and the other to the civil authorities and to the *Bürger* [citizens]. It went off well; but the amount of speaking, as one must speak to all, and the effort to remember who they all were—they having been all presented at once—was no small exertion. . . .

Mayence: April 15.

. . . Lady Car. [Barrington] wrote to me how very grateful Mrs. Grey was to you for your great kindness and consideration.[6] In trouble no one can have a more true and sympathising friend than my beloved Mama always is. How many hearts has she not gained by this,

[6] General Grey, Her Majesty's private secretary, who died March 30.

and how many a poor sufferer's burdens has she not lightened! . . .

April 25.

Thousand thanks for your dear loving lines! I kissed them a thousand times, and thank you so much for the quite lovely statuette—a little gem, which everyone has been admiring this morning. The shawl and little ornament gave me also great pleasure, and the coloured photographs of the rooms—in short, all and anything from such dear hands must give pleasure. . . .

June 25.

. . . I am proud of my two girls, for they are warm-hearted and gifted, too, in appearance. Victoria's facility in learning is wonderful, and her lessons are her delight. Her English history and reading she has learned from me. I give her a lesson daily, and Bäuerlein [7] can tell you how much she has learned. . . .

I read a great deal, chiefly history and deeper works; and I have one or two very learned acquaintances with whom to read or to have books recommended by.

My two committees always give me no end of work, and I have tried to have many improvements made in the girls' schools of the different classes; and some of these things, by dint of a deal of trouble, are prospering, and I hope in time to come will prove their worth. There is a great deal to be done, and in the hospitals I have been able to get some very necessary changes made. I tell you all this, fancying it may perhaps interest you a little bit. . . .

July 2.

How grieved I am for your sake, above all, and for the poor Clarks and ourselves, that dear kind Sir James,[8] that

---

[7] Miss Bauer, the German governess of the Royal family.
[8] Sir James Clark died at Bagshot June 29, 1870.

true fatherly friend, is no more!! Many thanks for your last letter, which tells me of your last visit to him, which I am sure must be a great comfort to you. Oh! how sad to think how many are gone! And for you, dear Mama, this is quite dreadful. I can't say how I feel it for you!

Lord Clarendon's death[9] grieves me much also; and it was so sudden. Alice Skelmersdale wrote to me in the greatest distress; he had been a most loving father.

In the midst of life we are in death; and in our quiet and solitary existence out here, where we see no one, all accords with sad and serious feelings, which, amidst the many people and worry you live in, must jar with such feelings and make you wish for solitude. The accounts you give touch me so much. Many thanks for having written so much about dear Sir James; it is of great value to me. Louis begs me to say how he shares the grief you all and we must feel at such a loss.

What you say about the education of our girls I entirely agree with, and I strive to bring them up totally free from pride of their position, which is *nothing*, save what their personal worth can make it. I read it to the governess—who quite enters into all my wishes on that subject—thinking how good it would be for her to hear your opinion. . . . I feel so entirely as you do on the difference of rank, and how all-important it is for princes and princesses to know that they are nothing better or above others, save through their own merit; and that they have only the double duty of living for others and of being an example—good and modest. This I hope my children will grow up to.

July 26.

When I returned home last night really heartbroken, after having parted from my good and tenderly loved Louis,

[9] Died June 27, 1870.

I found your dear sympathising words, and I thank you a thousand times for them—they were a comfort and pleasure to me! I parted with dear Louis late in the evening, on the high road outside the village in which he was quartered for the night, and we looked back until nothing more was to be seen of each other. May the Almighty watch over his precious life, and bring him safe back again! All the pain and anxiety are forgotten and willingly borne if he is only left to me and to his children!

It is an awful time, and the provocation of a war such as this a crime that will have to be answered for, and for which there can be no justification. Everywhere troops and peasants are heard singing 'Die Wacht am Rhein' and 'Was ist des Deutschen Vaterland?' and there is a feeling of unity and standing by each other, forgetting all party quarrels, which makes one proud of the name of German. All women feel ashamed of complaining, when father, husband, or son goes, and so many as volunteers in the ranks. This war is felt to be national, and that the King had no other course left him to pursue with honour.

I must be in town by nine o'clock: so much rests on me, and there are so many to help—the poor forsaken soldiers' families amongst others! I have seen that all is ready to receive the wounded, and to send out help. I send out fourteen nurses for the Feld-Lazarethe [field-hospitals].

How much I feel for you now, for I know how truly you must feel for Germany; and *all* know that every good thing England does for Germany, and every evil she wards off her, is owing to your wisdom and experience, and to your true and just feelings. You would, I am sure, be pleased to hear how universally this is recognised and appreciated.

What would beloved Papa have thought of this war? The unity of Germany, which it has brought about, would please him, but never the shocking means!

July 28.

My darling Louis is at Worms, and Henry just in front of him. The enthusiasm all along the Rhine is wonderful. They are all hopeful, though knowing well what enormous sacrifices and struggles a victory will cost.

I cannot leave this place until our troops should have—which God prevent!—to retreat, and the French come! Now is the moment when a panic might overcome the people; and I think it my duty to remain at my post, as it gives the people courage and confidence. My parents-in-law, who have their three sons out, would feel my absence, and they have the first claim on me. I am in beloved Louis' home, and nearer to him, if I remain. Of course, with dear Vicky I should personally be far better off. But Fritz is not much exposed, and she has not that fearful anxiety to such an amount as I have for dear Louis, who, as commander of only a division, must be in the very midst of all. Day and night this thought is uppermost in my mind. I hope and pray for the best, and bear what is sent to me in common with so many others. Work is a *Zerstreuung* [distraction], and I know dear Louis would prefer knowing me here for the present, and that must be the first consideration to determine my actions.

Louis is well, and, now the dreadful parting is over, I am sure in better spirits, though work and anxiety weigh on him, poor love.

The children send their love. I am pretty well; able to do a great deal; headache and sleeplessness are but natural at this moment.

August 5.

Arrived in our house this morning, I was received with the news of dear Fritz's first victory,[1] and that 500 French prisoners had just passed through here by rail. I know none of ours can have been engaged, but we have not heard if there was an engagement elsewhere. The excitement and anxiety are quite dreadful! Please God, my darling is safe, and will pass safely through these dreadful dangers—and our many dear friends and acquaintances also! I am always sending off things for the wounded from our stores, and continue working and collecting, and all are most patriotic and united. It is a solemn and great time we live in, and there is something grand and elevating in the unity of high and low throughout this great nation, which makes one proud of belonging to it. If only all goes on well!

I am very sleepless, and never without headache, but one has neither time nor wish to think of oneself. My own Louis' safety is the all-engrossing thought; and I know, beloved Mama, that you love him truly, and share this anxiety with me. . . .

August 15.

A few words by messenger. I have sent a letter by Kanné,[2] who came here yesterday, having seen dear Louis the day before, which was the first direct news I have had from him. Yesterday morning he was at Faulquemont. Poor General von Manstein (our Chef), when he reached Saarbrück, found his son had been killed, and he had him taken out of the general grave and buried in the churchyard. . . . No less than forty French wounded I saw

---

[1] Victory of the Germans at Weissenburg over Marshal MacMahon, on August 4, 1870.   [2] The Queen's own courier.

this morning in our hospital, with some Turcos. Some can't speak in any known language, and the French dislike having these savages near them as much as we do; their physiognomies are horrid, and they steal and murder as *Handwerk* [their vocation].

So much going about—for I go to Darmstadt at half-past eight, and remain till half-past eleven, in the morning, and in the afternoon from five till eight—is getting very fatiguing to me; but the people have no time to come out here, and there is much to see to, and many to speak with.

August 19.

I have tried to write as often as I could, but I have only two hours to myself during the whole day, through driving in here twice a day. Besides the large Hülfsverein for the 'wounded and sick,' which is in our palace, I have daily to visit the four hospitals. There is very much to do; we are so near the seat of war. This morning we got two large waggons ready and sent off for Pont-à-Mousson, where they telegraph from the battlefield of the 16th they are in great want. My best nurses are out there; the others are in three hospitals: two of them—military ones—were not ready or organised when 150 wounded arrived a week ago. I have just had a telegram from dear Louis; he is well, and I hope in a day or two the least dangerously of the Hessian wounded will arrive.

Thank God, all goes on successfully; but, indeed, I hope I shall not live to see another such war—it is too shocking by far. We have over five hundred wounded; as soon as any are better, they are sent north, and worse ones fill the beds—French and German intermixed. I neither see nor smell anything else but wounds! and the first *Anblick* [sight], which sometimes one does not escape meeting, is very shocking! It was very late last night before I got home. I was stopped at one of the hospitals, as a poor soldier had had sudden violent bleeding, and was all but dead, as the doctor could not find the artery; but I sent my carriage for another surgeon, and I am happy to say he lives, and is recovering.

As Louis commands the whole of our little army, a great many things concerning the troops come to me from all parts of the country, and there is much to do—much more than in my present state is good for me; but it can't be helped.

I drive back to Kranichstein by one daily, and am here again before five, so I hope you will kindly forgive my writing seldomer. Becker is engrossed with his duties at the Hülfsverein; there is no other gentleman with me, and I have the household to look after, besides.

August 20.

My telegram will have told you that dear Louis is until now safe.[3] On the 16th, in the evening, and on the 17th and 18th, our troops were engaged, and yesterday evening late I drove to the station, to speak to General Kehrer, our commandant, and received a telegram of the last victory, near Metz—a battle of nine hours, very bloody —no mention of names. The people, all excited, crowded round my carriage, asked for news—which of our regiments had been under fire? I could tell them nothing, but pacified them, begging them to go to their homes—they

---

[3] On the 16th, Marshal Bazaine, while retreating from Metz to Verdun, was attacked by Prince Frederic Charles, between Vionville and Mars-la-Tour, and a severe engagement was fought. On the 17th and 18th occurred the battles of Rezonville and Gravelotte, in which the King of Prussia commanded, and defeated Marshal Bazaine. Prince Louis was engaged with his division in these battles.

should hear as soon as I had news. I drove home with an aching heart, and passed a dreadful night of suspense. At six this morning a telegram from Louis (19th); he and his two brothers safe; our loss enormous—seventy officers out of one division (ours is the 25th), and Oberlieutenant Möller, a great favourite, his adjutant since 1866, very badly wounded. I went at once to Darmstadt to Louis' parents. They were so overcome and thankful to hear of the safety of their children. This continual anxiety is fearful. Now to-day all the poor wives, mothers, sisters, come to me for news of their relations; it is heartrending! We sent off two large waggon-loads to Pont-à-Mousson again with provisions, bandages and medicaments, and mattresses to bring back all the wounded possible by rail. I went the round of the hospital, to have all the convalescent Prussians and French able to travel sent to their homes, so as to get room, and now we can await the sad arrivals. Oh, if it would but end! the misery of thousands is too awful!

Kranichstein: August 25.

Many thanks for your dear words of the 20th. God knows, I have suffered much, and the load of anxiety is great! But thousands of Germans bear this load in unity together for their Fatherland, and none murmur. Yesterday a poor woman came to me to ask me to help her to get to the battlefield, to have the body of her only son looked for and brought home; and she was so resigned and patient.

I see daily, in all classes, so much grief and suffering; so many acquaintances and friends have fallen! It is heartrending! I ought to be *very proud* though, and I am so, too, to hear from the mouths of so many wounded officers the loud praise of Louis' great bravery on the 16th and

18th. Always in front, encouraging his men where the battle raged fiercest and the balls fell thickest. He was near our troops, speaking to them, directing them, and right and left of him they fell in masses. This lasted eight hours!

. . . Hourly almost the trains bring in fresh wounded, and many and shocking are the sights one sees. I only returned here by one, having gone to town at half-past eight this morning, and have still three hospitals for this afternoon.

My nurses reached the battlefield in time, and were of great use. Louis telegraphed (yesterday's date) from Auboué, between Thionville and Metz, where they remain in bivouac. . . . It is ten days since Louis has been in a bed or under a roof. They have no water (it is kept for the wounded), and little to eat, but he is very well.

It is difficult to get news, and I can never send any that is not mostly ten days old ere it reaches him.

August 26.

. . . I had a telegram on the 25th from near Marengo, not far from Metz—all well. Louis has not been in bed or under a roof since the 16th, and it rains incessantly. I hope they won't all be ill. He writes mostly on cards, on the hilt of his sword, sitting on a box. They cook their own dinner, and on the 16th they were going to eat it, when orders came to turn the French left wing and go into battle. That night was awful, though the day of the 18th seems to have been the bloodiest ever known. Our wounded all tell me so.

My dear parents-in-law bear up well; but when we three get together we pour our hearts out to each other, and then tears which are full of anxiety will flow.

Kranichstein: September 2.

I went early to Homburg, as no trains go regularly now. I went by road from Frankfort, and found dear Vicky well—her little baby very pretty and healthy-looking; the other dear children also well.

How much we had to tell each other! How much to be proud of, and how many friends and acquaintances to mourn over! The few hours we had together flew by in no time, and at Frankfort the train was unpunctual—outside Darmstadt it waited nearly an hour. At our palace, where I arrived at ten in the evening, people who were going to our Hauptquartier [headquarters] were waiting. I scribbled a few words to my dear Louis (the first since he received the Iron Cross, a great distinction) and packed a few things for him—tea, &c.

September 15.

Though I am still forbidden to use my eyes, I must send you a few words of thanks for your dear letter and telegram. I had a violent inflammation of eyes and throat, with two days strong fever and neuralgia. I am recovering now, but feel the effects very much; my eyes are still bad, and it has reduced my strength, which I require so much. Dr. Weber has just lost his sister (whom he treated in her confinement) from puerperal fever, and he told me he thought he must have given it to her, from going to and fro to his wounded, for *Lazarethfieber* [hospital fever] and that were so closely akin. You can fancy that in Louis' absence, and with the prospect of being alone, without even a married experienced lady in the house, this prospect frightened me. It is unhealthy at any time to be for one's confinement in a town full of hospitals with wounded, and Weber could never give me as much attention as at another time, and, should I be very ill, there is no authority to say anything about what had best be done. On that account your telegram was a relief to me.

September 20.

. . . Daily I hear the muffled drums of the funeral of some soldier or officer being taken past my windows to his last resting-place. How deeply I do feel for the poor parents and widows!

My children are very well, but have absolutely no place where they can walk with safety from infection, for the mass of sick troops who get out and stop near the Exercirplatz [drill-ground], and the hospitals in town. The barrack at the foot of our garden contains 1,200 French prisoners, and many of them ill. It is much to be hoped that there will be soon an end to all these things. I feel for the Emperor and Empress very much. What ungrateful, vain, and untruthful people the French are! To expose Paris to a siege, now their armies are beaten, which they think through fine speeches and volunteers they can set right again.

September 22.

I received your letter through Kanné yesterday, and thank you many times for it; also for the little shawls and sash for Ernie. Every souvenir from dear Balmoral is a pleasure.

Good Dr. Hofmeister[4] will be very welcome, and I know he is very clever. Mrs. Clarke[5] is sure to get on well with him, and an older doctor just now, besides being an acquaintance of so many years, is to me indeed a comfort. I shall be able also to hear of all at home, and of so many

---

[4] Sent by the Queen to attend the Princess in her confinement.
[5] Nurse.

things that interest me. Thousand thanks from Louis and from myself for your sending him! . . .

ALL long for peace—the army and the nation—and I think so great a national war as this need not require part of the foes' territory. What little is necessary for the military frontier they must take; but the union of Germany under one head is a far greater and finer end to such a war than the annexation of land!

. . . War is the greatest scourge this world knows, and that we may not live to see it again, is my earnest prayer.

October 1.

. . . The children are all well, in spite of the bad air here. I send them out driving of an afternoon, when I can best, having only one coachman, as ours are with Louis. At present they can't manage it often. . . .

October 3.

. . . Dr. Hofmeister is to both of us a source of real confidence and comfort. I don't think anyone else would have been more welcome to me just now, and he can write daily to Louis, and letters go usually in two days now.

I go as little as possible to the hospital now, and, indeed, do nothing imprudent, you can be sure. . . .

November 12.

. . . The nerves of my forehead and eyes are still painful; and from all sides I am again called upon to look after, settle, and advise concerning many things. On that account Dr. Weber and my mother-in-law insist on my leaving Darmstadt for a total change of scene, &c., for three weeks. I have resisted as long as I could, as I so much dislike going from home now (though I do not feel up to the work, and yet cannot keep from doing it), but I have finally given in, and accepted Vicky's kind invitation to accompany her for three weeks to Berlin. The journey is long and cold, but her company when we are both alone is a pleasure to me, and I shall hear all news as directly there as here.

. . . Last night I was much overcome. I had been sitting at the bedside of one of my poor young friends, and he was gasping in a too-distressing way. The father held his hand, the tears streaming down his cheek, the son trying to say 'Weine nicht, Papa' ['Don't weep, Papa!]. The poor old father, so proud of his good and handsome child, is heartbroken, and they are touchingly united and full of feeling for each other. I would give anything to save his life; but all efforts will, I fear, be in vain. Though I have seen so many lately die hard deaths, and heard and seen the grief of many heartbroken widows and mothers, it makes my heart bleed anew in each fresh case, and curse the wickedness of war again and again.

Poor Baby can't be christened yet, as my parents-in-law think Louis would not like it during his absence, so I shall wait. . . .

November 17.

. . . How I rejoice to hear that Leopold gains so much strength, and that he can be about again as usual. Will you kindly tell him in Louis' name and mine (as I am still restricted in all writing and reading), that we beg him to stand godfather to our little son?[6] Baby is so nice and fat now, and thrives very well. I think you would

[6] Prince Frederick William, the 'Frittie' of these letters, born the 6th of the previous month of October, and who was killed by a fall from a window on the 29th of May, 1873.

admire him, his features are so pretty, and he is so pink, and looks so wide-awake and intelligent. Ernie, who in general is a rough boy, is most tender and gentle to his little brother, and not jealous. . . .

Berlin: December 5.

. . . Yesterday Fieldmarshal Wrangel came to see me, and his words were, 'Zu gratuliren dass Ihr Mann ein Held ist, und sich so superb geschlagen hat' ['Accept my congratulations that your husband is a hero, and has fought so magnificently']. I am very proud of all this, but I am too much a woman not to long above all things to have him safe home again.

. . . The evenings Vicky and I spend alone together, talking or writing our letters. There is so much to speak of and think about, of the present and the future, that it is to me a great comfort to be with dear Vicky. It is nearly five months since Louis left, and we lead such single existences that a sister is inexpressibly dear when all closer intercourse is so wanting! There is so much, beloved Mama, I should like to speak to you about. . . .

The girls are quite well, and very happy with their grandparents. The governess—who in the end did not suit for the children—as the six months' trial is over, will not remain, and I am looking for another one.

Darmstadt: December 18.

. . . The children and I bore the journey well, and it was not cold. Parting from dear Vicky was a hard moment, and I shall feel the loneliness here so much, and miss my dear good Louis more than ever. The children are, of course, at such a time the greatest blessing. There is so much to do for them and to look after for them; and mine are dear good children, and do not give over-much trouble.

Letters I have again received speak of the amount of danger Louis has again been daily exposed to, and how his personal courage and daring have given the victory in many a fight. God protect him! I live in fear and trembling for his precious life, and after I hear of his being safe through one battle, I take it as a fresh present from the Almighty, and breathe freer again, though the fear soon enough gets the upper hand again.

I have asked Uncle Louis to allow his *Berichte* [reports] to be copied for you. Louis has Köhler and another footman with him, that is all—and two coachmen. He rides at all battles the horse you gave him in 1866, which he rode during that campaign, and which is quite invaluable. It would interest Colonel Maude [7] to know this, as he bought the horse. My nursery is in very good order, and they are all invaluable in their way.

How is good Dr. Hofmeister's family? Please say many kind things to him from me, and tell him that the Baby is getting so nice and fat, and is so healthy in spite of all troubles. Here is a photograph of him, but not at all flattered. Please give Dr. Hofmeister one of them!

I have this instant received a letter from Louis dated the 11th! I will have an extract made for you. I think it might interest Bertie to hear something of Louis, whom he can be proud to have as a brother-in-law, for I hear his praises continually. He has been throughout the war, as every other General has been, without a carriage, &c., like other Princes, and has gained the respect and devotion of his troops.

[7] Crown Equerry to the Queen.

Darmstadt: December 19.

... I hope for this last time, if we are spared and live to come over together once more, we may have the joy of showing their dear Grandmama the whole little band. Of course, no thoughts of plans can be entertained, and I know, after so very long a separation, Louis would not be willing again to part from his children.

My wounded were so pleased to see me again yesterday. Alas! many in bed, and so ill still! My two in the house are much better, and the one who during six weeks lay at death's door is recovering. I have seldom experienced so great a satisfaction as seeing this young man recover, and the doctors say I have been the means of saving his life.

The joy of the old parents will be very great. Since I left, there are new widows and fresh parents bereft of only children; it is a most painful duty to go to them. But I know the comfort of sympathy is the only one in deep grief.

December 23.

My warmest and tenderest thanks for your dear and loving letter, with so many expressions of a mother's love and sympathy, which do my heart good, now that I feel so lonely and anxious. It seems too great a happiness to think of, that of our being allowed to come with our children to you, and to Scotland; and you know the smallest corner is enough for us, who are by no means particular—neither are our people. If I write this to Louis, it will be something for him to look forward to, to cheer him and reward him after so hard a time, which he bears so bravely and uncomplainingly. This morning I have been at the Alice Hospital, which is prospering. I have been taking my gifts for Christmas to one hospital after another. Your two capes have delighted the poor sufferers, and the one wounded for the second time is very bad, alas! My wounded officer in the house is recovering, next to a miracle. For the two wounded in the house, the children, our household, and the children of our servants at the war, I arrange Christmas trees.

We grown-up ones of the family have given up keeping Christmas for ourselves. We have too much to do for others, and my parents-in-law, like me, feel the absence of the dear ones who are always here for Christmas.

I am superintending Victoria and Ella's letters to you, which have not achieved the perfection wished for. As they are to be quite their own, I hope you will excuse their arriving a little later.

Darmstadt: December 27.

... Louis telegraphed on Christmas day from Orleans, where I had sent Christa's brother with a box of eatables and woollen things for his people, and a tiny Christmas tree with little lights for the whole party. Louis has sent me a photograph of himself and staff done at Orleans, and I have sent for a copy for you, as it is very good. On Christmas day it was five months since Louis and the troops left. The charming stockings you sent, I have sent off in part to-day to Louis to give to his Stabswache [Staff-guard]; the other things I divide among the wounded and sick.

My children are all well. The little one sits up, and, though not very fat, is round and firm, with rosy cheeks and the brightest eyes possible. He is very healthy and strong, and in fact the prettiest of all my babies. The three girls are so grown, particularly the two eldest, you would scarcely know them. They are both very tall for their age. Victoria is the height of Vicky's Charlotte, and Ella not much less. They are thin, and a change of air would be very beneficial.

1871

Darmstadt: January 7.

... In England people are, I fear, becoming unjust towards the German troops. Such a long and bloody war must demoralise the best army; and I only say, in such a position how would the French have behaved? Many French officers say the same, and how greatly they respect the German soldier. Hundreds of French officers and two generals have broken their word of honour, and run away. I doubt whether *one* in the German army would do such a thing. The French peasants, often women, murder our soldiers in their beds, and the wounded they have used too horribly many a time. Is it a wonder, then, when the men let a feeling of revenge lay hold of them? A guerilla war is always horrid, and no words can say how all Germans feel and deplore the present phase of the war! I hope and trust that the end may not be far distant.

One of the poor wounded soldiers whom I gave your cape to is dying, and the poor boy won't part from it for an instant, and holds it tight round himself.

Louis continues at Orleans, where they have entrenched themselves, and await with impatience news from Paris which must be of great influence for the continuation or ending of the war.

My days fly past. The children take much of my time —so, too, the house, my two wounded in the house, and the hospitals, to one of which I go daily.

Darmstadt: January 14.

... How kind of you to work something for Louis; he will wear it with such pleasure. Prince Frederick Carl's recent victories[8] and the fresh hosts of prisoners must help to bring the war to an end. Germany does not wish to go on, but the French won't see that they are beaten, and they will have to accept the visitors, who must increase in numbers the longer the French refuse to accede to the German demands.

I am so low, so deeply grieved for the misery entailed on both sides, and feel for the French so much. Our troops do not pillage in the way described in English papers. I have read far worse accounts of what the French soldiers and *francs-tireurs* do in their French villages.

The poor soldier who had your cape is dead. He died with it round him. I was with him in the afternoon, and he had tears in his eyes, and was very low. In the night he died. This morning I was at the station to give things to the wounded and sick who came through—a sorry sight. This afternoon I am going to a poor soldier's widow who has just had twins. The distress on all sides is great. I help where I can. Becker tears his hair. The two wounded in the house cost so much. So does everything else; but as long as I can, through sparing on myself, help others, I must do it—though I have, as things are now, nothing left.

I will get a head of Ernest done for your bracelet, and another one, so that you may have something else of him. He is a magnificent boy, but so huge—such limbs! The Baby is not at all small, but near Ernest all the others look small.

He can't speak properly yet, but he understands everything, and has a wonderful ear for music. He sings the 'Guten Kameraden' without a fault in the time, and is passionately fond of dancing, which he also does in time.

Irène is growing fast also, but the two eldest are quite

---

[8] On the 10th, 11th, and 12th of January, 1871, before Le Mans.

big girls; it makes me feel old when I see them growing up to me so fast. Victoria has a very inquiring mind, and is studious, and learns easily and well. Since the middle of December I have been without a governess.

To-morrow I go to Mayence to see poor Woldemar[9] Holstein's sister. He is very bad, to the grief of all Mayence, and of all who know him.

Darmstadt: January 16.

My little Baby ought to be christened, but Louis and my parents-in-law always hope that the end of hostilities is near, and that Louis can then get leave. Baby's blue eyes are beginning to turn, and look almost as if they would be brown. Should dear Grandmama's and Grandpapa's eyes come up again amongst some of the grandchildren, how nice it would be!

I have but little news to give. I go about to the poor soldiers' widows and wives—no end of them, with new-born babies, in the greatest distress.

Yesterday I saw the mother of the poor young soldier who died. She keeps your cape as a precious relic, as it had given him such great pleasure.

January 30.

Your charming photograph and kind letter arrived this morning—thousand thanks for both! How like the photograph, and how pleasing! I am so glad to have it.

The armistice and capitulation of Paris are great events. The people are out of their minds with joy—flags all over the town, and the streets crowded.

I forgot to say in my last letter how grieved I was about Beaty Durham's[1] death. It is quite shocking! and those

---

[9] Prince Henry Charles Woldemar of Schleswig-Holstein, Governor of the fortress of Mayence. He died on the 20th of January, 1871.

[1] Daughter of the Duke of Abercorn.

numbers of children in so short a time. I earnestly hope none of us run such a chance, for on the whole our children have not been so close together. My last came sooner than I wished, and is smaller than his brother, but I hope now for a long rest. I have Baby fed, besides, so as not to try my strength. He is very healthy and strong, and is more like Victoria and my brothers and sisters than my other children, and his eyes remind me of Uncle Ernest's, and seem turning brown, which would be very pretty, as he is very fair otherwise.

Your pretty photograph is standing before me, and makes me quite absent. I catch myself continually staring at it, instead of writing my letters.

Darmstadt: February 2.

. . . All the many French here are pleased at the capitulation of Paris, and hope that peace is certain. Louis writes to me that the inhabitants of Orleans were equally pleased, and consider the war over. I earnestly pray it may be so. How greatly relieved and thankful all Germany would be!

Louis telegraphed to-day. He has no leave as yet, though he hopes for it. Now that there is a prospect of peace, and that the fighting is momentarily over, I feel quite a collapse of my nerves, after the strain that has been on them for six whole months. I can scarcely imagine what it will be when my beloved Louis is at home again; it seems *too great* a joy! Rest and quiet together are what I long for; and I fear in the first weeks he will have so much to do, and there will be much going on.

He speaks with the greatest hope of going to Scotland this autumn; and, if we are spared to do so, it will be such a rest, and do good to our healths, which must feel the wear and tear sooner or later.

February 11.

Many thanks for your last kind letter. I thought so much of you yesterday, spending the dear 10th for the first time again at Windsor. To-day our little son is to be christened, but only the family will be present, and my ladies and the two wounded gentlemen, who can get about on crutches now. When I think that the one owes his life to being here, it always gives me pleasure.

Two nights ago I was awakened by a dreadful noise, the whole house and my bed rocking from it; and twice again, though less violently. It was an earthquake, and I think too unpleasant. It frightens one so; the doors and windows rattle and shake. To-night two slight shocks, and one during the day yesterday.

How I shall miss dear Louis to-day! The seven months will be round ere we meet, I fear, and he has never seen his dear little boy. It always makes me sad to look at him, though now I have every reason to hope—please God—that I shall have the joy of seeing Louis come home, and of placing his baby in his arms. My heart is full, as you can fancy, and, much as I long to see Louis, I almost dread the moment—the emotion will be so great, and the long pent-up feelings will find vent.

I pray that peace may be restored, and that I may not live to see *such* a war again, or to see my sons have to go to it.

I will tell Christa to write an account to you of the christening, for Leopold to see also, as he will be godfather. Frederic William Augustus (after the Empress) Victor (victory) Louis will be his names. Fritz and Vicky, the Empress and Fritz Carl, are godparents.

Darmstadt: February 14.

My bad eyes must again excuse the shortness of these lines, which are to thank you many times for your last dear letter.

Christa will have sent you the account of little Fritz's christening, which was a sad day for me, and will have been so for dear Louis likewise. We have added dear Leopold's name to the others, as his sad life, and the anxiety his health has so often caused us all, endear him particularly, and we hoped it would give him pleasure, dear boy.

The elections in the provinces are all for peace, and only the towns for war and a republic. This week is one of intense and anxious expectation; though the greater portion believe in the restoration of peace, yet we have no security for it.

March 6.

. . . Now dear Louise's marriage draws near, how much you must feel it! I think so much of her, of your and of my dear home. I trust she will be very happy, which with such an amiable young man she must be.

Louis has received the Order 'Pour le mérite,' which I am so glad of for him. The Emperor telegraphed the announcement to my mother-in-law, with many complimentary words about her sons. To have the three sons safe is something to be thankful for, for they were much and continually exposed. I know nothing of Louis' coming. The troops march home, and it will take at least six weeks. I hope so much that he may have leave for a fortnight, and then return to the troops, to lead them home.

To-night are the peace illuminations here, which will be very pretty. Our house will also be illuminated, and I take the two eldest girls out with me to-night to see it all. It is a thing for them never to forget, this great and glorious, though too horrid, war.

March 13.

I know nothing as yet of Louis' return. I fear I must wait a few weeks longer. On Wednesday the Emperor,

Fritz, and some of the Princes pass through Frankfort, and I am going there with my parents-in-law to see them.

The Paris news is not very edifying, and I fear France has not seen the worst yet, for there seems to be a fearful state of anarchy there.

I have no news to give, save that Frittie has his first tooth. He is between Victoria and Irène, but not like Ernie—not near so big, which is really not necessary. I think he is the sort of baby you admire. I go on looking after my hospitals, and now the trains, full of Landwehr returning home cheering and singing, begin to pass. Now good-bye, darling Mama. I am in thought daily with you during these days, and only wish it had been in my power to be of any use or comfort to you just now.

Darmstadt: April 8.

... We had the pleasure of catching a glimpse of Louise and Lorne on their way through, but their stay was too short to be able to say more than a few words. They can scarcely help passing through here, as they can't go through France, on their way back; and if you would allow them *quite incognito* on their way back to pass a day here, it would give both Louise and me the greatest pleasure, and entail no other visits.

The Emperor, who kindly gave Louis leave, prolonged it till Monday, when he leaves, and for how long is quite undecided. If I could only go with him! Marie of Saxony has joined George: so has Carola [the Crown Princess of Saxony] her husband; but our division, which is near Chaumont, is in too bad and close quarters to admit of my living there.

Should Louis have to remain very long, I still hope to rejoin him—I don't care about the little discomfort.

The new governess, Frl. Kitz, comes on Thursday. She is not young, but pleasing-looking—said to be very amiable, and a good governess; has been for eighteen years in England, first with Lady Palk, and then for ten years with Herr Kleinwart—a rich German banker in London—where she brought up the two daughters.

Darmstadt: April 13.

... Ernie's kilt was sent him by Mr. Mitchell.[2] He admired Ernie so much at Berlin, that he said he would send him a Scotch dress, and I could not refuse. It is rather small as it is, and I hope that you will still give him one, as from his Grandmama it would be doubly valuable.

Louis has arrived safely at his destination—Donjeux; and we both feel the separation very much after having had the happiness of being together again.

The Paris battles are too dreadful, and the end seems some way off yet.

May 27.

My thoughts cannot leave unfortunate Paris! What horrors, and enacted so close by in the centre of the civilised world! It seems incredible; and what a lesson for those who wish to learn by it!

Darmstadt: June 8.

Louise and Lorne are just gone, and it rains and blows, and is dreadful. Their visit was so pleasant, so *gemüthlich*, and I think Louise looks well and happy. She had much to tell of their journey, which seems to have been very interesting. I could show them almost nothing, as the weather was so bad. We three went yesterday evening to my parents-in-law, who were most kind to them, as they always are to all my relations.

---

[2] The late Mr. John Mitchell, the librarian of Old Bond Street.

Their short stay was a great *great* pleasure to me, so cut off from home as I have been since three long years.

Louis will be here in a few days, and we go together to Berlin for four days; Louis insists on my accompanying him. On the 24th the entry of the troops will be here.

Seeheim : June 14.

... I am so glad that the poor Emperor and Empress are so kindly treated. They deserve to be well used by England, for the Emperor did so much to bring France and England together. How shamefully the French treat them, and speak of them, is not to be told; for the French consider themselves blameless, and always betrayed by others, whom they had made almost their gods of as long as all went well.

Dear Frittie is getting better—principally his looks, but the illness is not overcome yet. I have been so anxious about him. The country here is more beautiful than ever, and country air and flowers are a great enjoyment. Every little walk is up and down hill, little brooks, rocks, small green valleys, fine woods, &c. I have not lived here since 1865, when Ella was a baby. The children are beside themselves with pleasure at the pretty country and the scrambling walks, but above all at the wild flowers, in which they are getting quite learned. I find them in a book for them, and even Ernie knows some names, and never calls them wrong. All my children are great lovers of nature, and I develop this as much as I can. It makes life so rich, and they can never feel dull anywhere, if they know to seek and find around them the thousand beauties and wonders of nature. They are very happy and contented, and always see, the less people have the less they want, and the greater is the enjoyment of that which they have. I bring my children up as simply and with as few wants as I can, and, above all, teach them to help themselves and others, so as to become independent.

Darmstadt: June 20.

Thousand thanks for your dear letter received before our departure from Potsdam! Our journey was dreadful. We left in the evening, and were to have been here at 11 A.M., and through the irregularity of the trains we only got here at four in the afternoon. I am quite done up. The fatigues at Berlin were incessant. Anything more grand, more imposing or touching and *erhebend* [elevating] than the entry of the troops in Berlin I never saw. It was a wonderful sight to drive for three-quarters of an hour through rows of French cannon! The decorations were so artistic, so handsome, and the enthusiasm of the dense crowds quite enormous. I am glad to have been there: it will be a thing to recollect. The old Emperor, surrounded by the many princes and by his great generals, looked so noble riding at the head of his glorious troops. Deputations of all the German troops were there.

It was very hot, and we had to drive every day to Berlin, and back in the evening.

Alas! it is rainy here, and the town is so beautifully decorated: three large triumphal arches, and the houses covered with garlands and flags.

I found the dear children well, though rather pale from the heat.

Louis left again this morning, but after to-morrow remains here for good, which will indeed be a pleasure after such endless separations.

Darmstadt: June 27.

. . . To-day Aunt Marie[3] of Russia and her children were here. Aunt Marie looks thinner than ever, but well; and Marie dear and nice, with such a kind fresh face, so simple and girlish. She gives her brothers music lessons during the journey, which she is very proud of. She is very fond of children, and of a quiet country life—that is the ideal she looks for. The Emperor of Russia comes here on the 5th, to join Aunt Marie at Petersthal. Louis' work is incessant—the selling off of horses, the changing garrisons of the regiments, the new formation of our division, causes almost more work than the *Mobilmachung* [mobilisation]. The entry was very beautiful: the decorations of the town most tasteful; not a house or the smallest street which was not covered with garlands, flags, and emblems. There were large groups of the captured guns, and the names of the battles on shields around. Unfortunately, it poured nearly all the time, and we were quite drenched. I had the five children in my carriage, and Irène gave wreaths to her godfathers of the cavalry brigade. Two days ago we gave a large military dinner, and have several soirées of that sort to give before we can go into the country, which I am longing for. We shall probably go to Seeheim, as the summer seems too damp for Kranichstein.

The middle of August we shall go to Blankenberghe, near Ostend, as the doctors wish sea-bathing for Louis, and sea air for me and for some of the children, which is very necessary to set us up before going to Scotland. We want to remain one or two days and one night in London. We require a few things, which make a stay necessary. If we

---

[3] Empress of Russia, mother of the Duchess of Edinburgh, and aunt of Prince Louis of Hesse.

might be at Balmoral on the 10th, as Louis's birthday is on the 12th, would that suit you?

Please let me know in time if you think our plans good. This will enable us to settle when to go to Blankenberghe, as we can't be there longer than three weeks.

How I look forward to seeing you again, and to come home once more! It is so kind of you to let us bring the children. The arrangement of the rooms will do perfectly, and we don't care how we are put up, and above all things don't wish to be in the way.

The weather is horrid—rain and wind incessantly—after having been tremendously hot. These sudden changes upset everyone, and Frittie has had a very slight return of his illness.

August 13.

We leave at eight to-morrow morning, reach Cologne at one o'clock, and wait there till ten in the evening, when we continue our journey and reach Blankenberghe at eight next morning. Will you kindly send a gentleman to Gravesend, who can remain with us in London, as we are quite alone?

Uncle George, Aunt Cambridge, and Mary dined with us at Frankfort two days ago. Mary I had not seen for three years; she was looking very handsome.

Blankenberghe: August 17.

Only two words to say that we arrived safe and well here yesterday after a very hot journey. The hotel is on the beach, where we sit all day; there are no walks or anything save the beach, and no trees. Our rooms are very small and not very clean; but the heavenly sea air and the wind refresh one, and the sands are very long. One can ride on donkeys which enchants young and old children.

Everyone bathes together, and one has to take a little run before the waves cover one. We bathed with the three girls this morning, but I felt quite shy, for all the people sit round and look on, and there are great numbers of people here. Our children play about with others and dig in the sand. Frittie sleeps so well since he has been here; his colour is beginning to return.

We have one small sitting-room, which is our dining-room, and Louis's dressing-room.

I was so sad and upset at taking leave of my dear Marie [1] Grancy the other day; a kind true friend and companion has she been to me these nine years, and during the war she was quite invaluable to me. I hope she will be as happy as she deserves to be.

Buckingham Palace: September 10.

The pleasure of seeing your dear handwriting again has been so great! Thank God that you are going on well. I do feel *so much* for you, and for all you have had to suffer in every way! I trust entire quiet and rest of mind and body, and any little attention that I may be able to offer for your comfort, will make the autumn of real benefit for your health. How I do look forward to seeing you again, I can't say. . . .

We propose leaving the evening of the 13th. Bertie and Uncle George have arranged for our going to Aldershot on Monday and Tuesday, which interests Louis above all things, and I fancied this arrangement would suit you best.

The journey has quite cured Frittie, without any medicine, and the heat is over.

. . . I took Victoria and Ella to the Exhibition, and what enchanted Ella most was a policeman, who was, as she said, 'so very kind' in keeping the crowd off. It

---

[1] Lady in Waiting to the Princess, married to General v. Hesse.

reminded me of 'Susy Pusy,' which dear Papa used to tease me with as a child.

We dined and lunched with Bertie, who had only just arrived, and is gone again. Dear Arthur of course I have not seen.

Bram's Hill Park Camp, Cavalry Brigade, 2nd Division:
September 12.

In Bertie's tent I write these few lines to thank you in Louis's name and my own a thousand times for your dear kind letter. Every loving word is so precious to us, and the presents you so kindly gave Louis enchanted him. The pin, unfortunately, did not arrive.

How I regret each time I hear you speak of your illness! I have been so anxious about you. Uncle Louis and my parents-in-law, in their telegram of to-day, inquire after you.

We have had two such interesting days; the country too lovely, each day in a quite different part. We accompanied Uncle George, and in this way have seen the two Divisions, and through sleeping here will be enabled to see the third Division to-morrow before returning to town.

I saw dear Arthur yesterday. He rode with me all the time, and to-day we met him marching with his company. How I have enjoyed seeing your splendid troops again, I can't tell you; but I shall reserve all news till we meet.

Louis thanks you again and again for your kindness, and only regrets not having seen you himself, but is very grateful that we were allowed to stay a few days at Buckingham Palace, through which we were enabled to come here, which to him as a soldier is of the very greatest interest. Bertie is full of his work, and I think it interests him immensely. He has charming officers about him, to help and show him what to do. To our great disappointment we did not see the 42nd Highlanders, the 'Black Watch,' to-day; but yesterday we saw the Argyleshire 91st Highlanders, who gave Louise the present. Bertie lent me a charming little horse, but the ground is dreadful, and not having ridden for so long, and being on horseback so many hours, makes me feel quite stiff.

Dunrobin Castle, Sutherland: October 19.

I wish your telegram had brought me better new of you. I really can't bear to think of you suffering, and so much alone. I feel it quite wrong to have left you, and my thoughts and wishes are continually with you, and distract my attention from all I see here. I can't tell you how much I feel for you at being so helpless. It is such a trial to anyone so active as yourself; but your trial must be drawing to a close, and you will be rewarded in the end, I am sure, by feeling perhaps even better and stronger than you did before all your troubles.

I was nearly sick in the train, which is the slowest I was ever in in my life, and was unable to go to dinner; but a long walk by the sea this morning has quite set me up in spite of the extraordinary warmth.

Sandringham: November 9.

It is the first time since eleven years that I have spent Bertie's birthday with him, and though we are only three of our own family together, still that is better than nothing, and makes it seem more like birthday. Bertie and Alix are so kind, and give us so warm a welcome, showing how they like having us, that it feels quite home. Indeed I pray earnestly that God's blessing may rest on him, and that he may be guided to do what is wise and right, so that he may tide safely through the anxious times that are before him, and in which we now live. They are both charming hosts, and all the party suit well together. The Westminsters and Brownlows are here; Lady B. is so very handsome.

We joined the shooting party for luncheon, and the last beats out to-day and yesterday; and the weather is beautiful, though cold—a very bracing air, like Scotland.

1872

Darmstadt: January 21.

. . . Louis returns to-morrow from Berlin. He was the first to be invested by the Emperor, and has met with great kindness. He was very glad to have been there with dear Arthur, who seems to please everyone.

February 5.

. . . It is a great pleasure to have dear Arthur here. He is so amiable, civil, and nice, and takes interest in all he sees, and is so pleasant to have in the house. His visit will be very short, as he gives up two days to go to Baden.

We gave small suppers on two evenings for Arthur, and yesterday evening a celebrated most excellent violinist played quite as well as Joachim: a friend of his, and a pupil of Spohr's. This afternoon he is going to play some of Bach's celebrated sonatas with and to me. Arthur enjoys music very much, and keeps up his playing.

There is a dance at Uncle Alexander's to-night, on Wednesday a Court ball, and on Friday one at my parents-in-law. I can't stand the heat at all of an evening, and the rooms are very hot. Louis, who has an awful cold, took Arthur to see the barracks, as all military things give him pleasure.

It is heavenly sunny weather, having been quite dark and foggy all day yesterday.

June 17.

Many thanks for your dear letter and kind wishes for the birth of our Baby[5]—a nice little thing, like Ella, only smaller and with finer features, though the nose promises to be long. . . .

Kind Dr. Hofmeister was most attentive; and of course having him was far pleasanter than not, and we owe you great thanks for having sent him. Mrs. Clarke has been all one could wish.

Louis wrote as soon as he could, but this last week he has only been home just before his dinner, and was so tired that he invariably fell asleep. He has gone out at six, returning at twelve, and has had to be out before four in the afternoon, returning at eight. He is away again to-day. Until the 15th of September his duty will be important, and he has all the office work besides. It is double this year to what it usually is, as all people and things are new since the war.

How sad the loss of those two poor children is,[6] and the sweet little 'bairnie' of three! The unfortunate mother to lose two in so dreadful a way! I am sure it touched Beatrice much to see the poor little one; and in a child death so often loses everything that is painful.

We think of calling our little girl 'Alix' (Alice they pronounce too dreadfully in German) 'Helena Louise Beatrice,' and, if Beatrice may, we would much like to have her as godmother.

---

[5] Princess Alix, born on the 6th of June.

[6] Two children who were carried away by a 'spate' while playing in Monaltrie Burn, near Balmoral (11th of June, 1872), and swept into the river Dee and drowned. See *More Leaves from a Journal of a Life in the Highlands*, p. 156 et seq.

Darmstadt: June 24.

... We both felt so truly for you when we heard of dear Dr. Macleod's death, knowing what a kind and valued friend of yours he was, and how fate seems to take one friend after another, and before age can claim its right. He indeed deserves his rest, for he did so much good in his life!

I feel rather weaker than usual this time, and sitting and walking, though only a few steps, tries me a good deal. I was out for half an hour yesterday, and I think the air will do me good.

Louis left at half-past five this morning, and will be back by seven, I hope, this evening; to-morrow the same.

I will add Vicky's name to Baby's others, as you propose; and 'Alix' we gave for 'Alice,' as they murder my name here: 'Aliicé' they pronounce it, so we thought 'Alix' could not so easily be spoilt.

Uncle Alexander is coming back shortly, and says the Empress is not to return to Russia this winter, and will be sent to Italy for the whole winter.

The heat has been quite dreadful; there is a little air to-day, though.

August 14.

... Baby is like Ella, only smaller features, and still darker eyes with very black lashes, and reddish-brown hair. She is a sweet, merry little person, always laughing, with a deep dimple in one cheek just like Ernie.

We are going to Frankfort to-day to give Uncle George [7] and Fritz Strelitz [8] a luncheon in our Palais there. Hélène Reuter comes to us for a month to-morrow as lady.

---

[7] Duke of Cambridge. [8] Grand Duke of Mecklenburg Strelitz.

I hope your Edinburgh visit will go off well. You have never lived in Holyrood since 1861, have you?

How I shall think of you at dear Balmoral, and this time capable of enjoying it—not like last time, when you had to suffer so much, and were unable to do anything. It quite spoiled our visit to see you an invalid. Remember me to all old friends there—to Brown's kind old mother, and any who ask after us.

I shall think of you on dear Grandmama's birthday. She is never forgotten by any of us, and lives on as a dearly-cherished memory of all that was good and loving, and so kind. My children have her picture in their room, and I often tell them of her.

Kranichstein: August 20.

I am very grateful for your telegrams from Edinburgh, and for Flora [9] [MacDonald's] letter. It interests me so much to know what you did there, and I am very glad all went off so well. The people will have been too delighted to have had you in their midst again, and I am sure you enjoyed the beauty of your fine northern capital anew after not having seen it for so long a time. Beatrice seems delighted with what she saw. I recollect those many interesting and beautiful spots so well.[1]

The 18th was the anniversary of the dreadful battle of Gravelotte, which cost so many lives, to our division especially. We drove into town to the military church, which was full of officers and men, at half-past seven in the morning, and thought much of the friends and acquaintances in their distant graves, and of the desolate homes, until that day so bright. My heart felt too full when we were singing

---

[9] Maid of Honour to the Queen, now Bedchamber Woman.

[1] For an account of this visit, see *More Leaves from a Journal*, pp. 164 *et seq.*

Ein' feste Burg, and I had my husband at my side, whom the Almighty had graciously spared to my children and myself. Gratitude seems barely enough to express the intense depth of what I feel when I think of that time, and how again and again I long to give all and all to my good dear Louis and to our children, for he is all that is good and true and pure.

. . . The children were much distressed at the sad fate of my poor little bullfinch, who piped beautifully. Louis had caught an owl and put it in a wooden sort of cage in the room where my bird was. In the night it broke the bars and got loose and tore the bullfinch's tail out, and the poor little thing died in consequence.

Of our quiet country life there is little to tell. We are a good deal out always with our little people, their pets—dogs, cats, ponies, donkeys; it is rather like a menagerie.

Schloss Kranichstein : September 17.

On the 9th there is a large meeting here of the different associations existing throughout Germany for the bettering of women's education and social position (of the middle class especially with regard to trade). Some English ladies are coming, some Swiss and Dutch. It will last four days, and be very fatiguing. The programme I arranged with my two committees here and the gentlemen at Berlin, and they wanted to force me to preside; but for so large an assemblage—to me nearly all strangers—I positively refused. I do that in my own Associations, but not where there are so many strangers, who all want to talk, and all to cross purposes. It is difficult enough to keep one's own people in order when they disagree. I hope and trust I have prevented *all* exaggerated and unfeminine views being brought up, which to me are dreadful. These Associations, if not reasonably led, tend too easily to the ridiculous. My Associations take a great deal of my time and thought, and require a good amount of study. I hope and trust that what we are doing here is the right thing. We have already had some satisfactory results in the class of the workwomen, and in the reform of the schools; but there are many open questions yet, which I hope this meeting, with others who work in the same field, may help us to solve.

Will you look through the programme? It would please me so much if I thought you took a little interest in my endeavours here in a very small way to follow in a slight degree part of dear Papa's great works for the good of others.

Kranichstein: September 25.

. . . . *All* sympathise with you, and feel what a loss to you darling Aunt[2] must be—how great the gap in your life, how painful the absence of that sympathy and love which united her life and yours so closely.

Darling, kind Mama, I feel so acutely for you, that my thoughts are incessantly with you, and my prayers for comfort and support to be granted you in the heavy trial are warm indeed. You have borne so many hard losses with courage and resignation, that for darling Aunt's sake you will do so again, and knowing her at rest and peace will in time reconcile you to the loss—all the more as her passing from this world to another was so touchingly peaceful. Dear Augusta [Stanley] wrote to me, which was a great consolation, and we intend going to Baden to pay our last token of respect and love.

---

[2] The Queen's half-sister, Feodore, Princess of Hohenlohe-Langenburg, who died on the 23rd of September, 1872, at Baden-Baden.

Darmstadt: October 13.

... A few words about our doings here may be of interest to you. The meeting went off well, was very large, the subjects discussed to the purpose and important, and not one word of the emancipated political side of the question was touched upon by anyone. Schools (those of the lower, middle, and higher classes) for girls were the principal theme; the employment of women for post and telegraph offices, &c.; the improvement necessary in the education of nursery-maids, and the knowledge of mothers in the treatment of little children; the question of nurses and nursing institutes.

The committees of the fifteen Associations met Wednesday afternoon, and in the evening thirteen of the members came to us to supper.

The public meeting on the following day lasted from nine to two with a small interruption; a committee meeting in the afternoon; and that evening all the members and guests came to us—nearly fifty in number. The following day the meetings lasted even longer, and the English ladies were kind enough to speak—only think, old Miss Carpenter, on all relating to women's work in England (she is our guest here). Her account of the Queen's Institute at Dublin was most interesting. Miss Hill (also our guest), about the boarding-out system for orphans. Miss C. Winkworth, about higher education in England. She mentioned also the new institution to which Louise now belongs, and is a member of it herself. The ladies all spoke very well; the German ones remarkably so.

There was a good deal of work to finish afterwards, and a good many members to see. They came from all parts of Germany—many kind-hearted, noble, self-denying women. The presence of the English ladies—above all, of one such as Miss Carpenter, who has done such good works for the reformation of convicts—greatly enhanced the importance of the meeting, and her great experience has been of value to us all. She means still to give a lecture on India and the state of the native schools there, before leaving us.

I have still so much work in hand, that I fear my letter is hurried and ill-written, but I hope you will kindly excuse this.

To-morrow I am taking Miss Carpenter to all our different schools, that she may see how the different systems in use work. Some are good, but none particularly so; there is much to improve.

Louis is gone to Mayence to-day for the inauguration of the Memorial which the town has erected to the memory of dear excellent Woldemar Holstein, for so many years its beloved Governor.

Darmstadt: October 24.

You must indeed miss dear Aunt much, and feel your thoughts drawn to her, whose precious intercourse was such a solace and comfort to you. It is nice for you to have Louise a little to yourself. . . .

You ask, if my mother-in-law talks with me about the different woman's work in which I am interested. Of course she does. We are so intimate together, that even where we differ in opinion we yet talk of everything freely, and her opinion is of the greatest value to me. She has ever been a most kind, true, and loving mother, whom I respect and love more and more. She was much pleased and interested in the success of the meeting, but is of course as averse as myself to all extreme views on such subjects.

I have joined to my Nursing Institute an Association for watching over the orphans who are boarded out by the State into families, where some poor children are unhappy and ill-used. The use of such meetings as this one was consists mainly in the interchange of experience made in the different branches in other places, which it is impossible to carry on by correspondence.

The schools are entirely different throughout Germany—good and indifferent; and those here do not count among the best, as everything, through the long misrule of the late Government, is not what it ought to be.

Darmstadt: November 3.

Ella is writing to you herself to thank you for the lovely bracelet, which gave me as much pleasure as it did her. To think that she is already eight! She is handsomer than she was, and a dear child. . . . They all give me pleasure, dear children, though of course they have as many faults as others; but they are truthful and contented, and very affectionate. Having them much with me, watching and guiding their education—which, through our quiet and regular life, is possible—I am able to know and understand their different characters, for not one is like the other.

Darmstadt: November 12.

. . . We have the same weather here which you seem to have, which for our long journey was not pleasant. We took nearly twelve hours going, and as much returning from Metz. For the inauguration itself the weather held up. The roads were dreadful, and the wide plateau looked dreary and sad—dotted all over with graves, like an enormous churchyard.

The Memorial is a dead lion in bronze, on a plain pedestal, bearing an inscription on black marble in front, and at the back all the names. Deputations of officers and men were present, besides the generals, &c., from Metz. The clergyman of the division read the prayers, preached a short and touching sermon, and the band played a chorale. Louis spoke a few words, ending with the usual 'Hoch' for the Emperor and Grand Duke. I then laid some wreaths at the foot of the Memorial from Louis's parents and ourselves, and we drove back to Metz across the different battlefields. The villages are all built up again, and re-inhabited, so that few traces of the dreadful struggle remain.

Darmstadt: December 12.

For the 14th I write a few words. From year to year they can but express the same: the grief at the loss of such a father, such a man, grows with me, and leaves a gap and a want that nothing on earth can ever fill up.

The deep, intense sympathy for what you, my poor dear Mama, went through then and since, in consequence of your bereavement, remains as vivid as ever. God heard our prayers, and sustained you, and through the healing hand of time softened your grief, and retained you for us, who were too young and too numerous to stand alone!

That our good sweet Alix should have been spared this terrible grief, when this time last year it seemed so imminent, fills my heart with gratitude for her dear sake, as for yours, his children, and ours. That time is as indelibly fixed on my memory as that of 1861, when the witnessing of your grief rent my heart so deeply. The 14th will now be a day of mixed recollections and feelings to us—a day *hallowed* in our family, when one great spirit ended his work on earth—though his work can never die, and generations will grow up and call his name blessed—and when another was left to fulfil his duty and mission, God grant, for the welfare of his own family and of thousands!

I have not time to write to dearest Bertie and Alix to-day; and as I love to think of them with you on the 14th, so I would ask you to let them share these lines full of sympathy for them, letting a remembrance of *me*, who suffered with them, mingle with your united prayers and thanks on this solemn day!

My little Fritz is at length better, but white and thin, in consequence of his illness.

Christmas Day.

Your dear presents gave me so much pleasure; I thank you again and again for them. The precious souvenir of dear Aunt, and my Ernie's picture delight me. I assure you, nothing has given me more pleasure this Christmas.

Let me also thank you, in Louis' and the children's names (meanwhile, until they do so themselves), for your kind gifts to them. It makes us all so happy and grateful, to be always so kindly remembered.

The boys were well enough to enjoy Christmas, though rather pale and pulled—above all, sweet Ernie.

We gave all our servants presents—the whole household and stable—under the Christmas-tree, which we made for the children; and when the tree is divided, the children of all our servants come and share it with ours. It keeps the household as a family, which is so important. We have fifty people to give to!

Dear Beatrice's wishes (cards) pleased the children very much, but Frittie lamented for a letter from Auntie ' for Frittie.' He talks quite well now.

On Saturday we shall go for the day to Vicky. I don't like leaving the boys for longer yet. I am so glad Vicky gave such a flattering account of Baby. She is quite the personification of her nickname ' Sunny '—much like Ella, but a smaller head, and livelier, with Ernie's dimple and expression.

1873

Darmstadt: January 12.

... We were both much shocked to hear of the death of the Emperor Napoleon, and I must say grieved; personally he was so amiable, and she is much to be pitied. That he should die an exile in England, as Louis Philippe did, is most striking. In England the sympathy shown must touch the poor Empress, and, as I telegraphed, we should be so grateful to you, if you would kindly be the medium through which both of us would like to express to her how much we feel for her. How proud you must ever be, in feeling that your country is the one always able to offer a home and hospitality for those driven away from their own countries! England is before all others in that; and its warm sympathy for those who are in misfortune is such a generous feeling.

February 1.

If anyone will feel with us, I know you will do so most. Since three days, with an interruption of one day, poor Frittie has been bleeding incessantly from a slight cut on his ear, which was nearly healed. Since yesterday evening we cannot stop it. All the usual remedies were used, but as yet unavailing. Just now the place has been touched again with caustic, and tightly bound, after we had with great trouble got rid of the quantity of dried blood from his hair, ear, neck, &c. He is horrified at the sight of so much blood, but shows great strength as yet in spite of so great a loss. He is of course very irritable, and, as he must not scream, one has to do whatever he wishes, which will spoil him dreadfully. I own I was much upset when I saw that he had this tendency to bleed, and the anxiety for the future, even if he gets well over this, will remain for years to come. All have their trials, one or another, and, please God, we shall bear whatever is sent without complaining. To see one's own child suffer is for a mother a great trial. With what pleasure one would change places with the little one, and bear its pain!

February 6.

. . . In the summer Fritz had a violent attack of dysentery, which was so prevalent at Darmstadt, and off and on for two months it continued, until Scotland stopped it; and this illness made him sensitive and delicate.

. . . What has caused him such great suffering has been that, what with the use of caustic, the tight bandaging and the iron, a quantity of small gatherings formed on his cheek and neck, causing such an amount of pain that he could not remain in bed or anywhere quiet for the two first days and nights. Now they are drying off, the itching is such that he don't know what to do with himself, and we have the greatest difficulty in keeping him from rubbing or scratching himself. The want of sleep through pain, &c., has excited him very much, so that he has been very difficult to manage. The bandages of course cannot be removed, and great care will be taken when they are removed, lest bleeding should recommence. He has been out twice a day as usual all along, and his skin never quite lost its pinkness and mottled appearance; all of which are signs that he has good blood and to spare, else he would look worse and have shown weakness, which after all he did not. . . .

He speaks well for his age, and is, alas! very wild, so that it will be impossible to keep him from having accidents. . . .

. . . I have been playing some lovely things (very difficult) of Chopin lately, which I know you would admire.

Darmstadt: February 19.

My best thanks for your dear letter! That I forgot to thank you at once for dear Grandmama's very beautiful print[3] came from my having the lithograph of that picture in my room always before me, and, though the print far surpasses it, I am so fond of the lithograph, that I forgot the print at the moment I was writing to you. Before that dear picture, the painting of which I recollect so well, my children often sit, and I tell them of her who was and ever will be so inexpressibly dear to us all. In the schoolroom, in my sitting-room, in the nursery, there is with the pictures of you and dear Papa always one of dear Grandmama, and, in my room and the schoolroom, the Duke of Kent also.

My sitting-room has only prints and lithographs, all Winterhalters, of the family: you and Papa, your receiving the Sacrament at the Coronation, Raphael's *Disputa* and *Belle Jardinière*, and the lovely little engraving of yourself from Winterhalter's picture in Papa's room at Windsor.[4]

Vicky is coming here on Wednesday. The Grand Duke of Weimar has kindly allowed Mr. Ruland[5] to join us as cicerone: which for galleries, &c., is very necessary, and we take no courier. Rome is our first halting-place in Italy, and for years it has been my dream and wish to be in that wonderful city, where the glorious monuments of antiquity and of the Middle Ages carry one back to those marvellous times.

I am learning Italian, and studying the history and art

---

[3] A private plate, engraved for the Queen by the late Mr. Francis Holl from a picture by Winterhalter.

[4] Also engraved by the late Mr. Francis Holl for the Queen from a picture given by Her Majesty to the Prince Consort on the 26th of August, 1843.

[5] Former German private secretary and librarian to the Prince Consort.

necessary to enable me, in the short time we have, to see and understand the finest and most important monuments. I am so entirely absorbed and interested in these studies just now, that I have not much time for other things. My father-in-law, perhaps Princess Charles too, will be with Aunt Marie of Russia at Sorrento then. William will probably join us at Rome; he is quite a connoisseur in art, and a good historian, quite at home in Rome, about which he raves. I must say that I look forward immensely to this journey; it opens a whole new life to one. . . .

Kanné has made all arrangements for us at Rome. We shall leave here about the 18th of March.

Rome, Hôtel d'Allemagne: March 27.

. . . We left the dear children well, but very sorry at parting. The two days at Munich were most interesting. The National Museum in its way surpasses any I have ever seen, and in originals is richer even than South Kensington. Aunt Mariechen was very kind and dear; the Moriers very amiable hosts, and we met some interesting people there. Two hours before we left, after eight in the evening, Ludwig and Otto[6] came to us and remained some time.

The Brenner, over which we came, was covered with snow—most beautiful scenery, like St. Moritz in the Engadine. The journey was very fatiguing. We had a morning for Bologna, and had to wait three hours at Florence for the night train—time enough to drive round and in the town, which is most lovely. What trees, mountains, colours! then the fine buildings!

The following morning at six we reached Rome. The

---

[6] The King of Bavaria and his brother, first cousins of Prince Louis Hesse.

sun was bright, the distance blue—the grand ruins dark and sharp against the sky, cypresses, stone-pines, large cork oaks, making up such a beautiful picture. Every day I admire the scenery more and more; every little bit of architecture, broken or whole, with a glimpse of the Campagna, a picturesque dirty peasant and a dark tree close by, is a picture in itself which one would like to frame and hang up in one's room. It is too, too beautiful! To tell you all we have seen and are seeing would tire you. Bertie and Arthur's descriptions, too, so lately have told you the same.

The Via Appia, the grand old road lined with ruins of splendid tombs, leading from Albano through the Campagna to Rome, along which St. Paul went, and the great kings and emperors made their triumphal entries, is a fit one to lead to such a city as Rome, which ruled the world.

The antique monuments, those of the Middle Ages, are so magnificent and interesting that as yet I don't know which to mention first or admire most!

Our incognito did not last long (though even now we maintain it), for the Crown Princess[7] heard of us and came to see us, as did the Crown Prince, and we had to go to the Quirinal, a morning visit without *entourage.*

Palm Sunday, Rome: April 6.

. . . We saw the beginning of Mass and blessing of the palms in St. Peter's this morning, with a procession and beautiful singing. Whilst the procession, with part of the choristers, go outside the church, some remain within, and they respond to each other, which produces a very striking effect. In spite of the bad style inside of

---

[7] Crown Princess of Italy, daughter of the Duke of Genoa, and granddaughter of late King of Saxony.

St. Peter's, as a whole it produces a marvellous effect through its wonderful size and richness of decoration.

I saw two convents yesterday: the Sepolte Vive, which Bertie and Alix saw, and where the nuns asked much after him, and said that he was *molto amabile*; and another equally strict one, but not austere, where the Superior told me that Aunt Feodore with Princess Hohenzollern had paid them a visit. Monsignore Howard was the only gentleman with me and the ladies, as they never see any men. Their idea is, that they spend the whole of their life in contemplation and prayer, so as to pray for those who cannot pray for themselves.

The museums of the Vatican and of the Capitol, with their enormous collection of antiques, are very fine. The celebrated Venus, Apollo Belvedere, the Torso (which Michael Angelo admired so much, and was taken to touch when he could no more see it), the wounded Gladiator, &c., are there. The Sistine Chapel, with Michael Angelo's frescoes, which are certainly the most marvellous pieces of painting and conception, is very dark, and the frescoes are suffering much from the smoke, dust, &c. Raphael's Stanze are far better preserved, and lighter than I had expected, and of such beauty!

I thought so often and so much of dear Papa when I saw the originals of all the pictures he so much admired and took such interest in. How this alone fascinates me I cannot tell you. In these galleries and churches there is only too much to be seen, besides the antique ruins, &c. You would be terrified to see how full our day is from before nine. Mr. Ruland is an excellent cicerone for pictures and sculptures. William is with us here since last Sunday.

We are going to the Villa Ludovisi this afternoon. The gardens of the Villa Doria Pamfili are most beautiful: the terraces there remind me of Osborne. I can see in many things where dear Papa got his ideas from for Osborne and for his decorations, which Professor Grüner understood so well to carry out.

Many thanks for your having told Lady Churchill to send me an account of your opening of the Park.[8] I am glad all went off so well, and that you were not the worse for it.

I have quite refused going to Naples. We shall arrange probably to go for two days to Castellamare (one hour from Naples); from thence to Sorrento and Pompeii, and return here. As yet it is not hot here at all.

Rome: April 9.

Let me thank you for your letter written on our dear Victoria's birthday. I have never been away from her on her birthday before, and though we see such fine interesting things, yet I feel very homesick for the dear children always. In three weeks or less I shall see them all again. I look forward to the time with perfect impatience, as I am so rarely separated from them, and we live so much together. Every other day Fräulein Kitz and Orchard write, so that I have news daily.

Louis's father wrote to me to-day, as his sister asks us to her house at Sorrento for one or two nights for the 12th; but as I was rather deranged from a sick headache yesterday, I shall wait a day before we decide. It is wet and quite cold to-day.

We visited San Clemente two days ago, and Father Mulooly took us through the three churches—one under the other. The antique one was full of water, and we

[8] The opening of Victoria Park, in the East End of London, on the 2nd of April.

walked about on rickety planks, each with a lighted taper, as it is quite dark there. It is most curious, and the old paintings on the walls telling the legend of St. Clement are wonderfully full of expression and feeling for the time they were done.

Rome: April 19.

... Our visit to Sorrento went off well. We got there at one on Monday morning for luncheon. The sun had given me a dreadful headache, which ended in sickness, so that I could not leave my room. Marie sat with me, and was very dear and kind. The next day, she and my Aunt, who seems tired and dispirited, had bad headaches. We went with my father-in-law and some of the ladies and gentlemen on the following afternoon in the Empress's yacht to Capri, close by, to see the blue grotto.

The Bay of Naples, particularly seen from Sorrento, is most lovely—like a beautiful dream—the colours, the outlines are so perfect.

We breakfasted together in the mornings with Aunt and Marie, and on Tuesday we took our leave.

We shall go to Florence the 23rd (the first station homewards); remain there three or four days; one night at Verona, and then home. It is a fatiguing journey, and we have so often had people in the carriage, which is very unpleasant—some very rude English, going to Sorrento; they did not know us.

Florence: April 25.

Your kind wishes I received early this morning. Thousand thanks for them, and for the presents which I shall find on getting home!

I shall be so glad to have a large photograph of yourself. Thirty years! Good-bye, youth! but I feel quite as old as I am, though the time has flown by so fast. I would it had flown as well as it has fast! I look back to the past with great gratitude to the Almighty for innumerable blessings, and pray our life may continue so blest. I have a very bad headache—neuralgia; I have it continually, and the journey is very long and tiring. Darling Ernie wanted to buy something for my birthday, and he thought a china doll with a bath would be the best. I am glad Victoria remembered to write to Beatrice as I told her; they are very fond of their Auntie.

Florence seems a beautiful town, and the situation amongst the hills, over which the suburbs spread, is most picturesque.

Darmstadt: June 9.

Tender thanks for your last letter, and for every word of sympathy! The weary days drag on, and bring much pain at times, though there are moments of comfort, and even consolation.

The horror of my Darling's sudden death [9] at times torments me too much, particularly waking of a morning; but when I think he is at rest, free from the sorrow we are suffering, and from every evil to come, I feel quite resigned. He was such a bright child. It seems so quiet next door; I miss the little feet, the coming to me, for we lived so much together, and Ernie feels so lost, poor love.

We were at the Mausoleum with all the children yesterday evening. It is a quiet spot amidst trees and flowers, with a lovely view towards the hills and plain. He loved flowers so much. I can't see one along the roadside without wishing to pick it for him.

There is a young sculptor from Stuttgart, who was accidentally here, and, meeting the children, had asked

---

[9] The allusion is to the death of the little Prince Frederick, who was killed on the 29th of the previous month by a fall from a window.

permission to make medallions of them. The *last* afternoon sweet Frittie had sat to him, and he is now making a lovely bust of him, which is getting very like.

On Wednesday my mother-in-law, with her three sons, goes to Berlin; on Thursday Uncle Adalbert[1] will be buried in the Dom.

We shan't be able to go to Seeheim until Saturday.

How *too kind* of you to have asked us to Osborne! How a rest and home air would have revived me—and the pleasure of seeing you again; but Louis cannot leave until after his birthday. If he did get leave, it would so throw him out before he has to command; and, having been absent this spring, he feels it an impossibility, and this I am sure you will understand. I could not leave him or the children. Our circle has grown smaller, and drawn us all the more together with a dread of parting from each other. We thank you a thousand times for the kind offer.

Seeheim : June 22.

. . . I do earnestly hope that too long a time may not elapse before we meet.

It is very hot, and I feel very low and unhappy.

To-morrow this house will be full, and all the Russians, &c., close by. Had there only been any other quiet country place to be at, how gladly would I have escaped this!

. . . It is only three weeks to-day since we took our darling to his last resting-place! I wish I could go there to-day, but it is too hot and too far.

Fritz and Louise of Baden came two days ago to Darmstadt, to see my parents-in-law and us.

Dr. Macleod's letter is very kind.

I enclose two photographs of dear Frittie out of groups,

---

[1] Princess Charles's brother, Prince Adalbert of Prussia.

the negative of one of which unluckily does not exist any more. The little blouse is the one he had on on that terrible day. My darling sweet child—to have lost him so! To my grave shall I carry this sorrow with me.

In the book you sent me there is a fine poem by Miss Procter, ' Our grief, our friend,' called *Friend sorrow*, which expresses so much what I myself feel about a deep grief.

Seeheim : June 27.

. . . It was just four weeks yesterday since our darling died, and we went to the Mausoleum. I felt the whole weight of my sorrow, and the terrible shock doubly again. But the precious child does not—that is a comfort. He is happy and at rest, whilst we grieve and mourn. Ernie always prays for Frittie, and talks to me of him when we walk together.

Aunt Marie arrived at two on Monday, and a few hours later came to see me, and was so sympathising, motherly, and loving; it touched me much. At such moments she is peculiarly soft and womanly, and she loves her own children so tenderly. She cried much, and told me of the sad death of her eldest girl, who was seven, and of the terrible, irreparable loss her eldest son was to her. She has such a religious, truly resigned way of looking at great sorrows such as these. In the room I am now living in Aunt Marie had seen Frittie in his bath two years ago, and she remembered all about him. She is coming to ' Sunshine's ' toilet this evening; it always amuses her, and she is very fond of the children.

Seeheim : July 9.

. . . There are days which seem harder than others, and when I feel very heartsick, prayer and quiet and solitude do me good.

I hear Affie[2] comes on Thursday night. This evening the Emperor arrives. Poor Marie[3] is very happy, and so quiet. . . . How I feel for the parents, this only daughter (a character of *Hingebung* [perfect devotion] to those she loves), the last child entirely at home, as the parents are so much away that the two youngest, on account of their studies, no more travel about.

Seeheim : July 26.

. . . I am glad that you have a little coloured picture of my darling. I feel lower and sadder than ever, and miss him so much, so continually. There is such a gap between Ernie and Sunny, and the two boys were such a pretty pair, and were become such companions. Having so many girls, I was so proud of our two boys! The pleasure did not last long, but he is *mine* more than ever now. He seems near me always, and I carry his precious image in my heart everywhere. That can never fade or die!

Seeheim : August 2.

Many thanks for your dear letter! I am feeling so low and weak to-day that kind words are doubly soothing. You feel so with me, when you understand how long and deep my grief must be. And does one not grow to love one's grief, as having become part of the being one loved— as if through *this* one could still pay a tribute of love to them, to make up for the terrible loss, and missing of not being able to do anything for the beloved one any more?[4]

---

[2] Duke of Edinburgh.

[3] The Grand Duchess Marie, who was engaged on the 11th of July to the Duke of Edinburgh.

[4] How these words recall those of Constance (*King John*, act iii. scene 4) :—

> Grief fills the room up of my absent child,
> Lies in his bed, walks up and down with me,

I am so much with my children, and am so accustomed to care for them and their wants daily, that I miss not having Frittie, the object of our greatest care, far more than words can describe; and in the quiet of our everyday life, where we have only the children around us, it is doubly and trebly felt, and is a sorrow that has entered into the very heart of our existence.

May the hour of trial and grief bring its blessing with it, and not have come in vain! The day passes so quickly, when one can do good and make others happy, and one leaves always so much undone. I feel more than ever, one should put nothing off; and children grow up so quickly and leave one, and I would long that mine should take nothing but the recollection of love and happiness from their home with them into the world's fight, knowing that they have there *always* a safe harbour, and open arms to comfort and encourage them when they are in trouble. I do hope that this may become the case, though the lesson for parents is so difficult, being continually *giving*, without always finding the return.

Dear Fanny Baillie[5] has been a few days here, and goes to England to-day. I shall miss her so much. I am so very fond of her. I hope you will see her; she will bring you many messages from us.

Seeheim: August 16.

... Louis joins with me in saying that we shall gratefully accept your wish that we should come to Windsor, and he trusts there will be no difficulties for leave then. ...

> Puts on his pretty looks, repeats his words,
> Remembers me of all his gracious parts,
> Stuffs out his vacant garments with his form;
> Then have I reason to be fond of grief.

[5] Lady Frances Baillie, sister of Lady Augusta Stanley and late Earl of Elgin.

Seeheim: September 7.

. . . You ask if I can play yet? I feel as if I could not, and I have not yet done so. In my own house it seems to me, as if I never could play again on that piano, where little hands were nearly always thrust when I wanted to play. Away from home—in England—much sooner. I had played so often lately that splendid, touching funeral march of Chopin's, and I remember it is the last thing I played, and then the boys were running in the room.

Mary Teck came to see me and remained two nights, so warm-hearted and sympathising. I like to talk of him to those who love children, and can understand how great the gap, how intense the pain, the ending of a little bright existence causes.

Heiden, Appenzell: October 7.

How kind of you to remember our darling's birthday; we both thank you for this. Sad and many are our thoughts. I think of my loneliness and anxiety when he was born, with Louis far away in the midst of danger—a sad and awful time to come into the world; but sweet Frittie was my comfort and occupation, a second son, a pleasure to us both! Now all this is wiped out, and our parents' hearts are sore, and asking for the dear bright face we miss so much from amongst our circle of children! He ended his fight very soon. May we all follow in a way as peaceful, with as little struggle and pain, and leave an image of as much love and brightness behind, to be a blessed remembrance for the rest of our lives!

I can't write on any other subject to-day, therefore close these short lines with much love from your devoted child,

ALICE.

Beloved Mama,   Buckingham Palace: December 20.

How much I thank you for your dear precious letter, and for all the true love and considerate sympathy you showed me during our visit! It has soothed and comforted me, I assure you, and will be a pleasure and satisfaction for me to look back to the many pleasant talks we had together.

Louis, who has always been so devoted to you, was touched to tears, as I was, by your expressions of love to us and to our children.

Thank you also for all advice, which is so precious to me, and in following it I shall like to think that I am doing something that you told me.

How much I felt in parting from you I cannot say. Neither did I like to speak of it, for it was too much, and the harder things in life are better borne in silence, as none can bear them for one, and they must be fought out by oneself.

Ernie and Irène send endless loves to you, to Uncle and Auntie. Sunny's hand is better.

Tilla came to see me yesterday, and we both drove with her to the Memorial.[6]

. . . There is so much I would run on about, now the dear habit of intercourse together has once more become so natural to me. Writing is at best a poor *remplaçant*.

Once more from both of us warm and tender thanks for so much love and kindness! Love to Leopold and Beatrice; kind remembrances to all who surround you!

From your grateful and devoted child,

ALICE.

---

[6] To the Prince Consort in Hyde Park.

Buckingham Palace: December 21.

. . . It is fine and warm and still. I hope it will be so early to-morrow when we cross over. I shall telegraph how the passage has been.

Please thank Brown for his kind wishes. I am so sorry that I missed saying good-bye to several. To say the truth, I dreaded it. It is always so painful. The old Baron's[7] way of disappearing was almost the best.

1874

Darmstadt: January 12.

. . . *How* low and miserable I am at times in these rooms, particularly when I go to bed, I cannot tell you! The impression of *all* is so vivid and heartrending. I could cry out for pain sometimes.

Till the first year is round this will often return, I know, and must be borne as part of the sorrow!

January 16.

. . . I know well what your grief and your bereavement were compared to mine; but they are such different sorrows, I don't think one can well compare them. Your life was broken—upset: altered from the very roots, through the one you lost; my life is unchanged, save in the mother's heart the blank, the pain which thousands of little things awaken—which by the world, even by the family, are scarcely felt; and this ofttimes loneliness of

---

[7] Baron Stockmar had such a dislike of leave-takings that he never let it be known when he was going away from the English Court. The first intimation of his intention was—that he was already gone.

sentiment clouds one's life over with a quiet sorrow which is felt in *everything*. . . .

Darmstadt: January 23.

On our dear Affie's [Prince Alfred's] wedding-day, a few tender words. It must seem so strange to you not to be near him. My thoughts are constantly with them all, and we have only the *Times'* account, for no one writes here—they are all too busy, and of course all news comes to you. What has Augusta [Lady Augusta Stanley] written, and Vicky and Bertie? Any extracts or other newspaper accounts but what we see would be most welcome.

We give a dinner to-night to the family and *entourage*, and Russian and English legations. . . .

Louis sends you his love and warmest wishes for yourself and the happiness of the dear pair, in which I most earnestly join. God bless and protect them, and may all turn out well!

Darmstadt: January 28.

. . . Dear Marie [the Duchess of Edinburgh] seems to make the same impression on *all*. How glad I am she is so quite what I thought and hoped. Such a wife must make Affie happy, and do him good, and be a great pleasure to yourself, which I always like to think. I shall read to my mother-in-law the letters, and show them to Bäuerlein. Both will be very grateful for being allowed to see them.

We are going from Saturday to Monday to Carlsruhe. The eldest girls and Bäuerlein, who is going to take charge of them for a week, are going with us.

. . . One day we have six degrees of heat, the next two or four of cold; it is very unwholesome.

Carlsruhe: February 2.

I have a little time before breakfast to thank you so very much for the enclosures, also the Dean's [Stanley] letter through dear Beatrice. We are most grateful for being allowed to hear these most interesting reports. It brings everything so much nearer. How pleasant it is to receive only satisfactory reports! I fear Aunt Marie is far from well. I should be very anxious, for she is like a fading flower.

All the family, Hohenlohes and Holsteins, send their duty. All their respective children and ours were together yesterday afternoon. I hope not to seem vain, if it strikes me that amongst all the children my girls usually carry away the palm. Victoria is in such good looks at present; they are both natural and real children, and as such I hope to be able to retain them long.

Sophie Weiss [8] came to see me yesterday. I was very glad to be able to give her so good an account of you, and how young you looked when I had that great happiness of those few short days at Windsor, which did me good in *every* respect. Old Frau von Bunsen, now eighty-three, I went to see—such a charming old lady, fresh in her mind, with snow-white hair. You and Papa were the topic she enjoyed speaking about, and our brothers and sisters.

Darmstadt: March 11.

. . . I hope you were not the worse for all your exertions. The *Times'* accounts are charming. Such a warm reception must have touched Marie, and shown how the English cling to their Sovereign and her house.

We have cold, snow and dust, after quite warm weather. I trust you will have sunshine to-morrow.

This last fortnight the news from Ashantee has so absorbed our thoughts. It has been an arduous undertaking, and one's heart warms to our dear troops, who under all difficulties sustain their old name for bravery and endur-

[8] A former Dresser of the Queen's.

ance. The poor 42nd [Regiment] lost many through illness, too; and I see they entered Coomassie playing the bagpipes!

Louis is just reading to me Sir Hope Grant's book on the Indian Mutiny, which he kindly sent me, and which is interesting and pleasant to read.

I am taking the first snowdrops to sweet Frittie's grave. *How* the first flowers he so dearly loved bring tears to my eyes, and recollections which wring my heart anew! I dread these two next months with their flowers and their birds. Good-bye, darling Mama.

Darmstadt: April 7.

. . . Surely Marie must feel it very deeply, for to leave so delicate and loving a mother must seem almost wrong. How strange this side of human nature always seems—leaving all you love most, know best, owe all debts of gratitude to, for the comparatively unknown! The lot of parents is indeed hard, and of such self-sacrifice.

April 11.

. . . The children are too much an object here: they have too little to compare with; they would be benefited by a change, seeing other things and people, else they get into a groove, which I know is not good. They are very unspoilt in their tastes, and simple and quiet children, which I think of the greatest importance.

Louis Battenberg[9] has passed a first-rate examination. The parents are so happy, and the influence the good conduct and steady work of the elder brother has on the younger is of the greatest use, as they wish to follow him,

---

[9] Eldest son of Prince Alexander of Hesse and Princess Battenberg married on the 30th of April, 1884, to Princess Victoria of Hesse, and brother to the present Prince of Bulgaria and Prince Henry of Battenberg.

and be as well spoken of, and please their parents, as he does. . . .

April 15.

My best thanks for your dear letter of the 13th. You say rightly, what a fault it is of parents to bring up their daughters with the main object of marrying them. This is said to be a too prominent feature in the modern English education of the higher classes. . . . I want to strive to bring up the girls without *seeking* this as the sole object for the future—to feel they can fill up their lives so well otherwise. . . . A marriage for the *sake* of marriage is surely the greatest mistake a woman can make. . . . I know what an absorbing feeling that of devotion to one's parent is. When I was at home, it filled my whole soul. It does still in a great degree, and *Heimweh* [home-sickness] does not cease after ever so long an absence. . . .

Darmstadt: April 23.

. . . I thought so much of your remarks about daughters, &c., and do think it *so* natural and dutiful to remain with one's parent as long as one is wanted. Is it not a duty when no one else can take one's place? I should feel it so.

April 26.

I thank you most tenderly for your loving wishes for my birthday, received on getting up yesterday morning. You can understand that the day was inexpressibly sad, that the fair head missing in our circle was painfully felt, and that all these recollections caused me endless tears and heartache—though not for him, sweet precious child.

As you say, life at best is a struggle: happy those who can lie down to rest, having fought their battle well; or those who have been spared fighting it at all, and have remained pure and untouched, barely touching this earth, so mixed up with grief and sin!

Let me thank you for the charming photographs, and for the present towards the layette—a most kind assistance.

. . . We went to the Mausoleum. The children had made me wreaths to take there, and we all went together. How often and tenderly Ernie speaks of Frittie! It is very touching, and speaks of his deep and warm heart. He said the other day—for the recollection of death has left such a deep impression, and he cannot reconcile it with life, it pains him—'When I die, you must die too, and all the others; why can't all die together? I don't like to die alone, like Frittie.' Poor child! the wish that *all* have, who love their own, so early expressed. . . .

May 4.

Many thanks for your last dear letter written on dear Arthur's birthday, of which, though late, I wish you joy. Such a good, steady, excellent boy as he is! What a comfort it must be to you, never to have had any cause of uneasiness or annoyance in his conduct! He is so much respected, which for one so young is doubly praiseworthy. From St. Petersburg, as from Vienna, we heard the same account of the steady line he holds to, in spite of all chaffing, &c., from others; which shows character.

My mother-in-law tells me that since Miechen has been allowed to retain her religion, this right will of course be conceded to all Princesses in future. What a good thing, for the changing I always thought too bad, and nowadays so intolerant and narrow. . . . To think of Mr. Van de Weyer also leaving this world! To you he will be a loss, and to all who knew him. Old friends are precious landmarks in the history of one's life, and not to be replaced by new ones; and it is sad, how time reduces the number as one gets on in life. How deeply you must feel this with each fresh loss! I feel much for you. . . .

Beloved Mama, Darmstadt: June 5.

. . . The day (Whitsunday, and dear Frittie's burial-day) of Baby's[1] birth would have been too sad, had not the fact of its being your birthday given a double significance; but when I heard those bells, and became conscious again of everything, my feelings were deep and mingled beyond expression.

. . . With repeated tender thanks, your most loving child,

ALICE.

June 11.

. . . Having no cow, or country place to keep one, in this tremendous heat where one can't keep milk, and dysentery carries off so many babies, it would not be fair to deprive the poor little thing of its natural and safest nourishment till the hot months are over.

July 13.

The christening went off very well. Baby looked really pretty for so young an individual. It was in a large room. Marie [Duchess of Edinburgh], quite in pink, held her godchild; and my mother-in-law, with her best love, begs me to tell you, it had pleased her so much that you had asked her to represent you. My three older girls looked very nice, I thought, in lavender silk (your Christmas present). I had the same colour, and 'Sunny,' in pink, was immensely admired. She is still improving in looks since you saw her.

---

[1] Princess May, born on the 24th of May, 1874.

I was glad it was another place, in different circumstances from the last christening. As it was, it moved me much. The last time I heard these words darling Frittie was with us, and now the chain has a gap!

... We can get nothing at Scheveningen except at exorbitant prices, so we go to that dreadful Blankenberghe —without tree or bush, nothing but a beach and sand banks.

Blankenberghe : July 24.

The sea air is doing all good, the children especially, the heat had pulled them so.

I have bathed once, and hope it will agree. ... My cough and relaxed throat are getting better.

The rooms are small and few, but clean, and the cooking good, and we are quite satisfied. There is not a soul one knows.

Blankenberghe : August 16.

This day makes me think of our dear kind Grandmama, whose image still dwells amongst us! None who ever knew her can forget how truly loveable she was; and we grandchildren will ever retain such a bright recollection of her. So many little attentions, small souvenirs, kind letters, all tokens of affection *so* pleasing to the receivers.

Yesterday Louis saved a lady from drowning. He was bathing. The waves were high, and he heard a cry for help, and saw a bather struggling. She had lost her footing. Her husband tried to help her, but was exhausted and let her go; equally so the brother-in-law, and Louis felt he was losing his strength, but she kept her presence of mind and floated. He let her go once till a wave brought her near him again, and he caught her hand and brought her in, feeling quite done himself. I was not in the sea at the time, for the waves were so tremendous that I lost my footing several times, and had come out, fearing an accident. The lady is a Mrs. T. Sligo, a Scotchwoman, and she has just written to me to thank Louis. He is a good swimmer, and very strong. The gentlemen are two grey-haired Scotchmen.

Ella has so wonderfully improved since she has been here. She is no more pale and languid, and Ernie is another child also.

Luckily it has not been warm, so the air and baths are doubly efficacious. They have done me a world of good. I feel quite different to what I have done ever since Sunny's birth. I believe the sea to be the only thing for such a relaxed state, and, being strong and healthy by nature, I can't bear not being well and feeling so weak. Miss Graves[2] has returned, but the girls have been very good—no trouble at all.

Kranichstein: August 26.

On dear Papa's birthday I must send you a few lines. The past is ever bright and vivid in my mind, though year after year intervenes. How must it be for you, who live surrounded by such precious recollections of the happy past!

Kranichstein: September 1.

. . . I shall get a comforter done for good Mrs. Brown, kind old woman. I am glad she does not forget me, and shall be pleased to do any little thing that can give her pleasure. Will you tell her, the plaid she made me still goes everywhere with me? How is Mrs. Grant?

Louis is gone, and I have a good deal to do every day. We breakfast at half-past eight, then I have Baby and take the children out till eleven. I then have business, Baby, and, at one, the elder girls alternately for French reading.

---

[2] Governess to Princess Alice's children.

After luncheon I write my letters, &c., and before five go out. In the evenings I read, and have supper at eight with the two ladies.

Ella is another child since she has been at the seaside—fine colour, no longer pale and languid, learns well, and is quite different. Ernie the same, bright and fresh; while before they had been looking pulled and weak, outgrowing their strength.

'Sunny' is the picture of robust health, and sweet little 'sister Maly' sits up quite alone, and is very neat and rosy, with such quick eyes, and two deep dimples in her cheeks—a great pet, and so like my poor Frittie.

The return here has been very painful, and days of great depression still come, when I am tormented with the dreadful remembrance of the day I lost him. Too cruel and agonising are those thoughts. I dwell on *his* rest and peace, and that our sufferings he cannot know. What might not life have brought him? Better so! but hard to say, 'God's will be done.'

Kranichstein: September 15.

. . . ———'s conversion has created no smaller sensation with us than elsewhere, and the *Times* criticised his step so sharply. It remains a retrograde movement for any Protestant, how much more so for a man of his stamp! Quite incomprehensible to me.

. . . This Catholic movement is *so un-English*. I think, among those Ritualists there are *bonâ fide* Catholics who help to convert. . . .

I will send you sweet little Maly's photograph next time. . . . Baby has a very fair skin, light-brown hair and deep blue eyes with marked eyebrows, not much colour in her cheeks, but pink and healthy-looking altogether.

Kranichstein: September 24.

... People with strong feelings and of nervous temperament, for which one is no more responsible than for the colour of one's eyes, have things to fight against and to put up with, unknown to those of quiet equable dispositions, who are free from violent emotions, and have consequently no feeling of nerves—still less, of irritable nerves. If I did not control mine as much as I could, they would be dreadful. ... One can overcome a great deal—but *alter* oneself one cannot. ...

October 31.

... I always think, that in the end children educate the parents. For their sakes there is so much one must do: one must forget oneself, if everything is as it ought to be. It is doubly so, if one has the misfortune to lose a precious child. Rückert's lovely lines are so true (after the loss of two of his children):

Nun hat euch Gott verliehen, was wir euch wollten thun,
Wir wollten euch erziehen, und ihr erzieht uns nun.
O Kinder, ihr erziehet mit Schmerz die Eltern jetzt;
Ihr zieht an uns, und ziehet uns auf zu euch zuletzt.[3]

Yesterday Ernie was telling Orchard that I was going to plant some Spanish chestnuts, and she said, 'Oh, I shall be dead and gone before they are big; what a pity we had none sooner!' and Ernie burst out crying and said, 'No, you must not die alone—I don't like people to die alone; we must die all together!' He has said the same to me before, poor darling. After Lenchen's [Princess Christian's]

---

[3] Now unto you the Lord has done what we had wished to do;
We would have train'd you up, and now 'tis we are train'd by you.
With grief and tears, O children, do you your parents train,
And lure us on and up to you, to meet in heaven again.

boys were gone, and he had seen Eddy and Georgy [sons of Prince of Wales], his own loss came fresh upon him, and he cried for his little brother! It is the remaining behind the loss, the missing of the dear ones, that is the cruel thing to bear. Only time can teach one that, and resignation to a Higher Will. . . .

November 16.

Many thanks for your dear letter, and for the advice, which, as a mark of your interest in our children, is very precious, besides being so good! What you mention I have never lost sight of, and there is, as you say, nothing more injurious for children than that they should be made a fuss about. I want to make them unselfish, unspoiled, and contented; as yet this is the case. That they take a greater place in my life than is often the case in *our* families, comes from my not being able to have enough persons of a responsible sort to take charge of them always; certain things remain undone from that reason, if I do not do them, and *they* would be the losers. I certainly do not belong by nature to those women who are above all *wife*; but circumstances have forced me to be the mother in the real sense, as in a private family, and I had to school myself to it, I assure you, for many small self-denials have been necessary. Baby-worship, or having the children indiscriminately about one, is not at all the right thing, and a perpetual talk about one's children makes some women intolerable. I hope I steer clear of these faults—at least I try to do so, for I can only agree in *every* word you say, as does Louis, to whom I read it; and he added when I was reading your remarks, ' Das thust Du aber nicht. Die Kinder und andere Menschen wissen gar nicht, was Du für sie thust ' [' But you don't do so. Neither the children nor anybody else knows what you do for them ']. He has often complained that I would not have the children enough in my room, but, being of your opinion, where it was not necessary, I thought it better not. . . .

December 12.

I enclose a few lines to Mr. Martin.[4] I have only had time to look at the preface, and am very glad to hear that you are satisfied.

With what interest shall I read it! You will receive these lines on the 14th. Last year I had the comfort of being near you. It did me real good then, and I thank you again for those short and quiet days, where the intercourse with you was so soothing to my aching heart. There is no *Umgang* [intercourse] I know, that gives me more happiness than when I can be with you—above all, in quiet. The return to the so-called world I have barely made. Life is serious—a journey to another end. The flowers God sends to brighten our path I take with gratitude and enjoy; but much that was dearest, most precious, which this day *commemorates*, is in the grave; part of my heart is there too, though their spirits, adored Papa's, live on with me, the holiest and brightest part of life, a star to lead us, were we but equal to following it! The older I grow the more perfect, the more touching and good, dear Papa's image stands before me. Such an *entire* life for duty, so joyously and unpretendingly borne out, remains for all times something inexpressibly fine and grand! With it how tender, loveable, gay, he was! I can never talk of him to others who have not known him, without tears in my eyes—as I have them now. He *was* and *is* my ideal. I never knew a man fit to place beside him, or so made to be devotedly loved and admired. . . .

[4] The first volume of whose *Life of the Prince Consort* had just been published.

December 14.

Before this day is over, I must write a few words—my thoughts are so much with you and with the past, the bright happy past of my childhood, where beloved Papa was the centre of this rich and happy existence. I have spent nearly the whole day with the precious volume which speaks so much of you and of him.

What a man in every sense of the word; what a Prince he was—so entirely what the dear old Baron [Stockmar] urged him always to be! Life with him must have seemed to you so secure and well-guarded. How you must have loved him! It makes one's heart ache again and again, in reading and thinking of all dear Papa was to you, that you should have had to part from him in the heat of the day, when he was so necessary. *Ihm ist wohl* [With him it is well]. A life like his was a whole long lifetime, though only forty-two years, and he well deserved his rest!

The hour is nearing when we last held and pressed his hand in life, now thirteen years ago. How well I recollect that last sunrise, and then the dreadful night with you that followed on that too awful day! But it is not well to dwell on these things, when we have the bright sunny past to look back to. Tennyson's beautiful Dedication [5] expresses all one feels and would wish to say. I can only add, with a heavy-drawn sigh, 'Oh, to be worthier of *such* a Father!' How far beneath him, if not always in aims, at least in their fulfilment, have I always remained!

December 17.

My best thanks for the letter of the 15th. Poor Colonel Grey's [6] death is shocking, and Bertie and Alix are

---

[5] To *The Idylls of the King*.

[6] Only child of Sir George Grey, and Equerry to the Prince of Wales. He died at Sandringham of inflammation of the lungs.

sure to have felt it deeply. Dear Bertie's true and constant heart suffers on such occasions, for he can be constant in friendship, and all who serve him serve him with warm attachment. I hope he won't give way to the idea of Sandringham being unlucky, though so much that has been trying and sad has happened to them there! Superstition is surely a thing to fight against; above all, with the feeling that all is in God's hands, not in ours!

How interesting the book is [*Life of the Prince Consort*]! I have finished it, and am *befriedigt* [satisfied]. It was a difficult undertaking, but Mr. Martin seems to have done it very well.

I am sure dear Osborne is charming as ever, but I can't think of that large house so empty; no children any more; it must seem so forsaken in our old wing. I have such a *Heimweh* [yearning] to see Osborne again after more than six years! . . .

1875

[The following two letters refer to an opinion held and expressed in certain quarters, that the publication of the Prince Consort's *Life* had taken place too soon after the occurrence of many of the events which are dealt with in it.]

Darmstadt: January 3, 1875.

. . . It is touching and fine in you to allow the world to have so much insight into your private life, and allow others to have what has been only *your* property and our inheritance.

People can only be the better for reading about dear

Papa, such as he was, and such as so feelingly and delicately Mr. Theodore Martin places him before them. To me the volume is inexpressibly precious, and opens a field for thought in various senses.

To this letter Her Majesty replied :—

Dearest Alice,   Osborne : January 12, 1875.

. . . Now as regards the book. If you will reflect a few minutes, you will see, how I owed it to beloved Papa to let his noble character be known and understood, as it now is, and that to wait longer, when those who knew him best—his own wife, and a few (very few there are) remaining friends—were all gone, or too old, and too far removed from that time, to be able to present a really true picture of his most ideal and remarkable character, would have been really wrong.

He must be known, for his own sake, for the good of England and of his family, and of the world at large. Countless people write to say, what good it does and will do. And it is already thirteen years since he left us!

Then you must also remember, that endless false and untrue things have been written and said about us, public and private, and that in these days people will write and will know: therefore the only way to counteract this is to let the real, full truth be known, and as much be told as can be told with prudence and discretion, and then no harm, but good, will be done. Nothing will help me more, than that my people should see what I have lost! Numbers of people we knew have had their Lives and Memoirs published, and some beautiful ones: Bunsen's, by his wife; Lord Elgin's, by his (very touching and interesting); Lord Palmerston's; &c. &c.

The Early Years volume was begun for private circulation only, and then General Grey and many of Papa's friends and advisers begged me to have it published. This was done. The work was most popular, and greatly liked. General Grey could not go on with it, and asked me to ask Sir A. Helps to continue it, and he said that he could not, but recommended Mr. Theodore Martin as one of the most eminent writers of the day, and hoped I could prevail on him to undertake this great national work. I did succeed, and he has taken seven years to prepare the whole, supplied by me with every letter and extract; and a deal of time it took, but I felt it would be a national sacred work. You must, I think, see I am right now; Papa and I too would have suffered otherwise. I think even the German side of his character will be understood.

One of the things that pleases people most is the beautiful way in which he took all good Stockmar's often very severe observations. And they also admire so much good old Stockmar's honesty, fearlessness, and are pleased to be shown what a dear warm-hearted old man he was. Your devoted Mama,

V. R.

January 27.

. . . My little May has such a cold, which lessens her usual smiles. She is a fine strong child, more like what Victoria was, but marked eyebrows, with the fair hair and such speaking eyes. She and Aliky are a pretty contrast!

February 14.

You say of the drains just what I have said from year to year; and this summer—if we can get away in the spring, when it is most unwholesome—what can be done is to be done, and I hope with better success than what has hitherto been attempted.

My little May cannot get rid of her cough, though she looks pink and smiling. I shall be so glad to show her to you—she is so pretty and dear.

My father-in-law has for the first time got the gout in his feet, and is so depressed. Uncle Louis suffers dreadfully from oppression at night, so that he can't remain in bed. He is a good deal aged, and stoops dreadfully. . . .

March 14.

Louis gave me a dreadful fright last week by suddenly breaking through the ice, and at a very deep place. He laid his arms over the thicker ice, and managed to keep above water till some one was near enough to help him out. He said the water drew immensely, and he feared getting under the ice. The gentleman, who is very tall, lay down and stretched his arms out to Louis, another man holding the former; and so he got out without ill effects. As it was at Kranichstein, he undressed and rubbed himself before the stove in the Verwalter's [land-steward's] room; and he came home in the Verwalter's clothes, which looked very funny. . . .

Marlborough House : May 15.

I did not half thank you yesterday for our pleasant visit. I could not trust myself to speak. I felt leaving you again so much. It has been a great happiness to me, so *wohlthuend* [doing me so much good] to have been with you, and I can never express what I feel, as I would, nor how deep and tender my love and gratitude to you are! The older I grow, the more precious the *Verhältniss* [relation] to a mother becomes to me, and how doubly so to you!

Louis feels as I do; his love to you has always been as to his own mother; and my tears begin to run, when I recall your dear face and voice, which to see and hear again has seemed so natural, so as it ought to be! that it is quite difficult to accustom myself to the thought that only in memory can I enjoy them now.

How I do love you, sweet Mama! There is no sacrifice I would not make for you! and as our meetings are of late years so fleeting and far between, when they are over, I feel the separation very much. . . .

Marlborough House: June 15.

. . . God bless you, my precious Mother, watch over and guard you; and let your blessing and motherly interest accompany us and our children! Louis' tenderest love; many, many kisses from all children, and William's respectful duty!

Kranichstein: June 20.

. . . All Victoria and Ella tell me of their stay at Balmoral—the many things you gave them and their people—touches me so much: let me thank you so many times again. I feel I did not say half enough, but you know *how much* I feel it!

Our journey did very well; no one was ill, after that dreadful storm—a piece of luck. You are now again at Windsor. How much I think of you and of dear Beatrice!

Kranichstein: October 7.

. . . To-day my eyes will not remain dry: the recollection of five years ago, which brought us joy and promise of more in our sweet second boy, is painful in the extreme. The sudden ending of that young life; the gap this has left; the recollections that are now but to be enjoyed in silent memory, will leave a heart-ache and a sore place, beside where there is much happiness and cause of gratitude. The six children and we, with endless flowers and tears, decked his little grave this morning, and some sad lines of Byron's struck me as having much truth in the pain of such moments—

> But when I stood beneath the fresh green tree,
> Which living waves where thou didst cease to live,
> And saw around me the wide field revive
> With fruits and fertile promise, and the Spring
> Come forth her work of gladness to contrive,
> With all her reckless birds upon the wing,
> I turn'd from all she brought, to those she could not bring.[7]

The weather is fine; it was much like this five years ago, but round Metz it rained. Louis was turning into quarters with his troops from a sortie, and he called the news out to the regiments as he rode along, and they gave a cheer for their little Prince!

It was a dreadful time of trial and separation for both of us, and Frittie was such a comfort and consolation to me in all my loneliness.

How sorry I am for poor Alix at this long separation![8] For her sake I grieve at the impossibility of her accompanying him.

We hope to get back to our house by the 19th, though there will be an end of nice walks for the next eight months—the town grows so, and is all railroad and coal-heaps where we had our walks formerly, and the town pavement in the streets is most unpleasant walking. . . .

---

[7] *Childe Harold*, canto iii. stanza 30.
[8] During the visit of the Prince of Wales to India.

Schloss Kranichstein: October 16.

For your dear letter and for the enclosures I am so grateful, but distressed beyond measure at dear Fanny's [Lady Frances Baillie]. I had a long letter from her some weeks back, when she was more hopeful about dear Augusta [Stanley]. This is too much sorrow for them all! Fanny I love as a sister, and dear Augusta's devotion and self-sacrifice to you, and even to us in those dreadful years, was something rare and beautiful. Her whole soul and heart were in the duty, which to her was a sacred one. The good, excellent Dean! My sympathy is so great with these three kind and good people so sorely tried. I grieve for you, too! God help them!

October 26.

How sorry I am for dear good old Mrs. Brown and for her sons![9] Please say something sympathising from me; her blindness is such a trial, poor soul, at that age. How gloomily life must close for her!

1876

January 18, 1876.

No words can express how deep my sympathy and grief is for what our dear Augusta and the Dean[1] have to go through. With her warm, large heart, which ever lived and suffered for others, how great must her pain be in having to leave him! I can positively think of nothing else lately, as you know my love for Augusta, the General [her

---

[9] Her husband, the father of the Queen's personal attendant, John Brown, had just died. See *More Leaves from a Journal*, p. 319.

[1] Lady Augusta Stanley's life was at this time despaired of. She died on the 1st of March.

brother, General Bruce] and Fanny has always been great; and when I think back of them in former times, and in the year 1861, my heart aches and my tears flow—feeling what you and we shall lose in dear Augusta. My pity for the dear good kind Dean is so deep. I sent him a few words again to-day, in the hope he may still say a few words of love and gratitude to dear Augusta from me.

Darmstadt: January 22.

... Yesterday morning Ernie came in to me and said, 'Mama, I had a beautiful dream; shall I tell you? I dreamt that I was dead and was gone up to Heaven, and there I asked God to let me have Frittie again; and he came to me and took my hand. You were in bed, and saw a great light, and were so frightened, and I said, "It is Ernie and Frittie." You were so astonished! The next night Frittie and I went with a great light to sisters.' Is it not touching? He says such beautiful things, and has such deep poetic thought, yet with it all so full of fun and romping.

February 9.

... I am so sorry and shocked about excellent Mr. Harrison.[2] *What* a loss! He was so obliging and kind always in the many commissions for us children. Poor Kräuslach,[3] too—so sad! It is too grievous; how one well-known face—with its many associations—after another, is called away; and on looking back, how short a space of time they seem to have filled!

[2] Secretary in the office of the Privy Purse.
[3] The Prince Consort's head groom, who had come over with him to England.

Darmstadt: June 23.

... How sorry I am for good kind old Mrs. Brown! —to be blind with old age seems so hard, so cruel; but I am sure with your so loving heart you have brightened her latter years in many kind ways. It is such a pleasure to do anything for the aged; one has such a feeling of respect for those who have the experience of a long life, and are nearing the goal.

September 5.

It is long since I have felt such pain as the death (to me really sudden and unexpected, in spite of the danger inherent in her case) of my good, devoted, kind Emily[4] has caused me. My tears won't cease. Louis, the children, the whole household, all mourn and grieve with me. She was singularly beloved, and richly deserved to be so! Her devotion and affection to me really knew no bounds. I cannot think what it will be to miss her. I have *never* been served as she served me, and probably never shall be so again. It is a wrench that only those can estimate who knew her well—like poor Mary Hardinge. She came first in Emily's heart, and the loss for her is quite, QUITE irreparable! Had I but seen dear Emily again! This sudden, cruel sort of death shocks me so.

How I should have nursed and comforted her had I been near her! She always wished this, and told me she had such a fear of death. There never breathed a more unselfish, generous, good character.

September 6.

... I fear you will find me so dull, tired, and useless. I can do next to nothing of late, and must rest so

---

[4] The Hon. Emily Caroline Hardinge, the Princess's Lady-in-Waiting, died in London on the 4th of September, 1876.

much. Poor Emily! My thoughts never leave her. I cannot yet get accustomed to the thought of her loss.

P.S.—Just received your dear note. The accounts of my dear Emily's sad end have just reached me, and I am terribly upset. You can hardly estimate the gap, the blank she will leave—my only lady, and in many ways *homme d'affaires*. We had been so much together this last waiting; everything reminds me of her, and of the touching love she bore me. Surely some years more she would have lived.

Darling Mama, I don't think you quite know how far from well I am, and how absurdly wanting in strength. I only mention it, that you should know that until the good air has set me up I am good for next to nothing; and I fear I shan't be able to come to dinner the first evenings. I hope you won't mind. I have never in my life been like this before. I live on my sofa, and in the air, and see no one, and yet go on losing strength. Of course this unexpected shock has done me harm too, and has entailed more sad things. . . .

Douglas's Hotel, Edinburgh: September 11, Sunday.

. . . I hear Ernie is still so dull and melancholy at missing me; he always feels it most, with that tender loving heart of his. God preserve and guard this to me so inexpressibly precious child! I fancy that seldom a mother and child so understood each other, and loved each other, as we two do. It requires no words; he reads in my eyes, as I do in his what is in his little heart.

It is so wonderfully still here, not a soul in the streets. The people of the house have sent up several times to inquire when and to what church I was going; so I shall go, as it seems to shock them, one's staying away. I shall see the Monument this afternoon, and go and see Holyrood again. The whole journey here brought back with the well-remembered scenery the recollection of my childhood, all the happy journeys with dear Papa and you. How the treasured remembrance, with the deep love, lives on, when all else belongs to the past!

I seem, in returning here, so near you and him and former happy years, when my home was in this beloved country. No home in the world can quite become what the home of one's parents and childhood was. There is a sacredness about it, a feeling of gratitude and love for the great mercies one had there. You, who never left country, *Geschwister* [kindred], or home, can scarcely enter into this feeling.

In the hopes of meeting you soon, kissing your dear hands, with thanks for all goodness, and many excuses for having caused so much trouble. . . .

Buckingham Palace: October 19.

I was so sad at parting with you yesterday. I could not half thank you for all your love and kindness during those weeks. But you know how deeply I feel it; how truly grateful I am to you; how happy and contented I am to be allowed to be near you as in old days. Darling Mama, once more, a thousand thanks for all and for everything!

The journey went quite well, and I am not particularly tired.

Buckingham Palace: November 19.

Thousand thanks for your dear letter received this morning! I feel leaving dear England, as always, though the pleasure of being near the dear children again is very great.

Let me thank you once more from my heart, darling Mama, for all your great kindness, and for having enabled me to do what was thought necessary and best. I return so much stronger and better than I came, in every way—refreshed by the pleasant stay in dear Balmoral with you, and then much better for the time here. I feel morally refreshed, too, with the entire change, the many interests to be met with here, which is always so beneficial, and will help me in every way when I get back to Darmstadt. All this I have to thank you for, and do so most warmly.

Louis, who, as you know, is full of love and affection for you, is very grateful for your kind words, and has likewise derived profit and enjoyment from his stay in England.

. . . My colour and strength have so much returned, that I do not doubt being well again this winter.

I went with Dean Stanley to see Mr. Carlyle, who was most interesting, and talked for nearly an hour. Had I had time, I would have written down the conversation. The Dean said he would try and do so.

With Louise I visited Mr. Motley also, who in his way is equally interesting, and has a great charm. . . .

Darmstadt: November 26.

Many thanks for your last letter from Balmoral, received yesterday morning! I *know* you feel leaving the dear place, but without going away there is no *Wiedersehen* [meeting again]. The happiness of our meeting with the dear children was very great on all sides—they eat me up!

They had made wreaths over the doors, and had no end of things to tell me. We arrived at three, and there was not a moment's rest till they were all in bed, and I had heard the different prayers and hymns of the six, with all the little different confidences they had to make. My heart was full of joy and gratitude at being with them once more, and I prayed God to make me fit to be their real friend and stay as long as they require me, and to have the insight into their different characters to guide them aright, and to understand their different wants and feelings. This is so difficult always.

Victoria is immensely grown, and her figure is forming. She is changing so much—beginning to leave the child and grow into the girl. I hear she has been good and desirous of doing what is right; and she has more to contend with than Ella, therefore double merit in any little thing she overcomes, and any self-sacrifice she makes.

Ernie is very well, and his birthday was a great delight. Sweet little May is enchanting,—'my *weet* heart,' as she calls me. Aliky is very handsome and dear.

Darmstadt: December 12.

I see this letter will just arrive on the 14th—day never to be forgotten! How deeply it is graven in my heart—with letters of blood; for the pain of losing *him*, and of witnessing your grief, was as sharp as anything any child can go through for its beloved parents. Yet, God's mercy is to be found through all, and one learns to say 'Thy will be done,' hard though it is. . . .

1877

Darmstadt: January 1.

. . . How beautifully Max Müller's letter[5] is written and expressed, and how touchingly and truly he puts the point of view on which we all should learn to stand! To become again pure as children, with a child's faith and trust—there where our human intellect will *ever* stand still!

[5] Written after the death of his daughter.

I have been reading some of Robertson's sermons again, and I think his view of Christianity one of the truest, warmest, and most beautiful I know. . . .

Darmstadt: March 23.

Thank you so much for your dear and sympathising letter. These have been most painful—most distressing days—so harrowing.[6]

The recollections of 1861, of dear Frittie's death, when my dear father-in-law was so tender and kind, were painfully vivid. My mother-in-law's resignation and touching goodness, doing all that she could during the illness and since for all arrangements, is very beautiful!

The poor sons gave way to bursts of tears during those agonising hours; yet they held their father alternately with me, and were quiet and helpful for their mother and for him, just as their simple quiet natures teach them. I begged Bäuerlein to write to you meanwhile. I am feeling so exhausted, and there is so much to do, and we are always going from one house to the other.

It was heartrending from Monday morn till Tuesday eve, to see the painful alteration in the dear well-known features augmenting from hour to hour, though I believe he did not suffer latterly. He was not conscious, unless spoken to, or called very directly.

My mother-in-law never left his bedside day or night, and we were only a few hours absent on Monday night. Before we went home, she called our names distinctly to him as we kissed him, and he seemed to notice it; then she knelt down, and distinctly, but choked with tears, prayed the Lord's Prayer for him, calling him gently.

The next day at six we were there again, and till half

---

[6] Illness and death of Prince Charles of Hesse, father of Prince Louis.

past six in the evening never left the bedside. She repeated occasionally, as long as she thought he might hear, a short verse—*so* touching! and once said, 'Bist Du traurig? es ist ja nicht auf lange, dann sind wir wieder zusammen!' ['Art thou sad? It is not for long, and then we shall be together again'] kissing and stroking his hands. It was very distressing.

When all was over we four were close to her, and she threw herself on him, and then clasped her sons to her heart with words of such grief, as you so well understand!

Early the next morning we went with her to his room. He lay on his bed, very peaceful, in his uniform. Louis had clasped the hands together when he died, and I arranged flowers on the bed and in the room round him.

There is a terrible deal to do and to arrange, and many people come, and we are much with my poor mother-in-law. Yesterday afternoon we went for the last time, to see the remains of what had been so precious. She read a *Lied* [a hymn], and then kissed him so long, and took with us the last look. Yesterday evening the coffin was closed in presence of the sons.

We are going to the Rosenhöhe [the Mausoleum] now, before going to Louis' mother, to put things straight there, and see if one can get by dear Frittie—it is *so* small.

The three brothers are dreadfully upset, but able to arrange and see after what is necessary. Aunt Marie [the Empress of Russia] wanted to come, and is in terrible distress; she loved that brother beyond anything. In her last letter to my mother-in-law she says, 'Ich habe solche Sehnsucht nach dem alten Bruder' ['I have such a yearning after my old brother].

His was a singularly delicate-minded, pure, true, unselfish nature, so full of consideration for others, so kind. My tears flow incessantly, for I loved him very dearly.

My dear mother-in-law has such a broken ruined existence now—all turned round him! She knows where to find strength and comfort—it will not fail her. . . .

Darmstadt: June 7.

. . . We are going through a dreadful ordeal. The whole of Monday and Monday night, with a heat beyond words, dreading the worst. Now there has been a slight rally.[7] Whether it will continue to-morrow is doubtful. He is always conscious, makes his little jokes, but the pulse is very low and intermits. I was there early this morning with Louis. . . .

The questions, long discussions between Louis and some people, as to complication and difficulty of every kind that will at once fall upon us, are really dreadful, and I so unfit just now! The confusion will be dreadful. . . .

I am so dreading everything, and above all the responsibility of being the first in everything, and people are not *bienveillant*.

I shall send you news whenever I can, but I am so worn out. I shall not be able to do so much myself.

I know your thoughts and wishes are with us at so hard a time. God grant we may do all aright! . . .

Telegrams.

June 7.

Going to Seeheim, as great weakness has come on. Am much tired by all that lies before us, and not feeling well.

[7] The Grand Duke of Hesse was alarmingly ill.

Seeheim: 13th.

Dear Uncle Louis is no more. We arrived too late.

Darmstadt: 6.20 o'clock, 13th.

Such press of business and decisions. Feel very tired.

15th.

We are both so over-tired; the press of business and decisions is so wearing, with the new responsibility.

18th.

Last ceremony over! All went off well, and was very moving.

ALICE.

Darmstadt: June 19.

Only two words of thanks from both of us for your kind wishes and letters! Christian and Colonel Gardiner bring you news of everything that has been and is still going on. But we are overwhelmed, over-tired, and the heat is getting very bad again.

. . . Will tell you what a very difficult position we are in. It is too dreadful to think that I am forced to leave Louis in a few weeks under present circumstances, but, if he wishes to keep me at all, I must leave everything and this heat for a time. These next weeks here will be very anxious and difficult. God grant we may do the right things!

June 28.

. . . To have to go away just now, when the refreshment of family life is so doubly pleasant to Louis after his work, I am too sorry for. If I were only better; if I only thought that I shall have the chance of rest, and what is necessary to regain my health! Now it will be more difficult than ever, and I see Louis has the fear, which I also have, that I shall not hold out very long.

July 15.

. . . I leave on Tuesday, but stop on the way. The children go direct and join me in Paris, when we go on together on Friday or Saturday to Houlgate. The trains don't fit, and one has some way to drive from Trouville.

Houlgate : July 25.

. . . This place is quite charming—real country, so green, so picturesque—a beautiful coast; the nicest sea-place I have been at yet. Our house is 'wee' for so many, and the first days it was very noisy: and it was so dirty. The maids and nurses had to scrub and sweep; the one French housemaid was not up to it. All is better now, and quite comfortable enough. The air is doing me good, and the complete change. I have bathed twice, and the sea revives me.

I follow as eagerly as any in England the advance of the Russians, and with cordial dislike. *They* can never be redressers of wrongs or promoters of civilisation and Christianity. What I fear is, even if they don't take Constantinople, and make no large demands as the price of their victories now, the declaration of the independence of Bulgaria will make that country to them in future what Roumania has been for Russia now, and therefore in twenty years hence they will get all they want, unless the other Powers at this late hour can bring about a change. It is bad for England, for Austria, for Germany, if this Russian Slav element should preponderate in Europe; and the other countries must sooner or later act against this in self-preservation.

What do the friends of the 'Atrocity Meetings' say now? How difficult it has been made for the Government through them, and how blind they have been! All this must be a constant worry and anxiety for you!

The children are so happy here—the sea does them such good. I am very glad I brought them.

Houlgate: July 28.

... Though we have rain off and on, still the weather is very pleasant, and we are all of us charmed with the place, and the beautiful, picturesque, fertile country. The life is so pleasant—real country—which I have never yet found at any bathing-place abroad yet. I have bathed every other day—swim, and it does me good. I feel it already. Ella is getting her colour back, and the little ones look much better.

I send you the last photos done of the children; Ella's is not favourable, nor Irène's, but all in all they are a pretty set. May has not such fat cheeks in reality; still it is very dear. The two little girlies are so sweet, so dear, merry and nice. I don't know which is dearest, they are both so captivating.

I have been to an old tumble-down church at Dives—close by here—where William the Conqueror is said to have been before starting for England. His name and those of all his followers are inscribed there—names of so many families now existing in England. It was very interesting.

August 22.

... How difficult it is to know one's children well! to develop and train the characters according to their different peculiarities and requirements! ...

Darmstadt: September 9.

. . . I must tell you now, how very heartily and enthusiastically the whole population, high and low, received us yesterday. It was entirely spontaneous, and, as such, of course so very pleasing. . . . I was really touched, for it rained, and yet all were so joyous—flags out, bells ringing, people bombarding us with beautiful nosegays; all the schools out, even the higher ones, the girls all dressed in white. The Kriegerverein, Louis' old soldiers, singing, &c. In the evening all the Gesangvereine joined together and sang under our windows.

We are very glad to be at home again, and, please God, with earnest will and thought for others, we together shall in our different ways be able to live for the good of the people entrusted to our care! May God's blessing rest on our joint endeavours to do the best, and may we meet with kindness and forbearance where we fall short of our duties!

Darmstadt: October 30.

. . . I had to receive sixty-five ladies—amongst them my nurses—and some doctors from here and other towns, all belonging to my Nursing Society, which has now existed ten years. Then I was at the opening of my Industrial Girls' School, where girls from all parts of the country come, and which is a great success. I started it two years ago. On Sunday I took the children to hear the Sunday school, which interested them very much.

I have been doing too much lately, though, and my nerves are beginning to feel the strain, for sleep and appetite are no longer good. Too much is demanded of one; and I have to do with so many things. It is more than my strength can stand in the long run. . . .

December 13.

For to-morrow, as ever, my tenderest sympathy! Time shows but more and more what we all lost in beloved Papa; and the older I grow, the more people I know, the more the remembrance of him shines bright as a star of purer lustre than any I have ever known. May but a small share of his light fall on some of us, who have remained so far beneath him, so little worthy of such a father! We can but admire, reverence, long to imitate, and yet not approach near to what he was!

We are going with the children to-day to Wiesbaden until Saturday; and I mean to tell Vicky that she had better give up the hope of my being able to come for the wedding.[8] I could not do it. I only trust the why will be understood. Do write to the dear Empress about it when next you write. *How* sorry I am to be absent at a moment when, as sister and a German Sovereign's wife, I should be there; but the doctor would not hear of it, so I gave it up. . . .

Darmstadt: December 21.

. . . You say all that happened after the dreadful 14th is effaced from your memory. How well I can imagine that! I remember saying my utmost to Sir Charles Phipps in remonstrance to your being wished to leave Windsor—it was so cruel, so very wrong. Uncle Leopold insisted; it all came from him, as he was alarmed lest you should fall ill.

How you suffered was dreadful to witness; never shall I forget what I went through for you then; it tore my heart in pieces; and my own grief was so great, too. Louis

---

[8] Of the Princess Charlotte of Prussia with the Hereditary Prince of Saxe-Meiningen.

thought I would not hold to my engagement then any more —for my heart was too filled with beloved, adored Papa, and with your anguish, to have room or wish for other thoughts.

God is very merciful in letting time temper the sharpness of one's grief, and letting sorrow find its natural place in our hearts, without withdrawing us from life!

1878

Darmstadt: January 26.

Though I have no letter, and expect none at such a moment, still I must send you a few lines to tell you how constantly I think of you, and of my own beloved and adored country. The anxiety you must be going through, and the feelings you must experience, I share with my whole heart. . . .

God grant it may be possible to do the right thing, for it is late, and the complication is dreadful!

I have barely any thoughts for anything else; and the Opposition seems to me to have been more wrong in its country's interest, and to have done her a greater harm than can ever be redressed. It is a serious, awful moment for Sovereign, country, and Government; and in your position none have to go through what you have—and after all so alone!

I hope your health bears up under the anxiety.

April 9.

. . . Angeli has arrived, and will begin at once. We thought Ernie and Ella—Victoria is too big, though she is the eldest and ought to be in the picture; she would be too preponderant. Angeli is quite lost in admiration of Aliky and May, who are, I must say myself, such a lovely little pair as one does not often see. He will begin our heads to-morrow. . . .

Darmstadt: November 6.

. . . I am but very middling, and leading a very quiet life, which is an absolute necessity. It is so depressing to be like this. But our home life is always pleasant —never dull, however quiet. Only a feeling of weariness and incapacity is in itself a trial.

Telegram. November 8.

Victoria has diphtheria since this morning. The fever is high. I am so anxious.

Telegram. November 10.

Victoria is out of danger.

Telegram. November 12.

This night my precious Aliky has been taken ill.

Darmstadt: November 12.

This is dreadful! my sweet, precious Aliky so ill! At three this morning Orchie called me, saying she thought the child was feverish: complaining of her throat. I went over to her, looked into her throat, and there were not only spots, but a thick covering on each side of her throat of that horrid white membrane. I got the steam inhaler, with chlorate of potash for her at once, but she was very unhappy, poor little thing. We sent for the doctor, who lives close by, and who saw at once that it was a severe case. We have put her upstairs near Victoria, who is quite convalescent, and have fumigated the nursery to try and spare May and the others. It is a *terrible* anxiety; it is such an acute, and often fatal, illness.... Victoria has been graciously preserved; may God preserve these [the younger ones] also in His mercy! My heart is sore; and I am so anxious.

Telegram. November 13.

Aliky tolerable. Darling May very ill; fever so high. Irène has got it too. I am miserable; such fear for the sweet little one!

On the 14th of November Prince Ernest and the Grand Duke were attacked with diphtheria, so that, up to that time, Princess Elizabeth only had escaped the infection. She was sent to her Grandmother's, Princess Charles of Hesse's palace.

Telegram. November 15.

My precious May no better; suffers so much. I am in such horrible fear. Irène and Ernie fever less. Ernie's throat very swelled. Louis no worse; almost no spots. Aliky recovering.

Evening.

Darling May's state unchanged; heartrending. Louis' fever and illness on the increase. The others, as one could expect; all severe cases. May's most alarming.

November 16.

.... Our sweet little one is taken. Broke it to my poor Louis this morning; he is better; Ernie very, very ill. In great anguish.

Telegram. November 16; evening.

The pain is beyond words, but 'God's will be done!' Our precious Ernie is still a source of such terrible fear. The others, though not safe, better.

Telegram. November 17.

Ernie decidedly better; full of gratitude.

Telegram. November 18.

My patients getting better; hope soon to have them better. Last painful parting at three o'clock.

Telegram. November 19.

The continued suspense almost beyond endurance. Ernie thought he was going to die in the night, and was in a dreadful state for some hours. Louis very nervous, too; but they are not worse. The six cases have been one worse than the other.

Later, November 19.

Ernie had a relapse, and our fears are increased. I am in an agony between hope and fear.

Beloved Mama, November 19.

Tender thanks for your dear, dear letter, soothing and comforting!

Our sweet May waits for us up there, and is not going through our agony, thank God! Her bright, happy, sunshiny existence has been a bright spot in our lives—but oh! how short! I don't touch on the anguish that fills me, for God in His mercy helps me, and it must be borne; but to-day, again, the fear and anxiety for Ernie is still greater. This is quite agonising to me; *how* I pray that he may be spared to me!

His voice is so thick; new membranes have appeared. He cries at times so bitterly, but he is gayer just now.

To a mother's heart, who would spare her children every pain, to have to witness what I have, and am still doing, knowing all these precious lives hanging on a thread, is an agony barely to be conceived, save by those who have gone through it.

. . . Your letter says so truly all I feel. I can but say, in all one's agony there is a mercy and a peace of God, which even now He has let me feel. . . .

P.S.—I mean to try and drive a little this afternoon. I shall go out with Orchie. Of my six children, since a week none more about me, and not my husband. It is like a very awful dream to me.

Beloved Mama,   November 22.

Many thanks for your dear letter, and for all the expressions of sympathy shown by so many! I am *very* grateful for it.

Dear Ernie having been preserved through the greatest danger is a source of such gratitude! These have been terrible days! He sent a book to May this morning. It made me almost sick to smile at the dear boy. But he must be spared yet awhile what to him will be such a sorrow.

For myself, darling Mama, God has given me comfort and help in all this trouble, and I am sure His Spirit will remain near us in the trials to come! Great sympathy, such as all show, is a balm; but I am very tired, and the pain is often very great; but pain can be turned into a blessing, and I pray this may be so. . . .

When alone, I rest; and writing even is a physical exertion. Those around me have spared me all they could, but one must bear the greater weight oneself.

May God spare you all future sorrow, and give you the peace which He alone can give!

P.S.—I finish these lines at my dear Louis' bed. He thanks you so much for your dear loving sympathy. Thank God, he is doing well. But the pain they have all gone through in their poor throats has been *awful*. The doctors and nurses—eight! for they have changed day and night, and had such constant attendance—have been *all* I could wish.

Your loving child,   ALICE.

Darmstadt: December 1.

. . . . Everyone shows great sympathy, I hear, everywhere. . . . All classes have shown a great attachment to us personally, and to the House, and amongst the common people—it goes home to them that our position does not separate us so very far from them, and that in death, danger, and sorrow the palace and the hut are visited alike.

So many deep and solemn lessons one learns in these times, and I believe all works together for good for those who believe in God. . . .

December 2.

So many pangs and pains come, and must yet for years to come. Still, gratitude for those left is *so* strong, and indeed resignation entire and complete to a higher will; and so we all feel together, and encourage each other. Life is *not* endless in this world, God be praised! There is much joy—but oh! so much trial and pain; and, as the number of those one loves increases in Heaven, it makes our passage easier—and *home* is there!

Ever your loving child,
ALICE.

December 6.

Louis and Ernie will go out in a shut carriage to-day, though it rains—but it is warm. Louis' strength returns *so* slowly. Of course he shuns the return to life, where our loss will be more realised; to him, shut off so long, it is more like a dream. I am so thankful they were all spared the dreadful realities I went through—and alone. My cup seemed very full, and yet I have been enabled to bear it. But daily I must struggle and pray for resignation; it is a cruel pain, and one that will last years, as I know but too well.

Ever your loving child,

A.

A Watcher by the Dead

A Watcher by the Dead.

[THE beautiful sketch which follows appeared in the *Darmstädter Zeitung*, dated 'Christmas Eve, 1878'; and the annexed translation of it, by Sir Theodore Martin, appeared a few days afterwards in the *Times*.]

A WATCHER BY THE DEAD.

LONG, long before daybreak on one of those gloomy December days of last week an officer made his way hurriedly along the empty, silent streets of the capital. He was in full uniform, but its pomp and splendour were shrouded in a thick covering of crape, for he was afoot thus early to do duty by the bier of the beloved Princess. Desolate were the streets, as of a city of the dead; desolate as though tenanted only by the dead was the lordly palace to which he bent his steps. The sentinels at the great gate stood motionless, despite the severe cold, as if they feared to disturb the repose of death. Here, where the inhabitants of the capital used to see all astir with the busy, cheerful life inseparable from the residence of a reigning Prince; here, where, in days but recently gone by, children, blooming and beautiful, the country's pride and the joy of their princely parents, gave animation to house and garden, all was silent and void; a deadly blast had swept over the till now so happy home. The country's young, idolised mother had closed her beautiful eyes, closed them for evermore, after doing and enduring nobly, after tasting the bitterness of great earthly sorrow. Many long and woeful days, many nights of even greater anguish, had she watched, trembled, and prayed by the couch of a husband sick unto death, and of five children beloved past telling. The sweet, youngest bud in the fair wreath of princely children had been torn from her bleeding heart, and tears—scalding tears—for the sweet little May-blossom, which she had herself put to its last sleep under chaplets of flowers, flowed fast, as she folded her hands in gratitude, when the peril of death had passed over the heads of her husband and her other children. 'Thus do we learn humility!' she said, with quivering lip, to a lady who stood beside her. 'God has called for one life, and has given me back five for it; how, then, should I mourn?' And now, when, with fear and trembling, joy seemed about to enter once more into that heavily-stricken home, again the dark pinions of the Angel of Death were heard upon the air, and he bore away the truest of wives, the most loving of mothers, a sacrifice to duty fulfilled with the noblest forgetfulness of self. These were the thoughts with which the solitary wayfarer went upon his sorrowful way, and crossed the threshold of the chamber of death. With light step and whispered words the watchers by the dead whom he relieved withdrew.

Overwhelmed by the majesty of death, which met him here in its most sombre form, the new-comer bent his head and continued long in silent prayer. The Princess lay on a bier in the great hall on the ground floor, where she had so often sat surrounded by a radiant circle of guests. What of her was earthly, cased in a triple cerement, was covered with a pall of black velvet, which, however, was almost hid from view beneath a mass of flowers and palms. Upon the head of the coffin stood a little, simple crucifix of perfect artistic workmanship. Six torches on pedestals, hung with black, stood round the bier, shedding but a feeble glimmer through the hall, scarcely brighter, indeed, than the scanty light of the dawning winter day. From the wall opposite the coffin the youthful image of her husband, painted in happier times, looked sadly down upon the loved one lost. Directly opposite hung the picture which the Hessian Division had had painted for their much-loved leader, in remembrance of the glorious day of Gravelotte—a picture of battle and of the wild *mêlée* of slaughter in the silent chamber of death. He who now watched by the coffin had played a part in the conflict of the memorable day which the picture was meant to perpetuate, and he knew how deeply it was interwoven with the life of the Princess who lay there in her long last sleep. Her dear husband had gone to the campaign with his faithful Hessians; she knew his precious life to be in hourly danger; but her own sorrows and cares were not her first thought. Helpful, comforting, encouraging, she gave at all times to those who were left behind a brilliant example of cheerful and devoted courage; and when the wounded and sick came back from the battlefields in ever-increasing numbers, she it was who everywhere took the lead with noblest self-abnegation and practical good sense. By the beds of the sick and dying she stood like a comforting angel, and the love of the Hessian people twined the fairest of all diadems, the aureole of the heroine, round her princely brows.

This grateful love, not only of those who bore arms, but of the citizen and artisan as well, for which these things laid the foundation, was now sincerely and unconstrainedly busy beside the bier of the princely sleeper. Servants came, with loads of wreaths and bouquets, and arranged them upon the coffin. But it was not the official tributes of flowers from Court and noble, from the deputations of regiments far and near, which were laid as a mournful homage at the feet of the dead mistress, that touched most deeply the heart of him who stood there on guard. No, the tear that stole down unbidden, the little trivial gift of the poor and humble who lived far away from Court favour, had a greater value in his eyes. It was still quite early morning when, with the first glimmer of day, came an old peasant woman from the Odenwald. Advancing timidly, she laid, with a murmured prayer, a little wreath of rosemary, with a couple of small white flowers, perhaps the only ornament of her poor little room at home, as a token of grateful affection down upon the velvet pall. Then, thinking herself unnoticed, she took a rosebud from one of the splendid wreaths, and hid it under the old woollen dress. Who could interfere to balk the impulse of genuine affection, that longed to carry off some slight memorial with it? And now the little flower is lying between the leaves of the old Bible, and in days to come the matron, when she turns the leaves of the sacred volume, will tell her daughters and granddaughters of the noble lady, too early snatched away from her people—of her, who never forgot the poorest and the humblest of them all.

Anon appeared the bearer of one of the proudest names in Hesse, who was attached to the personal service of the Princess. The official, stalwart bearing of the courtier was left outside, and, weeping hot unhidden tears, he lingered long by the bier. To what a lofty soul, to what goodness of heart, was he saying here a bitter farewell! He was followed by two little girls, poorly but cleanly dressed, and they, too, brought their tribute of gratitude—two little bunches of violets. Shyly, almost frightened, and yet with childish curiosity, they drew slowly nearer. They thought of another winter day, some years ago. Hungry, chilled to the heart, they were sitting in an empty attic; their parents were dead, and they ate among strangers bread that was hard and grudgingly given, when that great lady appeared who was now sleeping here under the flowers. From her, whose heart was ever yearning to the orphan's cry, they heard again, for the first time, gentle, loving words; by her provision was quickly made for their more kindly treatment, and gratitude was rooted firmly and for ever in their young souls.

A deputation from the Court Theatre laid upon the coffin a wreath intertwined with pale pink streamers. Art, too, had come to mourn for her noblest patroness, who had been ever ready with her fine, cultivated intelligence to advance whatever was great and good. A servant brought a beautiful cross, of dark foliage with white flowers. It was the gift of the Grand Duke's mother, anxious to testify by an outward sign her love for her dead daughter. In ever-growing numbers came the mourners, all visibly oppressed by the weight of the calamity which had fallen upon the country. Countless were the gifts of love, of gratitude, of respect, which, now beautiful and costly, now slight and simple, arched ever higher and higher the hill of flowers above the coffin. The ladies of the neighbouring towns sent cushions of dark violets, with chaplets of white flowers. Two ladies deeply veiled brought branches of palm, from the dark green of which gleamed a white scroll—a poetic farewell word of deep feeling:—

> A hurricane, charged with destruction,
>   O palm, swept o'er thee. The squall
> Crash'd through thy leaves, and tore from thee
>   The tenderest, sweetest of all.

> The clouds clear'd away in the distance,
>   The tempest seem'd over and past,
> When forth from the firmament darted
>   A lightning-bolt, fiery and fast.
>
> It struck thee, O noble one, struck thee!
>   It crush'd thee, and now thou art gone!
> Farewell! To our death-day thine image
>   Still, still in our hearts shall live on.

There was a second poem, enclosed in a heart-shaped framework of leaves, which gave expression to the grief of a devoted soul for the high-hearted lady.

But now the hour was come for another to take the post of honour by the bier of the Princess. Silently and sadly the two men saluted. He that left took away with him a deep and elevating impression of the general love and respect paid by the people of Hesse to their too-early departed Princess, and the remembrance of that silent watch by the dead will remain in his memory for ever. And he who now entered on that honourable duty could chronicle proofs of genuine grief, of true reverence and love, not fewer nor less touching. Whosoever is thus bewept has secured the best and fairest memorial in the hearts of her own people for all time—'The remembrance of the just abideth in blessing.'

SKETCH OF THE LIFE

OF

PRINCESS ALICE

BY

SIR THEODORE MARTIN

A SKETCH OF THE
LIFE OF PRINCESS ALICE,
By SIR THEODORE MARTIN.

> 'Oh, sir, the good die first,
> And those whose hearts are dry as summer dust
> Burn to the socket.'—*Wordsworth.*

December 14, 1878.

ON the 14th of December, seventeen years ago, a great sorrow fell upon England in the death of the Prince Consort, who, if he did not die too soon for his own happiness and fame, died at least, as all now feel, too soon for England. That memorable 14th of December has again come round, and again a great sorrow has fallen upon the country. The Princess has been taken to her rest who watched and soothed the Prince Consort in the last days of his fatal illness, and who by her fortitude and noble devotion helped materially, though then but a girl of seventeen, to sustain and comfort the widowed Queen in her measureless affliction. For the first time a breach—and such a breach—has been made in that family circle to which all who had the privilege to know it looked as the happiest in England—happiest, because mutual love and esteem bound all its members together by ties knit in childhood and never broken, and because the noble activity for good which had been set before them in the example of their parents kept their hearts fresh and their minds ever open. She who, while yet a girl, was called to play a woman's part by her father's deathbed, has been the first to follow him into the Silent Land.

No life could have opened more auspiciously than that of the second daughter of our Royal house.[1] From the first she gave great promise of beauty and of intelligence. The fine old English names of Alice and Maud, selected for her by her happy parents, seemed, as names sometimes do, to be particularly fitted to the winning, open character of her fair and finely-formed features, and their sound was one pleasant in the mouths, not only of those to whom she was known, but of the people, as she grew up and was seen in public by the eager and kindly eyes to whom the sight of the Royal children has always been welcome.

When the marriage of the Princess Royal took place in 1858, the Princess Alice was still only a girl of fifteen; but she had already developed qualities of mind and heart of no ordinary kind. She came by degrees to fill up in some measure the vacancy which had been created by the removal of her very gifted sister to Berlin. Naturally she was drawn nearer to the Prince Consort; and the influence of his character and the teachings of his affectionate wisdom sank deeply into her pure and highly intellectual nature.

[1] 'She is a pretty and large baby, and we think will be *la Beauté* of the family.'—*The Queen to King Leopold*, 9th May, 1843.

'Our little baby, whom I am really proud of, for she is so very forward for her age, is to be called *Alice*, an old English name; and the other names are to be *Maud* (another old English name, and the same as Matilda), and *Mary*, as she was born on Aunt Gloucester's birthday.'—*The same to the same*, 16th May, 1843.

'Our christening went off very brilliantly, and I wish you could have witnessed it. Nothing could be more *anständig*, and little Alice behaved extremely well.'—*The same to the same*, 6th June, 1843.

He looked forward to her future with the assurance that she would prove all he could wish a daughter to be. She, on the other hand, loved him with a devotion only tempered by profound reverence for the great qualities which she could then, perhaps, but dimly appreciate, but the true extent and worth of which her own subsequent experience and reflection taught her more thoroughly to measure. When in later years she spoke of the Prince, one saw that, as Ben Jonson said of Shakespeare, 'she honoured his memory, on this side idolatry, as much as any.'

The teaching of that beloved father was put to the proof in those sad days of patient watching which preceded his death. Things were told at the time of the devotion and the marvellous self-control of the young girl, called so sternly and so suddenly to face death in the person of a father, on whose life that of the Queen herself seemed to depend, and whose counsels she knew to be of inestimable value to the nation. A few days after the Prince's death, she was spoken of by the *Times* in these noticeable words: 'Of the devotion and strength of mind shown by the Princess Alice all through these trying scenes it is impossible to speak too highly. Her Royal Highness has, indeed, felt that it was her place to be a comfort and a support to her mother in her affliction, and to her dutiful care we may perhaps owe it that the Queen has borne her loss with exemplary resignation, and a composure which, under so sudden and terrible a bereavement, could not have been anticipated.' The knowledge of this fact—and it was a fact—sank deeply into people's minds. It was never forgotten, and from that day the name of the Princess Alice has been a cherished household word to all her countrymen and women.

When, in 1862, she married the husband of her choice

—a man whose sterling worth and manliness had satisfied even the critical judgment of parents jealous for the happiness of a daughter so justly dear—the affectionate good wishes of the Queen's subjects of all grades went with her to her new home. In that home, brightened and ennobled as it was by her presence, her love for the home and country of her youth burned with a steady and ever-deepening glow. It is only those who know how strong is the mutual love by which the children of Queen Victoria are bound to their parent and to each other, who can appreciate the passionate yearning towards England of the Princesses whose homes have been made elsewhere. England and all its interests held a foremost place in the heart of the Princess Alice; and no one watched more closely every phase of the changeful life of the busy land, which she loved and reverenced as the home of liberty and the pioneer of civilisation.

While fulfilling with exemplary devotion every duty as a wife and mother, the process of self-culture was never relaxed. Every refined taste was kept alive by fresh study, fresh practice, fresh observation; neither was any effort spared to keep abreast with all that the best intellects of the time were adding to the stores of invention, of discovery, of observation, and of thought. Each successive year taught her better to estimate the value of the principles in religion, in morals, and in politics in which she had been trained. As her knowledge of the world and of man grew, she could see the wide range of fact upon which they were based, and their fitness as guides amid the perplexing experiences of human life, which, however seemingly varied in different epochs, are ever essentially the same. Then the significance of the Prince Consort's habit of judging everything by some governing principle, and working always by strict method, became clear to her; and in a letter written in

January 1875, of which a copy is before us, the Princess writes with her accustomed modesty: 'Living with thinking and cultivated Germans, much in Papa has explained itself to me, which formerly I could less understand, or did not appreciate so much as I ought to have done.'

She inherited much of her father's practical good sense, and, like him, was ever ready to take part in any well-directed effort for raising the condition of the toilworn and the poor. How much of their misery, nay, of their evil ways, was due to their wretched habitations, she, like him, felt most keenly; and she gave her sympathy and support to every effort for their improvement. With this view she translated into German some of Miss Octavia Hill's essays *On the Homes of the London Poor*, and published them with a little preface of her own (to which only her initial A. was affixed), in the hope that the principles, which had been successfully applied in London by Miss Hill and her coadjutors, might be put into action in some of the German cities. No good work appealed to her in vain. The great exemplar of her father was always before her; and in the letter from which we have already quoted she speaks of his life 'spent in the highest aims, and with the noblest conception of duty,' as a 'leading star' to her own.

That sense of duty carried her to the bedside of the Prince of Wales when, at the end of 1871, he was struck down at Sandringham by the fell disease under which his father had sunk. There she fulfilled the same priceless offices which she had ten years before discharged at Windsor Castle. It pleased Heaven to spare her a renewal of the great affliction of 1861; and in the very days of December in which we are now living, the life of the much-loved brother, which had been well-nigh despaired of, came slowly back to requite her affection, and in answer to her prayers.

The trials of that time came, before the exhaustion had passed away both of body and mind which the Princess had undergone during the Franco-German war. Separated—and for the second time—by war from the Prince of Hesse, who was away in the thickest of the perils of that campaign, she was not a woman to give herself up to morbid brooding on the pangs and apprehensions under which, devoted wife as she was, she yet could not fail to suffer most acutely, for her feelings were warm, and her imagination active beyond that of most women. In the hospital at Darmstadt, crowded with the soldiers, French as well as German, who had come from the battlefields maimed and racked with pain, she was foremost with her bright intelligence, her helpful sympathy, and her tender hand, in soothing pain, and inspiring that sense of manly gratitude which is the best of panaceas to a soldier's sick-bed. What she was and what she did at that time have embalmed her image in many a heart, and will make the tears flow thick and fast in many manly eyes at the thought of the death of one so young, so good, so gifted, and so fair. To her it was merely duty—duty to be done at every cost; but how much it had cost to that finely touched spirit and to that delicate womanly frame might be read, by all who could look below the surface, in the deep earnestness of her eyes and the deeper earnestness of her thoughts. The pain of that terrible period would not let itself be forgotten even in the gratitude which she felt for the providence which restored her beloved husband to her side, and for the realisation of her father's cherished dream of an United Germany, which had been purchased by the valour and the sufferings of its sons.

The Princess's fortitude had already been severely tried in the war between Prussia and Austria in 1866. Hesse-Darmstadt was engaged upon the side of Austria, and her husband, Prince Louis, took the field with the troops of the Principality. At the very time his third daughter, the Princess Irène, was born, he was with the army; and the Princess Alice knew he was under fire but was unable to get any tidings from him. The victorious Prussians marched into Darmstadt, while the Princess, newly made a mother, was still confined to her room.

Of the sad aspects of life it had been her destiny to see much—as daughter, as sister, and as woman. In June 1873, a terrible calamity fell upon her as a mother. A child—one especially beloved—climbing to an open window in a room adjoining that in which she was, lost its balance, and was killed almost before her eyes, as she rushed in terror to call him back. This, too, had to be borne. It was borne nobly, and with Christian resignation. But such shocks tell upon the vital powers, and some trace of what had been 'undergone and overcome' seemed to be visible long afterwards in a perceptible bodily languor, and in a more spiritual beauty which had passed into her expressive face.

The thought of this sent an anxious thrill through the hearts of many, when it became known that the Princess was herself seized by the terrible malady which had prostrated her husband and five of her children, and taken from her the youngest of them all—the youngest, the brightest, the idol of her other children.[2] She had nursed them all through their time of danger, and now, spent with watching

---

[2] The struggle to conceal from the other children that their favourite was dead cost the Princess, down to the time of her own fatal seizure, such a daily and almost hourly effort as, in her weak state, she was ill able to bear. Her sufferings during her short illness, which lasted less than a week, were borne with exemplary patience, and an unselfish and even cheerful spirit which were truly admirable. The day before she died, she expressed to Sir William Jenner her regret that she should cause her mother so much anxiety.

and anxiety as she was, the malady had laid its fatal clutch upon herself. She that had cared and thought for all was soon past all human care to save. Thus she died as she had lived, devoted, self-sacrificing, purified by great pain and great love—a model daughter—wife—mother.

Of the loss of such a woman to the husband to whom she was the all-in-all, to the children to whose love she will respond no more, to the mother in whose thoughts she is interwoven with the sweetest, the saddest, the most sacred memories, to the brothers and sisters whom she loved and who loved her so truly, so tenderly, who dare trust himself to speak? It must be long before the grief can be assuaged, under which all these must now be suffering—before the 'Idea of her life can sweetly creep,' as something hallowed, 'into their study of imagination;' but the day will come when they will bless God, that theirs was a wife, a daughter, a sister, a mother, so good, so noble, and that, having fought her fight on earth valiantly, yet meekly, she has gone where there is no more sorrow, nor crying, and where the great mysteries of life alone find their solution.

THEODORE MARTIN.

INDEX.

ALBERT

ALBERT EDWARD, Prince of Wales, 4, 6, 14, 15, 16, 17; birth of first son, 86; visit of Princess Alice to, 92; visits to Darmstadt, 95, 158; to Kranichstein, 120, 204; severe illness of, at Sandringham, 33; Princess Alice with him during his illness, 33, 245; his recovery, 33; at Bram's Hill Park Camp, 214; visit to Rome, 261; Princess Alice's opinion of constancy of his friendship, 286; at the funeral of Princess Alice, 53; 329

Albert, Prince Consort, his care for the education of his children, 2, 3; anniversary of his wedding-day (1854), 5; his influence on the character and education of Princess Alice, 7; at her confirmation, 8, 9; letters on the subject of her marriage, 10, 11; at the deathbed of the Duchess of Kent, 11; his illness and death, 12, 325; his name the last on Princess Alice's lips, 52; bust of, by Mr. Theed, and statue of, by Marochetti, 59; his Addresses and Speeches, 63; his Farm Book, 77, 80; letters by Princess Alice on anniversary of his death, 85, 97; his admiration of Mendelssohn's *Elijah*, 103; of Schiller's *Braut von Messina*, 126; Raphael collection by, 165; review of his life, 175; likenesses of, 15, 259; Hyde Park Memorial, 271; 326, 327, 328

Aldershot, 128, 243

Alençon, Duke of, 119

Alexandra, Princess of Wales, 33; birth of first son, 86; visit of Princess Alice, to, 92; visit to Darmstadt, 95; visits Princess Alice at Kranichstein, 120

Alfred, Prince (Duke of Edinburgh), 4, 6, 14, 15, 16, 17, 96; accompanies Dr. Macleod to Darmstadt, 97; visits Princess Alice at Seeheim, 110; invests Grand Duke of Hesse with Garter, 111; engagement to Princess Marie, 268; his wedding, 273

ALICE

Alice Maud Mary, Princess of Hesse, Memoir of, by her sister, Princess Christian, 1-53; her birth and christening, 1; her character as a child, 1-4; early education, 3; takes part in juvenile theatricals, 4-6; her sweetness of disposition, 6; her home life in the Royal family, 7; her veneration for her father: its influence on her after life, 7, 327; as eldest daughter, after the Princess Royal's marriage, 7; her confirmation, 8; sixteenth birthday, 9; first meeting with Prince Louis of Hesse, 9; her betrothal, 10; at the deathbed of the Duchess of Kent, 11; announcement of her engagement to Parliament, 11; her love for her Scotch home, 12; preparations for the marriage, 12; interrupted by the death of her father, 12; her devotion and assistance to her mother in her bereavement, 12-13; her marriage, 13, 327; at St. Clare: last days in England, 17-18; departure for her new home, 18; reception at Darmstadt, 20; official duties, 20; meeting with her mother and brothers and sisters at Rheinhardsbrunn in Thuringia, 20; letters from and impressions of her new home, 56-69; revisits England: birth and christening of first daughter, at Windsor Castle, 20; returns to Germany, 20; love for her adopted country, 21; her interest in politics, 21; birth of a second daughter, 21, 97; plans and superintends the building of her own palace, 21; schemes for the welfare of the people of Hesse, 21; annual visits to England, 22; life at Kranichstein, 72, 77; visit to Lich, 77; to Giessen, Marburg, and Frankfort, 80; to Munich, 90; to Berlin, 101, 102; meeting with Emperor and Empress of Russia, 109, 110; arrangements for the Queen's visit to Kranichstein, 115, 116; tour in Switzerland, 115-118; Scotch tour, 120; at Sandringham,

ALICE

120; death of her uncle, the King of the Belgians, 22, 123; bazaar in her new palace, to found idiot asylum in Darmstadt, 22; war between Austria and Prussia: her husband takes the field, 23, 138; birth of Princess Irène, 23, 141; return of Prince Louis: visiting the sick and wounded, 24, 147, 153; christening of the baby Princess, 24; founds the 'Ladies' Union' for aid to the sick and wounded, 24; establishes a committee for encouragement of female industry, 25; the 'Alice Bazaar,' 25; endeavours to found a Frauenverein, 160; visit to Berlin, 162; to Paris, 166; to Switzerland, 167-174; anxiety on account of Prince Leopold, 182; suffering from neuralgia, 193; at Gotha with Crown Princess, 185; in England, 188; apprehensions of war, 25, 192; failing health, 26; birth of Prince Ernest, 27; first lengthened separation from her husband, 27; her self-sacrifice to his interests, 27; views on Irish Church question, 199; visits Potsdam, 201; at Industrial Exhibition at Mayence, 205; Prince Louis' proposed visit to the East, 205; at Cannes with Crown Princess, 27, 207-209; nurses Prince Louis and children through scarlet fever, 27, 210-214; becomes acquainted with Frederick David Strauss, 27; proposes that he should make notes on Voltaire, 27; Strauss reads his notes to her, 28; acceptance of his proposal to dedicate the work to her, 28; misconceptions as to her intercourse with Strauss, 28; his influence on her opinions, 29; her examination and rejection of Strauss' views, 30; her husband ordered to the front in the Franco-German war, 30, 216; visits to the hospitals and ambulances, 30; organises aid for the sick and wounded, 30-31; birth of Prince Frederick William, 31, 226; letters during the war: account of her life at Darmstadt, 30, 215-227; visits to Berlin, 31, 32; christening of the little Prince, 32; meeting with her husband after the war, 32; peace illuminations at Darmstadt, 236; at Berlin on triumphant entry of troops, 239, 240; visit to the Queen at Balmoral, 32; at Bram's Hill Park Camp, 244; in Scotland, 245; at Sandringham: illness of the Prince of Wales, 33; remains with her sister-in-law till his recovery, 33; birth of Princess Alix, 33, 247; at Kranichstein: anniversary of battle of Gravelotte, 249; at the funeral of Princess Hohenlohe-Langenburg, 251; at the general assembly of charitable societies at Darm-

BADEN

stadt, 252; the 'Ladies' Diet': letters explaining its objects, 33, 252; present at unveiling of monument to Hessian soldiers, 34, 254; visit to Italy, 259-265; returns to Darmstadt much fatigued, 35; accidental death of Prince Frederick, 35, 36, 265, 331; its effect on her health, 37, 38; on the proper training of children, 37, 276, 283; birth and christening of Princess Marie Victoria, 38, 278; continued failing health: visits to England, Scotland, and the Black Forest, 38; death of her father-in-law, 39, 299-301; illness and death of the Grand Duke, 39, 301-302; her husband succeeds as Grand Duke Louis IV., 39; increased responsibilities, 39, 302; visit to Houlgate, 303; her feelings regarding policy of Russia, 303; enthusiastic reception at Darmstadt, 305; thorough change ordered: summer at Eastbourne 39; visits the Albion Home at Brighton, and consents to become patroness of it, 39, 40; Princesses Victoria, Alix, Marie, and Irène, Prince Ernest, and the Grand Duke attacked with diphtheria, 41-50, 309-310; death of Princess Marie, 47, 310; the funeral, 48-50; is attacked with diphtheria, 51, 331; her last hours, death, and interment, 51-53; sketch by one of the watchers by her coffin, 318-322; sketch of her life and character, by Sir Theodore Martin, 325-332

Alsfeld, 79, 177, 199
Altenburg, 79
Amelung, Emily, 107, 212
Amorbach, 84, 95, 111, 142
Angeli, Heinrich von, 308
Antwerp, 68, 91, 176
Arneth, Herr von, 104
Arthur, Prince (Duke of Connaught), 5, 8; visit of, to Darmstadt, 67; to Seeheim, 110; ill with small-pox, 176; his birthday (1868), 185; Col. Elphinstone's high opinion of, 190; at Berlin, 246
Aschaffenburg, action at, 141, 145, 153
Auboué, 222
Auerbach, letters from, 62-66
Aumale, Lina, at St. Moritz, 169
Austria, Emperor of, visit to Frankfort and Kranichstein, 80; 132, 134, 207
Avignon, 209

BACH, 90, 246
Baden, 67, 113, 161, 206, 246
Baden, Frederick, Grand Duke of, visits of

INDEX.

BADEN

Prince and Princess of Hesse to, 67, 158; visit of, to Her Majesty, 68; troubles of, 157; at St. Moritz, 169; at Carlsruhe, 174; at Darmstadt, 266

Baden, Louise, Princess of Prussia, Grand Duchess of, visit of Prince Louis and Princess Alice to, at Baden, 67; visits of Princess Alice to, on Island of Mainau, 174; at St. Moritz, 169; visit of, to Darmstadt, 266

Baden, Sophia, Grand Duchess of, 13, 67

Baillie, Lady Frances, 77, 129, 158, 195, 269, 292, 293

Balmoral, 112, 120, 128, 150, 249; Princesses Victoria and Ella at, 290; Princess Alice at, 296

Barrington, Lady Caroline, 2, 5, 213

Battenberg, Henry, Prince of, 275

Battenberg, Julia, Princess of, at Darmstadt with Princess of Hesse, 82; letter by, to Princess Alice, 146

Battenberg, Louis, Prince of, 120, 275

Bauer, Miss, 9, 214, 273, 299

Bavaria, Adalbert, Prince of, 81

Bavaria, Ludwig II., King of, at Rome, 260

Bavaria, Marie, Queen of, sister of Princess Charles, 196, 202, 260

Bavaria, Otto, Prince of, 260

Bazaine, Marshal, 220

Beatrice, Princess, 14, 16, 17, 57, 92, 94, 102; illness of, 132

Beck, Louis, 115, 206

Becker, Dr., private secretary, 17, 68, 73; visit of Princess Alice to, 82; accompanies Prince Louis to Munich, 145

Belgians, Leopold, Crown Prince of, death of, 195

Belgians, Leopold, King of, letters by Her Majesty to, 1, 326; advises the Queen's removal to Osborne after the death of Prince Consort, 13; illness of, 122; his death, 22, 123

Belgians, Leopold II., King of, death of only son of, 195

Belgians, Marie, Duchess of Brabant, afterwards Queen of, 121

Bender, 108, 129

Berlin, triumphal entry of German troops into, June 16, 1871, 240

Bernard, Mademoiselle, 119

Berry, Dr., 169

Bessungen, 56

Biddulph, Colonel, 13

Bismarck, Prince, 134

Blanche, Princess of Orleans, 119

Blankenberghe, 241, 242, 279

DAWSON

Blücher, Countess, 67, 123, 177, 200, 207

Bologna, 260

Bormio, 173

Brabant, Duchess of, 121

Bram's Hill Park Camp, 244

Brand, Victoria, 114

Brown, Archibald, 183

Brown, John, 61, 96, 100, 112, 190, 272

Brown, Mrs., 280, 292, 294

Brown's, John, sister, 177

Brownlow, Lord and Lady, 246

Bruce, General, 292

Büchner, Fräulein Louise, 25

Bulgaria, Alexander, Prince of, 275

Bunsen, Baroness, 5, 274, 287

CAMBRIDGE, Duchess of, at Rumpenheim, 79; visit of Princess Alice to, 93; at Frankfort, 113, 205, 242

Cambridge, George, Duke of, at Kranichstein, 120; present of horse by, to Princess Alice, 176; meets her at Frankfort, 205, 242; visit of Prince and Princess to Aldershot in company with, 244; visits them at Frankfort, 248

Cambridge, Mary, Princess of, 79, 242

Campbell, Lady Emma Augusta, sister of Duke of Argyll, 208

Campbell, Lady Victoria, daughter of Duke of Argyll, 208

Canterbury, Archbishop of, 8, 14

Carlyle, Mr., 297

Carpenter, Miss Mary, 34, 253

Chopin, 258, 270

Churchill, Lady, 16, 58, 263

Clarendon, Lord, 9, 133, 215

Clark, Sir James, 69, 104; illness of, 185; his death, 214

Clarke, Mrs., nurse, 224, 247

Coburg, 61

Combe, Mrs. George, 69

Congress of German Princes at Frankfort, 21

Convention with Prussia, 26

Corbett, Annie, 76

Corbett, Mr., 76, 78

Courbold, Mr., 6

Cusins, Mr., 103

DADELSEN, Herr von, 42, 45

Dalhousie, Lady Christian, 209

Dalhousie, Lord, 208, 209

Dawson, Lady Anna Maria, 5

INDEX.

Derby, Lord, 9, 74
Dives, old church at, 304
Dunrobin, visit to, 245
Durham, Beatrix Frances, Countess of, daughter of Duke of Abercorn, 233

EASTBOURNE, Princess Alice at, 39
Ebury, Lord and Lady, 208, 209
Eigenbrodt, Dr., 45, 47
Elgin, Earl of, 269
Elgin, Lady, 287
Elphinstone, Major (Sir Howard, K.C.B.), 162, 176, 190
Ely, Lady, 136, 138, 139
Engeler, Adam, guide, 171

FAULQUEMONT, 218
Fife, Lady, 76
Fischbach, 201, 202
Frankfort, congress of German Princes at, 21
Frauenverein, attempt by Princess Alice to found a, at Darmstadt, 160
French, Eugénie, Empress of, distress of, at attempt on Emperor of Russia's life, 166; gift of Arenenberg by, to the Emperor Napoleon, 174; Franco-German War, 224; in England, 239; general sympathy with, on death of the Emperor, 257
French, Louis Napoleon, Emperor of, 174; Franco-German War, 224; treatment of, in England, 239; his death, 257
French, Louis Philippe, King of the, 257

GAINSBOROUGH, Lady, 9
Gardiner, Colonel, 302
George, Prince, son of Prince and Princess of Wales, 92, 283
Geyer, Mr., 178
Gibbs, Mr., 6
Gleichen, Laura, Countess, 170, 171, 172, 174
Gleichen, Victor, Count, 170, 171, 172, 173, 174
Gloucester, Duchess of, 101
Göben, General von, enters Darmstadt at head of Prussian troops, 23
Grancy, Marie, 100, 116, 243
Grant, Mrs., 280
Grant, John, 61
Grant, Sir Hope, his book on Indian Mutiny, 275
Granville, Lord, 206
Gravelotte, 220, 249

Graves, Miss, 280
Grey, Mrs., 213
Grey, Colonel, son of Sir George Grey, 5; his death, 285
Grey, General, 156
Grolmann, Adolphus, 107
Grosvenor, Miss (Oggie), daughter of Lord Ebury, 209
Grüner, Professor, 263

HALLNACHS, Dr., 82
Hamilton, Duchess of, 67
Harcourt, Colonel and Lady Catherine, 16
Hardinge, the Hon. Emily Caroline, death of, 294, 295
Harrison, Mr., 293
Helena, Princess, memoir of Princess Alice, by, 1–53; 4, 6, 14; betrothal of, 121; Prince Adalbert's praise of, 187
Helmsdörffer, Fräulein, 45, 49
Helps, Sir Arthur, 63
Hesse, Alexander, Prince of, 55, 57, 72, 76, 79, 132, 133, 136, 138, 146, 161, 246, 248, 275
Hesse, Alice, Grand Duchess of. See *Alice Maud Mary, Princess*
Hesse, Anna, Princess of, 14, 16, 79; death of, 107
Hesse, Charles, Prince of, father of Prince Louis, 16, 21, 24, 92, 96; grief at loss of his daughter, 107–109; his delicate state of health, 121; at blessing of Prince and Princess's new palace, 129; distress at position of his son, Prince Henry, during the German war, 139; Prince Louis' first son named after, 193; Prince and Princess guests of, at Castle Fischbach, 202; three sons in the war, 217; continual anxiety, 221, 222, 230; his reception of the Marquis and Marchioness of Lorne, 238; at Sorrento, 260, 263, 264; his death, 39, 299–301
Hesse, Princess Charles of, 16, 21, 24, 45, 55, 72, 92; her kindness to Princess Alice, 96; death of her daughter, Princess Anna, 107–109; at Kranichstein to meet Her Majesty, 114; Princess Alice's frequent vists to, at the Rosenhöhe, 119; present at the blessing of the new palace at Darmstadt, 129; helps in establishing Frauenverein, 161; proxy for Her Majesty at baptism of Prince Ernest, 194; original famous Holbein in Darmstadt Gallery, property of, 203; three sons in the war, 217, 221; complimentary message concerning her sons from Russian Emperor, 236; sympathy of, with Princess

INDEX.

HESSE

Alice in her various works, 253; death of her husband, 299, 301

Hesse, Elizabeth Alexandra Louise Alice, Princess of, birth of, 21; 42, 45, 86, 96, 97, 100, 104, 112, 113, 115, 125, 126, 140, 151, 154, 178, 194; her delicacy, 197, 210, 211; Christmas letter by, to the Queen, 230; birthday present from Her Majesty to, 254; visit of, to Balmoral, 290; sent to Princess Charles, and escapes infection, 309

Hesse, Ernest Louis Albert Charles William, Prince of, birth of, 27; christening, 31, 32; 193, 203, 206, 209, 210, 227, 232, 238, 239, 248; his grief for loss of his brother, Prince Frederick, 267, 277, 282, 293; his affectionate disposition, 295; in picture by Angeli, 308; attacked with diphtheria, 41-49, 309-313

Hesse, Frederick William, Landgrave of, 78

Hesse, Frederick, Prince of (brother of Landgrave), 78

Hesse, Frederick William I., Elector of, 161

Hesse, Frederick William Augustus Victor Louis, Prince of, 31, 35, 37, 226, 237, 242, 256, 257, 258; description of, 233, 237; death of, 35, 36; reminiscences of, 265, 266, 267, 270, 275, 276, 278, 290, 299

Hesse, General von, 243

Hesse, George, Prince of (brother of Landgrave), 79

Hesse, Henry, Prince of, 10, 15, 16, 78; his painful position during German war, 130, 132, 139; in the Franco-German war, at Worms, 217; at Berlin, for Prince Adalbert's funeral, 266; present at his father's death, 299-301

Hesse, Irène Louise Marie Anna, Princess of, birth of, 23-24; 141, 142, 147, 152, 154, 163, 175, 194, 232, 241, 271; attacked with diphtheria, 41-44, 309; 331

Hesse, Louise, Princess of (sister to the Duchess of Cambridge), 79

Hesse, Louis III., Grand Duke of (uncle of Prince Louis), 21, 23, 26; Prince's regiment inspected by, 66; his kindness to Prince and Princess, 71, 72, 81; meeting with Emperor and Empress of Russia, 109; receives the Garter, 111; his Palais at Frankfort, 113; Prince and Princess with him at Gotha, 126; 132, 136, 143; at Munich, 145; return, after war, to Darmstadt, 153; Princess Alice's son named Ernest Ludwig at his wish, 193; failing health, 289; death of, 39, 302

Hesse, Louis, Prince of, visits of to England, 10-12; first meeting with and betrothal to Princess Alice, 10; marrriage of, 13-16; in-

HESSE

vested with the Garter by the Queen, 17; departure from England, 18; reception of, at Darmstadt, 20; life there, 21, 55-61; stay at Auerbach, 63-66; visit to Baden, 67; again in England, 20; returns to Darmstadt, 23, 72; takes his seat in the Chambers, 72; his occupations, 73, 74; votes for alteration of Press Law, 76; visit to Lich, 76; to Giessen, 77; to England, 79; at his sister's funeral at Schwerin, 107; assists at investiture of the Grand Duke with Order of the Garter, 111; tour in Switzerland, 115, 119; military and other duties at Darmstadt, 122; visits Brussels for King Leopold's funeral, 123; takes the field in the war of 1866, 23; with the staff at Frankfort, 136; returns to Darmstadt on birth of Princess Irène, 141; departure for the front again: fighting at Aschaffenburg, 141; march to Odenwald and Amorbach, 142; hardships endured by, 143, 145; appointed to command of troops sent to Berlin, 146; visiting the sick and wounded with the Princess, 24, 147; at Nierstein, his farewell to Cavalry Brigade, 148; peace concluded, the terms, 151; enters Darmstadt at the head of the troops, 153; at Waldleiningen, 155; at Carlsruhe, 158; visit to Switzerland, 167-174; resigns his command in the Hessian army, 26; at Kranichstein: press of business, 191; birth of Prince Ernest Ludwig, 27, 193; inspects garrisons at Friedberg and Giessen, 199; Ludwigstag, 204; tour to the East with the Crown Prince of Prussia, 27, 205, 207; rejoins Princess at Cannes, 209; attacked with scarlet fever at Darmstadt, 28, 211-212; with the army of Prince Frederick Charles in Franco-German war, 30, 220; at Metz, Vionville, Rezonville, and Gravelotte, 220, 221; receives the Iron Cross, 223; Field Marshal Wrangel's high opinion of, 227; with head-quarters at Orleans on Christmas Day, 230; at Darmstadt on leave, 32, 237; receives Order of Merit, 236; at Donjeux, 238; at Berlin, triumphal entry of troops, 32, 239, 240; enters Darmstadt at head of his division, 240, 241; visit to the Queen at Balmoral with the Princess, 32; at Buckingham Palace, 243; at Sandringham, 245; invested with Order of Black Eagle at Berlin, 246; press of work, 247; anniversary of battle of Gravelotte, 249; at funeral of Princess Hohenlohe-Langenburg, 251; change of Ministry at Darmstadt, 253; present at unveiling of monument to Hessian soldiers, 34, 255;

HESSE

visit to Italy, 259; journey to Rome, 260; visit of Crown Prince and Princess of Italy to, 261; at Rome, 260-264; visit to Sorrento, 263; to Capri, Bay of Naples, Florence, 264; return to Darmstadt, death of little Prince Fritz, 36, 257, 265; visit to England, 271; to Blankenberghe: saves life of a lady while bathing, 279; accident on the ice at Kranichstein, 289; in England again, 289; at Darmstadt, 297; illness and death of his father, 39, 299, 301; illness and death of the Grand Duke, 39, 301-302; ascends the throne as Louis IV., 39; failing health of Grand Duchess, 303; enthusiastic reception at Darmstadt, 305; at Eastbourne with the Grand Duchess and children, 39; return to Darmstadt, 307; attacked with diphtheria, 41-50, 309; his recovery, 51, 311; illness and death of the Grand Duchess, 51-52; 330

Hesse, Marie Victoria Feodora Leopoldine, Princess of, birth of, 38; 41, 278, 280, 288, 298, 308; attacked with diphtheria, 42-46, 308; her death and funeral, 47-50, 309; 312

Hesse, Victoria Alberta Elizabeth Matilda, Princess of, birth and christening of, 20; 71, 75, 81, 83, 85, 86, 90, 104, 106, 112, 118, 121, 130, 149, 151, 155, 157, 178, 185, 189, 192, 193, 198, 204, 206, 211, 212, 214, 230, 233, 265, 275, 290; attacked with diphtheria, 41-44, 308; her recovery, 308

Hesse, Victoria Alix Hélène Louise Beatrice, Princess of, birth of, 33; attacked with diphtheria, 41-45; 247, 248, 256, 278, 280, 288, 298, 308, 309

Hesse, William, Prince of, 15, 16, 129, 138, 209, 260, 262, 290, 299, 300

Hessen-Homburg, Elizabeth, Landgravine of 129

Hessen-Homburg, Landgrave of, death of, 129

Hildyard, Miss, 6, 8, 9, 103, 271

Hill, Miss Florence, 34, 252

Hill, Miss Octavia, 40, 329

Hofmeister, Dr., 224, 225, 228, 247

Hohenlohe-Langenburg, Eliza, Princess of, 76

Hohenlohe-Langenburg, Feodora, Princess of (the Queen's half-sister), at Princess Alice's wedding, 15 17; bad health of, 177; mention of visit to convent at Rome by, 262

Hohenlohe-Langenburg, Hermann, Prince of, 274

Hohenlohe-Langenburg, Leopoldine, Princess of, 274

Hohenlohe, Prince of, 76

Hohenzollern, Princess of. 262

LEININGEN

Hohenzollern-Sigmaringen, Anton, Prince of, death of, 145; 195

Holl, Mr., 259

Holstein, Henry Charles Woldemar, Prince of, 233

Holyrood, 248

Holzei, Herr, 62

Houlgate, in Normandy, 303

Howard, Monsignor (Cardinal), 262

ITALY, Humbert, Prince of (now King), 261
Italy, Marguerita, Princess of (now Queen), 261

JACKSON, Miss, governess, 42, 45
Jäger, Catherine, 177
Jäger, servant, 115; illness of, 175, 177, 180; death of, 187, 188
Jenner, Dr. (Sir William), 52, 104, 137, 331
Joachim, Herr, 246
Jocelyn, Lady, 70
Joch Pass, 118
Jowett, Professor, 164

KANNÉ, M., 218, 224, 260
Kantner, Frau, 47
Kehrer, General, 220
Kent, Duchess of, 5, 8; failing health and death of, 11; remembrance of, by Princess Alice, 66; souvenirs of, at Amorbach, 84; anniversary of death, 89; of birthday, 172; 249, 279, 181, 233; engraving of portrait of, sent to Princess Alice, 259; Princess's loving recollections of, 279
Kerr, Lord Robert S., 78
Kingsley, Rev. C., his *Saint's Tragedy*, 80
Kinkel, Professor, 210
Kitz, Fräulein, governess, 238, 263
Kleinwart, Herr, 238
Knollys, Miss Charlotte, 176
Knollys, Lady, 176
Knollys, Sir William, 176
Köhler, 228
Kraus, architect, 82
Kräuslach, groom, 293

LANFREY, Life of Napoleon by, 208, 213
Lauchert, Amalie, Princess of Hohenlohe-Schillingsfürst, 162
Leiningen, Alberta, Princess of, 155
Leiningen, Charles, Prince of, 76, 84

INDEX.

Leiningen, Ernest, Prince of, 84, 93; visit of Princess Alice to, 155; at Osborne, 188
Leiningen, Marie, Princess of, 84, 155
Le Mans, 232
Leopold, Prince (Duke of Albany), 18, 32; the last to visit Princess Alice at Darmstadt, 41; at funeral of Princess Alice, 53; serious illness of, 182, 183; his confirmation, 196; delicate health of, 226, 236
Locock, Sir Charles, 70
Loftus, Lord Augustus, at Berlin, 200
Logoz, Sarah, nurse, 115, 168
Logoz, Theodore, 115
Lorne, Marquis of, marriage of, 236; at Darmstadt on wedding tour, 237, 238
Louise, Princess, 4, 6, 69, 132; letter to Princess Alice by, 182; Prince Adalbert's praise of, 187; her marriage, 236; wedding tour, 237, 238; present given to, by 91st Highlanders, 245; member of Institute, 252; visit to Mr. Motley with Princess Alice, 297
Lützow, Count, 74
Luxembourg question, 164, 165
Lyttelton, Lady, 2

MACBEAN, Miss, 41; account by of the attack with diphtheria of the Grand Duke of Hesse and his children: anxiety and devotion of the Princess Alice, 42–50
Macdonald, Miss Flora, 249
Macleod, Dr., 97, 99, 248
Mainau, 174
Manchester, Duchess of, 70
Manstein, General von, 218
Marie Amélie, Queen of the French, death of, 130
Marlborough House, 69, 92, 289
Marochetti, Baron, his statue of Prince Consort, 59
Martin, Mr. (Sir Theodore), his 'Prince Consort's Life,' 11; 284, 286, 287, 288; sketch of the life of Princess Alice by, 325–332
Mary, Princess (Duchess of Teck), 79, 93, 113, 114, 242, 270
Maude, Colonel, 228
McDonald, Annie, 190
Mecklenburg-Schwerin, Anna, Princess of Hesse, Grand Duchess of, 79; marriage of, 91; death of, 106–110
Mecklenburg-Schwerin, Frederick, Grand Duke of, marriage of, 91; 114
Mecklenburg-Strelitz, Adolphus, Grand Duke of, 79

Mecklenburg-Strelitz, Augusta, Princess, Grand Duchess of, 79, 205
Mecklenburg-Strelitz, Caroline, Duchess of, 79
Mecklenburg-Strelitz, Dowager Duchess of, 79
Mecklenburg-Strelitz, Frederick, Grand Duke of, 205, 248
Mendelssohn, his *Elijah*, 103
Mensdorff, Pouilly, Graf von, 132
Metz, battle near to, 220, 254
Meyer, Stallmeister, 175
Meyer, Superintendent, 62
Minter, Dr., 189
Mitchell, Mr., librarian, Old Bond Street, 238
Moffat, nurse of Princess Victoria of Hesse, 71, 81, 86, 115
Molin, Herr von, lecture on Art in Venice by, 163
Möller, Oberlieutenant, 221
Morier, Lady, 164, 178, 196, 260
Morier, Sir Robert, 28, 164, 178, 196, 210, 260
Motley, Mr. Lothrop, 297
Müller, Max, letter by, 398
Mulooly, Father, 263
Münchengratz, battle at, 141

NACHOD, defeat of Austrians at, 140
Nassau, Duke and Duchess of, 134
Nemours, Duke of, 15, 16, 119, 169
Netherlands, Prince and Princess Frederick of, 209
Nickel, Herr, 155

OBERHESSEN, 79, 106, 148, 154
Obernitz, Hugo von, 145
Orchard, nurse, 48, 164, 211, 263, 308, 311
Orleans, Marguerite, Princess of, 119

PAGET, Lord Alfred, 70
Palk, Lady, 238
Palmerston, Lady, 179, 287
Pauli, History of England by, 113
Perth, unveiling of statue of Prince Consort at, 93
Phipps, Sir Charles, 306
Playfair, Dr. Lyon, 114
Podoll, battle at, 141
Procter, Miss Adelaide, 267
Prothero, Mr., 14
Prussia, Adalbert, Prince of, 187, 196; death of, 266

PRUSSIA

Prussia, Augusta, Princess of (Queen of Prussia, Empress of Germany), at Baden, 67; proposed visit of Princess Alice to, 68; passes through Darmstadt, 71; visit to Princess Alice, 192; Prince Frederick William Augustus named after, 235; interchange of visits with Prince and Princess, 306

Prussia, Charlotte, Princess of (daughter of Crown Prince and Princess), marriage of, 306

Prussia, Frederick Charles, Prince of, in command of Second Army, 1870, 30, 220; victories of, 231; sponsor to Frederick William Augustus of Hesse, 235

Prussia, Frederick William, Crown Prince of (of Germany), 7; present at marriage of Princess Alice, 16; 23; visit of to Darmstadt, 95; there on anniversary of December 14 (1864), 97, 98; kindness of to Prince and Princess of Hesse, 100; hard work, 102; his sad position in case of war, 130; in Schleswig, 132; Prince Louis' interview with, 133; domestic trouble, 136; Queen Victoria writes to, 146; his kind reception of Prince Louis, 148; at Paris, 167; visit of to Darmstadt, 177; at Darmstadt on his return from Italy, 188; journey to the East with Prince Louis of Hesse, 27, 202, 205; at Cannes, 209; his first victory, 213; sponsor to Prince Frederick William of Hesse, 235; passes through Frankfort, 237

Prussia, Henry, Prince of (son of Crown Prince and Princess), in England with Her Majesty, 157

Prussia, Sigismund, Prince of (son of Crown Prince and Princess), Princess Alice's account of, 101; illness of, 135; death of, 140, 201

Prussia, Victoria, Crown Princess of (of Germany), on the character of Princess Alice as a child, 3; in juvenile theatricals in 1852 and 1854, 4, 5; marriage of, 7, 326; confirmation of, 8; visit of Princess Alice to, 27; desires the Princess to stay with her during Franco-German War, 30; at Darmstadt on anniversary (1864) of December 14, 98; Princess Alice's account of visit to, 100–102; at Kranichstein, 120; war a terrible prospect for, 130, 134; death of her son Prince Sigismund, 140; Prince Louis kindly received by, 148; accepts invitation to Paris Exhibition, 167; visit to Darmstadt, 177, 184; Princess Alice spends birthday with, 185; at Potsdam, 201, 202; with Princess Alice at Cannes, 208; visit of the Princess to, 223; together at Berlin, 226, 227; sponsor to Prince Frederick William of Hesse, 235; at Darmstadt, 256; 259, 273; at Wiesbaden, 306

Prussia, Victoria, Princess of (daughter of Crown Prince and Princess), 162

Prussia, Waldemar, Prince of (son of Crown Prince and Princess), 208

Prussia, William I., Prince of (King of Prussia, Emperor of Germany), 21, 26; refuses the meeting at Frankfort, 80; policy of, 134; at Paris, 167; sponsor to Prince Ernest of Hesse, 193, 195; in command at Rezonville and Gravelotte, 220; announcement by of Prince Louis having received Order of Merit, 236; passes through Frankfort, 237; at head of his troops at Berlin after the peace, 240, 254

Punch, sonnet in, on marriage of Princess Alice, 19

QUEEN

QUEEN VICTORIA, of England, 1; letters by to King of the Belgians describing the christening of Princess Alice, 1, 326; on the Princess's character as a child, 2, 3; plans for training her children, 2, 3; account of Princess Alice's acting in juvenile theatricals, 4, 5; anniversary (1854) of wedding, 5; shares in her children's occupations and amusements, 7; description by of Princess Alice's confirmation, 8, 9; of her sixteenth birthday, 9; of her betrothal, 10; at the deathbed of the Duchess of Kent, 11; announces to Parliament Princess Alice's contemplated marriage, 11; death of the Prince Consort, 12, 13; account by of the Princess Alice's marriage and her last days in England, 13, 18; invests Prince Louis of Hesse with the Garter, 17; at Rheinhardsbrunn, 20; receives Prince and Princess in England, 20, 32; anxiety of, during Prince Leopold's illness, 182; Princess Alice's recollections of first great sorrow of, 184, 185, 197; letter by, on Princess Victoria's birthday, 198; christening gift to Prince Ernest, 203; present of pony from, to the Princess's children, 204; visit of to Invertrossachs, 205; statuette of Prince Consort sent to Princess Alice by, 214; Princess's thanks for letters of sympathy from, during the war, 216, 221, 223, 224, 229, 235; illness of, 243–245; letters by, on birth of Princess Alix, 247; visit of to Edinburgh, 248;

INDEX.

QUEEN

death of her half-sister, 251–253; anniversary of Prince Consort's death (1872), 255; print of Winterhalter's picture of Duchess of Kent sent to Princess by, also engraving of picture of herself, 259; opening of Victoria Park by, 263; letters by, on Princess Alice's birthday, 264, 276; and after Prince Frederick's death, 265, 268; Prince and Princess's visit to, at Windsor, 269, 271; her birthday (1874), 278; Prince Consort's, 280; advice to Princess regarding the education of her children, given by, 283; letter by, on publication of Prince Consort's Life, 286, 287; Prince Alice's expressions of love for, 289, 295, 296; last letters to Princess, 310, 311; 325, 326, 327, 328

REUSS, Princess, 129
Reuter, Hélène, 248
Rezonville, 220
Riedesel, Herr von, 79
Rigi Kaltbad, 115
Robertson, Rev. Frederick William, his sermons, 95, 110
Rollande, Madame (Rollet), 208
Rome, 35, 209, 259; Princess Alice's visit to, 261–264
Rückert, Frederick, quotation from, 37, 282
Ruland, Mr. (Hofrath), catalogue of Prince Consort's Raphael collection by, 165; accompanies Princess Alice to Italy, 259, 262
Russell, Lord and Lady John, 207
Russia, Alexander II., Emperor of, visit of to Kranichstein, 93; leaves for Nice, 108; death of his son, 108, 109; visit to Jugenheim, 109; attempt on his life, 166; aged appearance of, 191; review at Darmstadt in honour of, 191; at Petersthal, 241; at Seeheim, 268
Russia, Marie, Empress of, gift to Princess Alice from, 71; death of her eldest son, 108, 109, 267; shock caused by attempt on Emperor's life, 166; visit of to Princess Alice at Darmstadt, 241; at Petersthal, 241; proposed winter in Italy, 248; visit to Sorrento, 260, 264; at Seeheim with Princess Alice, 267, 268; death of her eldest daughter, 267; failing health, 274; her grief at Prince Charles's death, 300, 301
Russia, Marie, Grand Duchess of (Duchess of Edinburgh), meets Princess Alice at Darmstadt railway station, 51; description of, by the Princess, 241; at Rome, 264; at Seeheim, engaged to Duke of Edinburgh,

STANLEY

268; reception of in England, 274; godmother to Princess Marie of Hesse, 278
Russia, Nicholas, Cesarewitch of, death of, 108, 109, 267
Russia, Serge, Grand Duke of, 21, 93

SADOWA, battle of, 141
Sahl, Mr. Hermann, 165, 182
Saxe-Coburg-Gotha, Duchess of, visits of Princess Alice to, 126, 185
Saxe-Coburg-Gotha, Ernest, Duke of, 8, 9; at Princess Alice's wedding, in her father's place, 15, 16; Princess Alice's visits to, 61, 62, 74, 126, 185; at Seeheim, 111; possible opposition to Hessians during the war, 140; 234
Saxe-Coburg-Gotha, Prince and Princess Augustus of, at Princess Alice's wedding, 15, 17
Saxony, Albert, Crown Prince of, 237
Saxony, Carola, Crown Princess of, 237
Saxony, George, Prince of, 237
Saxony, Marie, Princess of, 237
Schenck, Baron Alexander, sent to Orleans by Princess Alice during the war, 230
Schenck, Baroness Christa, Lady-in-Waiting to Princess Alice, 32, 65, 81, 82, 89; visits of Princess Alice to her parents, 91, 177; writes account of Princess Anna's wedding, 91; 95; 138
Schenck, Baron William, visit of Princess Alice to, 91
Schenck, Mademoiselle de, 16
Schleswig-Holstein, Adelaide, Duchess of, 274
Schleswig-Holstein, Frederick, Hereditary Prince of (later Duke of), 83, 86; meets Crown Prince at Carlsruhe, 274
Schleswig-Holstein, Princess Christian of. See *Helena, Princess*
Seymour, Miss, 74
Seymour, General (Marquis of Hertford), 16, 58, 198
Sidney, Lord, 55
Sillitoe, Mr., English chaplain at Darmstadt, 45
Skelmersdale, Alice (Lady Lathom), 215
Sligo, Mrs. T., 280
Sluggan, 122
Smiles, Dr. Samuel, *Lives of Engineers*, 99
Solms-Laubach, Princess, 77
Solms-Lich, Prince of, President of First Chamber, 75
Somerset, Lady Geraldine, 176
Spohr, 246
Stanley, Dean, 93; Her Majesty sends sermon

by to Princess Alice, 99; letter by to Princess Alice, 273; illness of his wife, Lady Augusta, 292-293; visit of to Carlyle with Princess Alice, 297

Stanley, Lady Augusta, 93, 95, 269, 273; illness of, 292-293

Stockmar, Baron, 5, 7, 12; Prince Louis and Princess Alice visit him at Coburg, 61, 62; his dislike to leave-taking, 272; the high standard placed by him before Prince Consort, 285; his relations with Prince Consort, 288

Strauss, David Frederick, becomes acquainted with Princess Alice, 27; reads to her his notes on Voltaire, 28; publication and dedication of the work to the Princess, 28; his influence on her opinions, 29

Strecker, Frau, 49

TENNYSON, his dedication to the *Idylls of the King*, 285

Theed, Mr., his bust of Prince Consort, 59

Thomas, Mr., 16

Thorburn, Mr., painter, 140

Times, extract from article in, on death of the Prince Consort, 12, 327

Townsend, Marchioness of, 76

Trautenau, battle at, 141

Tupper, Mr. Martin, 6

Turkey, Sultan of, visit of to England, 207

Tyndall, Professor, 172

USEDOM, Madame d', 169

VAN DE WEYER, Mr., his death, 277

Vicars, Mrs. Murray, 39

Victoria. See *Queen*

Vionville, battle of, 220

WALDECK, Princess of, 207

Wasa, Gustav, Prince, 81, 93

Weber, Dr. Carl, 74; Princess Alice's high opinion of, 91; 150, 184, 192, 211; death of his sister, 223, 225

Weber, P., painter, 112

Weimar, Grand Duke of, 76, 259

Weiss, Sophie, a former dresser of the Queen's, 274

Wellesley, Hon. and Very Rev. G., Dean of Windsor, 5, 8, 14, 16

Westerweller, Anthony von, 16, 48, 87, 105, 116, 118, 133

Westminster, Duke and Duchess of, 246

Willem, a Malay, Princess Alice's servant, 73; death of, 167; 170, 178, 180, 188

Winkworth, Miss C., 34, 252

Winterhalter, painter, 15, 67

Woodward, Mr., 165

Wrangel, Field-Marshal von, 227

YORK, Archbishop of, 14, 15

Ysenburg and Büdingen, Prince of, 205

Reprint Publishing

For People Who Go For Originals.

This book is a facsimile reprint of the original edition. The term refers to the facsimile with an original in size and design exactly matching simulation as photographic or scanned reproduction.

Facsimile editions offer us the chance to join in the library of historical, cultural and scientific history of mankind, and to rediscover.

The books of the facsimile edition may have marks, notations and other marginalia and pages with errors contained in the original volume. These traces of the past refers to the historical journey that has covered the book.

ISBN 978-3-95940-259-0

Facsimile reprint of the original edition
Copyright © 2018 Reprint Publishing
All rights reserved.

www.reprintpublishing.com

www.ingramcontent.com/pod-product-compliance
Lightning Source LLC
Chambersburg PA
CBHW080330170426
43194CB00014B/2516